Proofreading & Editing PRECISION

4th Edition

Larry G. Pagel
Assistant Professor
Walker L. Cisler College of Business
Northern Michigan University
Marquette, Michigan

Ellis Jones
Professor of Economics and Management, Emeritus
Gustavus Adolphus College
St. Peter, Minnesota

David Kane
Associate Professor of Business, Emeritus
Foothill College
Los Altos, California

VISIT US ON THE INTERNET
www.swep.com
www.thomsonlearning.com

Australia • Canada • Mexico • Singapore • Spain • United Kingdom • United States

Business Unit Director:	Peter D. McBride
Executive Editor:	Eve Lewis
Editor:	Timothy Bailey
Production Manager:	Patricia Matthews Boies
Manufacturing Manager:	Carol Chase
Manufacturing Coordinator:	Pam Wulf
Marketing Manager:	Mark Linton
Art & Design Coordinator:	Bill Spencer
Composition Services:	A. W. Kingston Publishing Services, LLC
Photo Credits:	All photos copyright PhotoDisc Inc. 1997-1999

ISBN: 0-538-69250-2

2 3 4 5 6 7 8 9 DR 08 07 06 05 04 03 02 01 00

PRINTED IN THE UNITED STATES OF AMERICA

For permission to use material from this text, contact us by

- Web: www.thomsonrights.com
- Phone: 1-800-730-2214
- Fax: 1-800-730-2215

PREFACE

For any businessperson whose daily activities involve working with written or printed communications, the ability to proofread and edit is most important. Proofreading and editing skills are critical for students, office workers, originators of documents, and other professional businesspeople who strive for excellence in their communications. Excellence is an attitude that must be developed. Excellence is accuracy, which is the most important standard in business.

Proofreading & Editing Precision, 4th Edition, is a comprehensive, activity-oriented text-workbook designed to sharpen proofreading and editing skills using hard copy (handwritten or printed) and computerized activities. It provides a thorough review of the rules governing language arts and document preparation and applies them in realistic business documents.

This text-workbook may be used effectively in any course that requires producing written communications. It may be used in courses including keyboarding, word/information processing, office procedures, business communications, or business English.

 SPECIAL FEATURES

Some of the special features in *Proofreading & Editing Precision,* 4th Edition, include the following:

- Full-color, engaging layout.
- A pretest and a posttest.
- Spotlight on Accuracy feature at the beginning of each chapter to highlight the importance of precision in written communications.
- E-mail activities integrated throughout.
- Tech Tips, provide guidance for composing documents on computer.
- Teamwork exercises identified throughout to build peer editing skills and foster collaborative learning.
- Foreign language proofreading exercises in new International Vocabulary activities.
- Cumulative Review Applications.
- Spelling and word usage reviews included in each chapter.
- A complete index.
- A list of proofreader marks for easy reference provided at the end of the text-workbook.

PREFACE

The Computerized Minisimulation has been completely revised for the 4th Edition. This Minisimulation provides practical, hands-on experience in proofreading, editing, and formatting. This optional activity consists of six business documents that are typically found in a business that utilizes the latest Internet technologies to conduct business. As an "employee," the student's responsibility is to proofread, edit, and format printed and online documents. The Minisimulation is divided into three parts, which gives students the option of completing the Minisimulation all at once, or in three stages.

CHAPTER PROFILE

Each chapter contains brief reviews of proofreading concepts in order of increasing difficulty. Concepts include keyboarding and spelling, word division, abbreviations, formatting business documents, sentence construction, punctuation, capitalization, number expression, and editing for errors in content, clarity, and conciseness. The last chapter in this edition is devoted exclusively to computer on-screen proofreading. This chapter includes information processing tools (spreadsheet, database, and voice recognition software) and e-mail.

To provide several opportunities for applying the principles reviewed in the chapter, each chapter includes the following:

- **Proofread and Mark.** These exercises immediately apply one rule or a short series of rules just presented.
- **Spelling and Word Usage Check.** A list of frequently misspelled words and three or four pairs of commonly misused words is given for identification and correction.
- **International Vocabulary:** A list of Spanish words for students to proofread. Students do not need to understand Spanish in order to complete these activities. Students will compare a list of correctly spelled Spanish words in the first column to a list of Spanish words that contain spelling errors in the second column. This is an excellent activity for building foreign language awareness as well as a means to focus students on the task of proofreading.
- **Proofreading Applications, Part A.** A business document is used to apply the concepts/rules covered within the chapter and in previous chapters.
- **Proofreading Applications, Part B.** Two realistic business documents are used to apply the concepts covered within the chapter and selected concepts from previous chapters.
- **Computerized Proofreading Applications.** This optional exercise consists of at least two business documents (on the Template CD-ROM) that provide extensive practice in loading, proofreading, formatting, and editing activities that occur in everyday business situations. This exercise also requires the printing, revising, and saving of documents. The first document was proofread and marked in Proofreading Applications, Part B. The other documents are new.

- **Cumulative Review Applications.** Five cumulative review exercises are interspersed throughout the text-workbook and are designed to provide additional practice and reinforcement in proofreading and editing.

SUPPLEMENTARY TEACHING AIDS

The following supplements are available to instructors for classroom use:

ANNOTATED INSTRUCTOR'S EDITION

The new Annotated Instructor's Edition (ISBN: 0-538-69252-9) provides the student edition in its entirety with answers overprinted to aid instruction and evaluation. Each chapter begins with a suggested completion time to aid in planning, and teaching suggestions are provided throughout the text as margin annotations.

In addition, the Annotated Instructor's Edition includes a suggested teaching schedule, evaluation and grading plans, quizzes for each chapter, a pretest and a posttest, and transparency masters. Solutions for all template CD activities, chapter quizzes, pretest, posttest, and the Computerized Minisimulation, are also included.

TEMPLATE CD-ROM

Word processing files for the documents in the Computerized Proofreading Applications are provided on the Template CD-ROM (ISBN: 0-538-69251-0) and are available for the following selected word/information processing software:

Windows: Word 6.0, Word97, WordPerfect 6.1, and Works 3.0

Mac: Word 6.0 and Works 3.0

ACKNOWLEDGMENTS

The authors extend thanks to the many instructors who have provided feedback and helpful suggestions for improving the content of *Proofreading & Editing Precision,* 4th Edition. Special thanks are extended to the following reviewers for their invaluable input in the preparation of the final manuscript:

- Jay Hutchinson, Nottingham High School, Hamilton, NJ
- Rochelle Kunkel, Kankakee Community College, Kankakee, IL
- Cathy Loftus, Toronto High School, Toronto, OH
- Dona Orr, College of Applied Technology, Boise State University, Boise, ID
- Katherine Ploeger, California State University Stanislaus, Turlock, CA
- Additional thanks are extended to Linda Barr (Business Writing Instructor, Otterbein College, Westerville, OH) who developed the Computerized Minisimulation for the 4th Edition.

CONTENTS

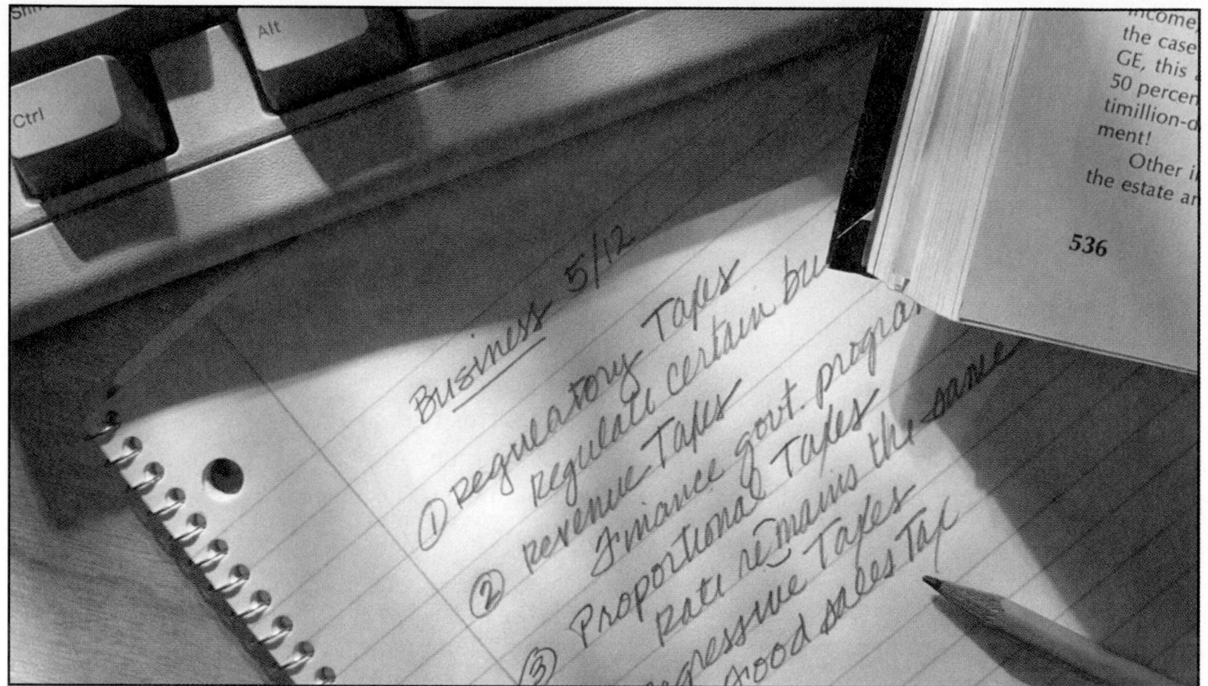

CHAPTER 1 Errors! Errors! Errors! 1

Importance of Proofreading **2** What Is Proofreading? **3** What Kinds of Errors Are Most Common? **4** Where Can a Proofreader Get Help? **6** Methods of Proofreading **6** What's Ahead? **8**

CHAPTER 2 Spelling Errors 9

Spelling Errors **10** Transposition Errors **10** Added Copy Errors **12** Incorrect Letters **13** Omitted Copy Errors **14** Numerical Errors **16** Spelling and Word Usage **17** Proofreading Applications **19** Computerized Proofreading Applications **23**

CHAPTER 3 Word Division Errors 25

The Nature of Word Division **26** Guidelines for Word Division **26** Proofreading Applications **34** Computerized Proofreading Applications **37**

Cumulative Review Applications No. 1 38

CHAPTER 4 Capitalization Errors 43

Capitalization **44** Proofreading Applications **51** Computerized Proofreading Applications **54**

CHAPTER 5 Abbreviation Errors and Rough Drafts 57

Abbreviations **58** Rough Drafts **63** Proofreading Applications **67** Computerized Proofreading Applications **70**

CHAPTER 6 Number Expression Errors 73

Numbers Expressed as Words **74** Numbers Expressed as Figures **76** ZIP Codes **78** Proofreading Applications **81** Computerized Proofreading Applications **87**

Cumulative Review Applications No. 2 89

CHAPTER 7 Sentence Construction Errors, Part 1 93

Sentence Structure **94** Sentence Fragments **96** Singular and Plural Nouns **97** Intervening Modifiers **98** Compound Subjects **99** Collective Nouns **100** Indefinite Pronouns **101** Proofreading Applications **105** Computerized Proofreading Applications **110**

CHAPTER 8 Sentence Construction Errors, Part 2 111

Pronoun and Antecedent Agreement **112** The Case of the Pronoun **115** Proofreading Applications **122** Computerized Proofreading Applications **126**

CHAPTER 9 Sentence Construction Errors, Part 3 127

Sentence Elements **128** Parallel Structure in Sentences **129** Dangling and Misplaced Modifiers **131** Bias-Free Language **132** Proofreading Applications **139** Computerized Proofreading Applications **144**

Cumulative Review Applications No. 3 145

CHAPTER 10 Comma Errors 147

The Importance of Punctuation Marks **148** The Comma **148** Other Comma Uses **154** Proofreading Applications **159** Computerized Proofreading Applications **162**

CHAPTER 11 Other Punctuation Errors 163

The Period, the Question Mark, and the Exclamation Mark **165** The Semicolon **166** The Colon **168** The Apostrophe **169** Underscoring and Italics **172** Quotation Marks **172** Proofreading Applications **175** Computerized Proofreading Applications **178**

Cumulative Review Applications No. 4 179

CHAPTER 12 Format Errors: Letters and Memos 183

Format **184** Letters **185** Interoffice Memorandums **196** Proofreading Applications **201** Computerized Proofreading Applications **204**

CONTENTS

CHAPTER 13 Format Errors: Reports and Job Search Documents 205

Reports **206** Job Search Documents **209** Proofreading Applications **216** Computerized Proofreading Applications **220**

CHAPTER 14 Editing for Content, Clarity, and Conciseness 223

What Is Editing? **224** Editing for Content **224** Editing for Clarity **228** Editing for Conciseness **232** Proofreading Applications **237** Computerized Proofreading Applications **242**

Cumulative Review Applications No. 5 243

CHAPTER 15 Proofreading and Editing on Computer 247

Introduction **248** On-Screen Proofreading **248** Information Processing Tools **250** Electronic Mail (E-Mail) **257**
Computerized Proofreading Applications **253**

Computerized Minisimulation: The Editor Online 261

Alternate Instructions for Computerized Proofreading Applications **273**

APPENDIX 275

Commonly Confused Words **275** Frequently Misspelled Words **277** Commonly Misspelled U.S. Cities **277** Spellings and Two-Letter Abbreviations of States and U.S. Territories **278** Letter Placement Guide and Report Formats **278**

Index 279
Proofreader Marks 281

CHAPTER 1

ERRORS ERRORS ERRORS!

Carl Sandburg urged care and caution in the use of words. What would life be like, he wondered, if we acted without a care for accuracy? Here are a few extreme examples of what life might be like if we were concerned with accuracy only 99.9 percent of the time:

- 50 newborn babies would be dropped at birth by doctors every day.
- 22,000 checks would be deducted from wrong bank accounts every hour.
- 16,000 pieces of mail would be lost by the U.S. Postal Service every hour.
- Two planes would not land safely at O'Hare International Airport in Chicago every day.

Source: Inc. Magazine, April 1989

Objectives

- Understand the importance of proofreading.
- Identify the most common types of errors when proofreading.
- Explain and apply the various methods of proofreading documents.
- Use reference sources to verify information when proofreading.

CHAPTER 1 ERRORS! ERRORS! ERRORS!

You receive a letter in the mail. You look at the envelope and what do you find? Errors! Your name is misspelled. Your house number is incorrect. Even your street name is misspelled. As if all that were not enough, your ZIP Code is wrong too. Wait! You still have to read the letter. You take a quick look and think to yourself, "Looks pretty good." Then you notice that "January" is spelled "J-a-n-a-r-y" and that the letter address is incorrect, just as it was on the envelope.

You wonder, "Why didn't someone proofread this letter? Who wrote this letter? Who signed the letter without first checking it for accuracy? What kind of employees does this company hire? Do I want to do business with this company?"

IMPORTANCE OF PROOFREADING

Documents that are error-free create a favorable impression. Letters that look attractive, contain no misspelled words, and use correct grammar and punctuation indicate to the reader that the sender is a competent person who is concerned about quality. The reader of such quality documents judges the individual to be a good person with whom he or she can conduct business.

On the other hand, errors reflect carelessness and incompetence. Most people are annoyed when their names are misspelled, even though they may not say so. Grammar errors, too, are very distracting, and the reader may assume that the sender is uneducated.

In business, people expect letters, memos, reports, and tables to have a certain "look." Readers expect documents to be prepared in a standard format, making them easy to read. Irregular formats are distracting because they cause the reader to think about how the letter looks rather than what it says.

Errors are inevitable. Everyone makes them. Errors can be found in all types of handwritten, keyed, and printed material. Errors occur in business letters, faxes, electronic mail, memorandums, reports, and other kinds of documents. Errors also occur in newspapers and in magazine headings, articles, and captions. Uncorrected errors are embarrassing; they may cause misunderstandings and confusion, and they may become expensive. Why? Errors cause delays in the delivery of goods or services. Apologies must be made when an incorrect price is quoted or an invoice total is wrong. Sometimes a phone call or follow-up message to explain how the error was made and how it will be corrected must be sent. All of these steps mean more time, more effort, and more expense. How the sender might wish he or she had taken the time to check for accuracy in the first place!

Today, computers, high-speed printers, and other electronic equipment enable documents to be produced faster than ever before. Form letters can be prepared for many people in an amazingly short period of time. If documents are not prepared correctly, however, this same equipment can produce errors just as quickly.

Accuracy is the most important standard in the business world. Businesses constantly seek qualified employees who pay attention to detail. Therefore, the ability to produce accurate documents is a necessity.

As a person who will soon be working in the business world, you must develop an attitude of excellence. You must not be satisfied until what you have produced is error-free. This means carefully checking names, numbers, dates, content, spelling, grammar, and punctuation. After all, you are responsible for the work that leaves your desk. Your image and that of the company depend on your ability to proofread well.

WHAT IS PROOFREADING?

Proofreading is the process of reading handwritten, keyed, or printed material and marking the errors to indicate the corrections that are required. Proofreading is thus essential to ensure the accuracy of your work.

As errors are identified, they are marked with special symbols called **proofreader marks**. Each symbol not only highlights the error but also indicates the correction to be made. Proofreader marks are standard symbols. They should be used by executives, managers, document specialists, and all other office workers who proofread and make corrections on an original document. The person who must make the corrections will then be able to interpret them accurately. The chapters in this text present the most common proofreader marks. A list of these also appears on the foldout at the back of this text.

Persons who are hired primarily to proofread are known as **proofreaders.** Proofreaders may also be responsible for setting format standards and training other office workers to follow the same standards.

Proofreading requires both knowledge and concentration. It demands patience and attention to detail. Information cannot be proofread by skimming. Many of us like to think that when we have finished composing or keying a document, it is correct. We say, "Well, I'll read it through quickly just in case I missed something." Or we might say, "I used the spell-check feature to search for errors, so I don't have to worry." Our task is not done, however, until we have carefully reread the document. Instead, we should say, "I know there is at least one error here; I just have to find it." In other words, we must develop the attitude that proofreading is vitally important in preparing documents.

Proofreading is an essential task that we need to take seriously. The more important the document, the more time we need to take proofreading to ensure accuracy. The best proofreaders are effective because they have these characteristics:

- **They pay attention to detail.**
- **They take time to proofread carefully.**
- **They recognize frequent types of errors.**
- **They use a variety of proofreading methods.**
- **They are good spellers.**
- **They know and apply the basics of good grammar and punctuation.**
- **They use appropriate reference materials to guarantee accuracy.**

WHAT KINDS OF ERRORS ARE MOST COMMON?

Errors may be classified as either mechanical or content. Because these are two very different kinds of errors, it is important to read the material once for mechanical errors and a second time for content errors. If the material is long and complex and has many numbers or other details, proofread the material a third time to ensure that all of the errors are found.

MECHANICAL ERRORS

Mechanical errors are those that can be recognized when looking at the material without specific reference to the meaning. These errors include transposition (reversing letters or words), capitalization, spacing, punctuation, and spelling errors. Can you find the mechanical errors in these three sentences?

1. Place thier agenda the in folder.

2. The color choices are red, blue and green

3. please send this to your assitant.

Proofreading for mechanical errors involves slow and careful reading. A proofreader card is an effective way to slow your rate of reading.

Concentrate on each detail. Carefully check each punctuation mark to be sure it is correct. Check capitalization and spelling. Check for correct number usage and word division.

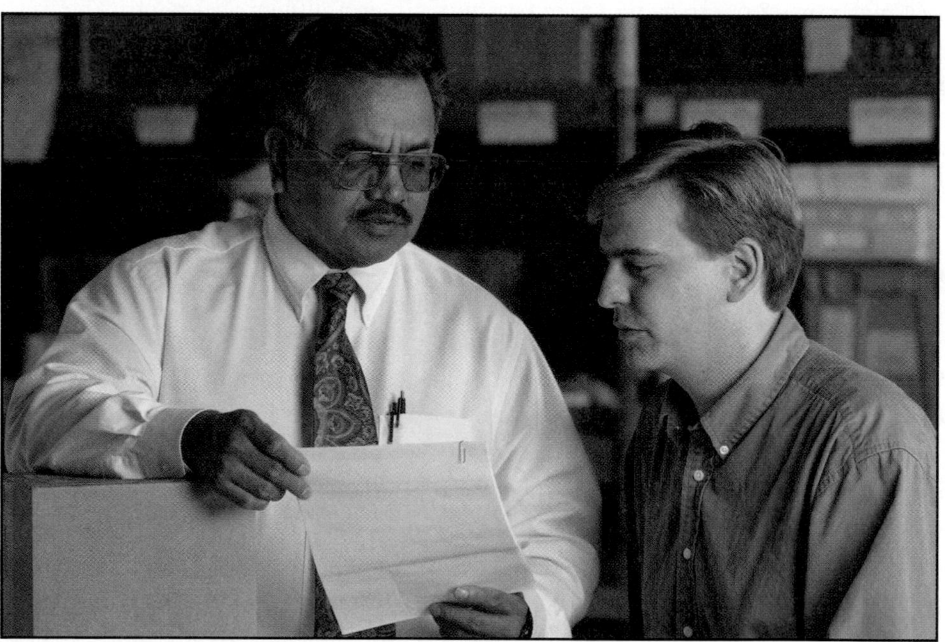

In sentence 1, *their* is misspelled, and the words *the* and *in* are reversed. In sentence 2, there should be a comma after *blue* and a period at the end of the sentence. In sentence 3, the first word should be capitalized, and the last word should be spelled *assistant*.

When proofreading for mechanical errors, slow your reading rate to "low gear." Read the copy letter by letter, word by word, phrase by phrase, or line by line, pronouncing each word as you read. Pronouncing each word forces you to slow your reading. It is the most effective way to proofread. Another procedure that can be used to slow down the reading rate is to place a proofreader card below the line that is being proofread. Figure 1-1 shows how a 3" × 5" card can be used as a proofreader card. To make a proofreader card, fold the card at the dashed line and place the top edge under the line you are reading. With a pen or pencil in the other hand, mark any errors you may locate.

Figure 1-1

Follow the instruction in this illustration to create your own proofreader card from a 3" × 5" card.

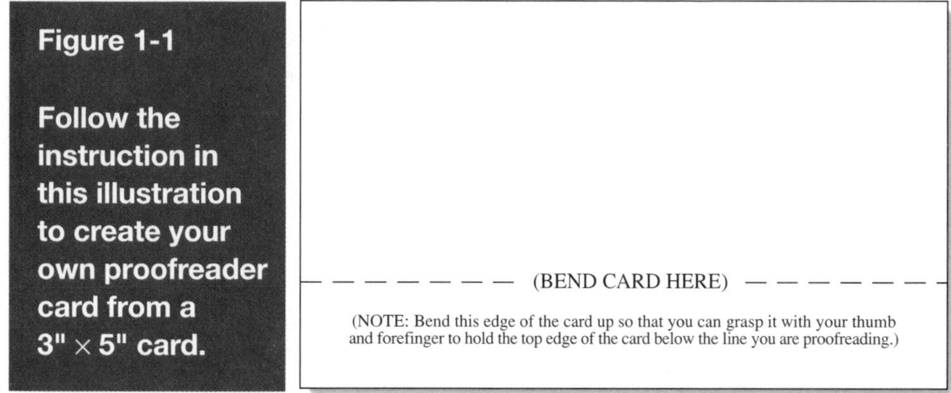

(BEND CARD HERE)
(NOTE: Bend this edge of the card up so that you can grasp it with your thumb and forefinger to hold the top edge of the card below the line you are proofreading.)

Another excellent proofreading technique is to read from right to left. This focuses attention on each word individually (checking for mechanical errors).

CONTENT ERRORS

Content errors are errors of information or fact. They are more difficult to locate than mechanical errors because, once information is in print, we tend to think of it as being correct. Content errors will cause confusion or misunderstanding.

To locate content errors, read the material much more slowly than your normal rate. Read complete sentences rather than reading word for word. Concentrate on the meaning of what you are reading. Ask yourself such questions as these:

- **Does it make sense?**
- **Are the facts accurate?**
- **Do I understand what the writer is trying to tell me?**
- **Do the subject and verb agree?**
- **Is there number agreement (singular versus plural)?**

When proofreading for content errors, particularly where there are dates, numbers, names, or other details or important facts in the copy, check the accuracy of the information against the original source. Always be ready to check references, such as those listed in the next section. Proofreading for content errors should be done at least twice, once for grammar errors and once for other content errors.

Can you find the content errors in the following sentences?

1. **The summer meeting in Des Moines will be on February 1.**
2. **On April 31 the tour will stop at Denver.**
3. **The flyers can be sent to the members which are orange.**

In sentence 1, a summer meeting in Des Moines would be in June or July. In sentence 2, the date is wrong because April has only *30* days, not 31. Sentence 3 needs a shifting of words because it sounds as if the members, not the flyers, are orange.

CHAPTER 1 ERRORS! ERRORS! ERRORS!

References are an invaluable aid to proofreaders.

WHERE CAN A PROOFREADER GET HELP?

A skillful proofreader does not simply rely on memory. Competent proofreaders verify facts and rules in a variety of sources. The first source should always be the copy from which the information was taken—the *original* source. The original source might include address files, price lists, sales receipts, vouchers, checkbook records, purchase orders, or invoices.

Use references such as these when you proofread:

- Atlases
- Calendars
- Dictionaries
- Office reference manuals
- Online reference works
- Spelling/word lists
- Statistical sources
- Thesauruses
- Word division guides

METHODS OF PROOFREADING

You can improve your proofreading by applying the methods described in this section. Use the first two methods when you are reading the material by yourself. Use the third method when you proofread with another person. Other helpful hints for proofreading are included in each chapter under the heading PEP (*P*roofreading and *E*diting *P*recision) TIPS.

COMPARATIVE PROOFREADING METHOD

The comparative proofreading method involves comparing one document with another. Follow these steps when using this method:

Step 1 Place the document to be proofread next to the original copy.

Step 2 Use a proofreader card under each line in the document as you proofread. At the same time, use another card to guide you through the second copy.

Step 3 Place the documents being compared as close to each other as possible. This decreases unnecessary eye and/or neck movement and allows for more accurate proofreading.

This method is especially useful when you proofread statistical or technical material that contains many numbers or specialized vocabulary, such as that found in medical, legal, or scientific material. This method can also be combined with the team method, which is explained later.

ON-SCREEN METHOD

When preparing documents on a microcomputer or word processor, you will need to proofread the documents before and after you print them. Follow these steps:

Step 1 Proofread on-screen once for mechanical errors and once for content errors. (Proofread sections of the document or one full screen at a time.)

Step 2 When proofreading for mechanical errors, move your cursor and carefully pronounce each word as you read.

Step 3 Hold a proofreader card directly on the screen under the line you are proofreading. Place another card under your original copy and compare word for word.

Step 4 Check for words that may have been omitted or added when copy was revised.

Step 5 Although most word processing software hyphenates words according to its built-in dictionary, check all the line endings for inaccuracies. Words are sometimes hyphenated in odd places. Also check to make sure that large gaps do not occur at the ends of lines because words have not been divided. Also check words that were hyphenated originally at the ends of lines but which are now in the middle of lines because of lengthy revisions that caused different word-wrapped paragraphs.

Step 6 If possible, spell-check your entire document from the beginning. (This procedure is discussed further in Chapter 2.)

Step 7 Print the document after you have proofread it.

Step 8 Using a proofreader card, reread the hard copy. It is sometimes easier to locate errors in hard copy than it is to find them on-screen.

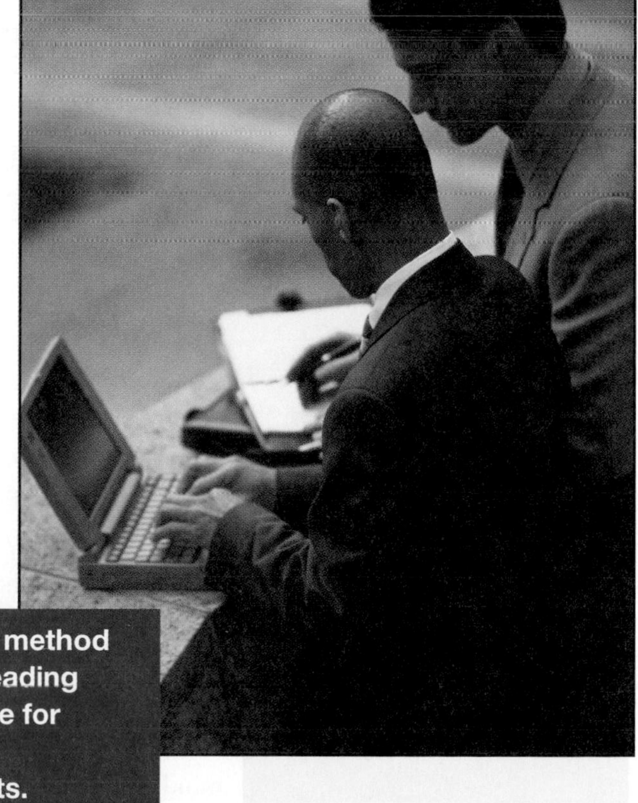

The team method of proofreading is effective for technical documents.

TEAM METHOD

As the name implies, the team method involves two persons. One person reads the draft or original copy aloud while another person follows along reading and marking the other copy. If the copy is quite long or complex, the two persons would take turns reading aloud and checking the copy. The team method is especially effective when checking the accuracy of technical or statistical copy or copy that has long lists, many names, or numbers. When using this method on lists of names, the readers *must* verify accuracy of spelling. The team method ensures that copy has been proofread carefully because two persons have checked it.

ERRORS! ERRORS! ERRORS!

✤ When proofreading for mechanical errors, read the material from right to left instead of the usual left-to-right method.

✤ Place a proofreader card, a ruler, or a piece of paper below the line you are reading. This will help slow your reading rate and focus your attention on the line you are reading.

WHAT'S AHEAD?

Beginning with Chapter 2, you will learn how to find specific kinds of errors and how to mark the errors using the correct proofreader marks. Errors will occur in spelling, word division, capitalization, number usage, punctuation, format, and content. You will also learn to make editing corrections.

Within each chapter, you will be introduced to several basic rules. You will then have an opportunity to test your understanding of the rules and to apply them in several ways:

- ***Proofread and Mark.*** Immediately following the introduction of specific rules, you will be asked to proofread in the context of short sentences.
- ***Spelling and Word Usage Check.*** Proofreading a special section in each chapter will help remind you of the correct spelling of ten commonly misspelled words as well as the use of commonly misused words.
- ***Proofreading Applications, Part A.*** You will proofread special documents that contain the types of errors introduced in the current chapter.
- ***Proofreading Applications, Part B.*** Each chapter will also contain two or more realistic business documents with proofreading errors. These errors may be from the current chapter or from preceding chapters.
- ***Computerized Proofreading Applications.*** A CD-ROM containing exercises similar to those in the Proofreading Applications is available. (Ask your instructor if you will be completing these exercises.) The purpose of these exercises is to provide additional proofreading and editing practice.
- ***Two or more documents are stored on the template CD.*** The first document will always relate to a document that you have already proofread within the chapter. A CD icon placed in the text will identify this document. The additional documents will be new documents that you have not proofread before. Specific directions are given within each chapter for completing these exercises.

As you complete the assignments in this text, read each item carefully. Keep in mind the importance of proofreading. With the proper attitude, you will succeed in developing good proofreading skills; and you will become a valuable, efficient, and productive employee.

CHAPTER 2

SPELLING ERRORS

If you are a bad speller, you may think you will always be a bad speller. There seems to be an exception to every rule, and the rules are not easy to remember. George Bernard Shaw demonstrated how ridiculous some spelling rules really are. By following these rules, he said, *fish* could be spelled *ghoti*. Pronouncing the "gh" as it sounds in enou<u>gh</u>, the "o" as it sounds in w<u>o</u>men, and the "ti" as it sounds in fic<u>ti</u>on would yield *fish*. With such rules to follow, no one should feel foolish for being a bad speller. The good news is that approximately 90 percent of all writing consists of 1,000 basic words, and that is a manageable number to learn.

Objectives

- Recognize transposition errors, added copy errors, omitted copy errors, incorrect letters, and numerical errors.
- Use appropriate proofreader marks to correct these errors.
- Spell correctly 12 frequently misspelled words.
- Use correctly 3 pairs of commonly misused words.

SPELLING ERRORS

The most frequent types of errors found in business documents are spelling errors. These errors result from either striking the wrong character on the keyboard or actually misspelling the word. Regardless of the cause, the proofreader's task is to locate the errors and indicate exactly what corrections are needed. In Chapter 2, you will learn to identify spelling errors that result from transpositions, additions of extra letters or spaces, omitted letters, and misstrokes.

To locate spelling errors, read very slowly, letter by letter. If the material has been keyed from another source, such as a handwritten document or a rough draft, use a proofreader card to check the final printed copy against the original copy. The card may also be used to proofread copy on the computer screen.

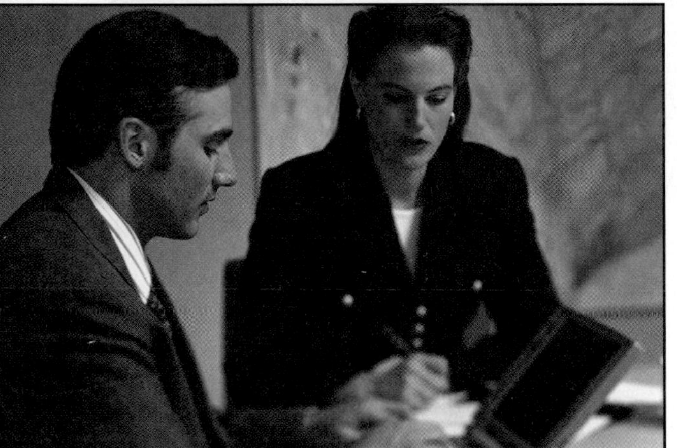

If you are using a word processing program equipped with a **spell-check** program, use it to check for spelling errors. The spell-check program compares each word in the document to the words in the program's electronic dictionary. Words that do not match the dictionary of the spell-check program are clearly marked on the screen. Although the spell-check program will identify errors such as *bisiness* or *oppertunity,* it will not recognize errors such as "when he *through* the ball" (should be *threw*) or "the third *addition* of the textbook" (should be *edition*). This is because some words are pronounced alike (called **homonyms**) but are spelled differently. In order to locate misused or inappropriate words, you must read the copy carefully.

TRANSPOSITION ERRORS

Letters, numbers, punctuation marks, words, or even sentences keyed out of order are called **transpositions**. Transpositions frequently occur in vowels (rec*ie*ve), short words (*adn*), and word endings (availab*el*). Letters that are adjacent on the keyboard, such as *r* and *t, v* and *b, n* and *m,* and *s* and *d,* are frequently transposed.

Sometimes transpositions result in words that look familiar. However, when the entire sentence is read for meaning, it becomes obvious that the word is used incorrectly. Careful proofreading is required to find transposition errors such as *form* for *from, board* for *broad, trail* for *trial, sacred* for *scared, sued* for *used, untied* for *united,* or *dairy* for *diary.*

To show any copy that is not in the correct sequence, use the transposition symbol. You should also write this symbol in the left or right margin of the document to alert the reader to an error in the line. Notice how the transposition symbol is used to mark errors in the following examples:

	MARKED COPY	CORRECTED COPY
Transpose (reverse order).	The handel is broken.	The handle is broken.
	"Start the meeting by noon".	"Start the meeting by noon."
	The report due is on Monday.	The report is due on Monday.

2-1

PROOFREAD AND MARK

Proofread these phrases for transposition errors. Use the transposition symbol to show corrections. If the phrase is correct, write **C** to the left of the number.

1. on Wedensday morning
2. quick answer is necesasry
3. the real prolbem
4. to be aware of the
5. frequent fylers
6. needless say to
7. a copy of the reciept
8. to cross street the

2-2

PROOFREAD AND MARK

Proofread the keyed copy for transposition errors by comparing it to the correct handwritten copy. Use the transposition symbol to show corrections. If the sentence is correct, write **C** to the left of the number.

1. Thank you for your response.	1. Thank you your for response.
2. The next meeting is in September.	2. The next meeting is ni September.
3. Call us before noon.	3. Call su before noon.
4. Our motto is "Friendly Service for All."	4. Our motto is "Freindly Service for All."
5. The committee meeting will be held on Tuesday.	5. The committee meeting be held on Tuesday.

ADDED COPY ERRORS

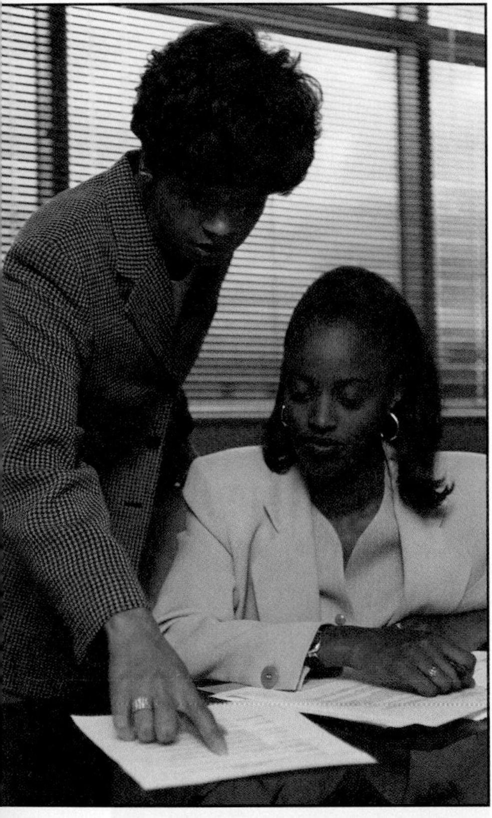

Another common spelling error is adding extra letters, spaces, numbers, or punctuation marks. Additions can be caused by faulty keying or by incorrect copying from the source document. Unnecessary words, phrases, and even sentences often occur in documents that have been composed and edited using a word processing software program. Writers may insert new text but fail to delete the old text. Similarly, when making changes in documents that have been printed on paper, writers often fail to cross out unwanted text.

As you proofread, be alert for the following added copy errors:

- **Words repeated at the beginning of a line (particularly small words such as *in, for, that, with, as*).**
- **Extra letters added in long words and words with double letters (*schedualed, immmediately, reccommend, tommorrow*).**
- **Words that may appear correct (singular vs. plural; homonyms) but are not because of an extra letter (office*s* for office, please for pleas, time*r* for time).**
- **Numbers repeated in a list.**
- **Phrases or an entire line of text repeated.**

When proofreading, use the delete symbol to show that the extra copy should be deleted and the close-up symbol to indicate that the extra space should be omitted. Use both the delete and close-up symbols when letters or characters should be deleted within a word.

	MARKED COPY	CORRECTED COPY
Delete or omit copy.	Purchase yourr supplies in Boston.	Purchase your supplies in Boston.
Close up space.	Hire four new employeees.	Hire four new employees.

2-3

PROOFREAD AND MARK

Proofread the following phrases for added copy errors. Use the delete and close-up symbols to show corrections. If the phrase is correct, write **C** to the left of the number.

1. an approppriate response

2. take a morning nap

3. some requirred reading

4. provided some an swers

5. discusssed the situation
6. a completed application
7. during our bussiness meeting
8. work with with the manager
9. lack of preparattion
10. one problems to settle

PROOFREAD AND MARK

Proofread the keyed copy for added copy errors by comparing it with the correct handwritten copy. Use the delete and close-up symbols to show corrections. If the sentence is correct, write **C** to the left of the number.

Handwritten copy	Keyed copy
1. Your tax return is due.	1. Your tax return is due.
2. Answer the customer's request.	2. Answer the cusstomer's request.
3. The decision by the faculty was final.	3. The deciscision by the faculty was final.
4. Preside over the meeting.	4. Preside over the the meeting
5. Clean the conference room.	5. Clean the conferrence room.

INCORRECT LETTERS

Keying an incorrect letter results in a misstroke. Misstrokes are easy to overlook in long words or in such words as "*q*uarantee" (incorrectly spelled with a *q*) for "*g*uarantee" (correctly spelled with a *g*). It would be easy to miss "chan*g*e" for "chan*c*e" because both of the words are spelled correctly. The meaning of the sentence determines which of the two words is correct. Proofread carefully for misstrokes in short words such as these:

o*f*, o*n*, o*r*	the*n*, the*m*, the*y*	th*a*n, th*e*n
no*t*, no*w*, n*e*w	th*e*se, th*o*se	

Use the straight diagonal line to mark a misstroke, and write the correct letter above the misstroke.

	MARKED COPY	CORRECTED COPY
Change letter. /	**It was a good opp**o/**ertunity.**	**It was a good opportunity.**

2-5

PROOFREAD AND MARK

Proofread the keyed copy for incorrect letters by comparing it with the correct handwritten copy. Use the straight diagonal line and proper letter to show corrections. If the sentence is correct, write **C** to the left of the number.

Handwritten copy	Keyed copy
1. Her name was added to the list.	**1.** Her name was added to the last.
2. She is our new manager.	**2.** She is our now manager.
3. Your help is sincerely appreciated.	**3.** Your help is sincerely apprediated.
4. Pay the insurance premium.	**4.** Pay the insurance primium.
5. They have increased their services.	**5.** They have increased their services.

OMITTED COPY ERRORS

Another common error is the omission of copy. Omissions occur whenever a space, character, or word is left out of a document. Entire lines and even entire sentences may also be omitted. Paired punctuation marks, such as brackets, parentheses, and quotation marks, are also common errors of omission.

Omissions of letters are common in long words, in words with silent letters (knowledg*e*able or temper*a*ment), and in words with double letters (o*cc*u*rr*ence or a*cc*o*mm*odate). Sometimes when you are scanning a document, the copy may appear to make sense, even though something has been omitted. An omission can change the meaning of copy—sometimes drastically. Note the difference an omission makes in the following examples:

OMISSION ERROR	CORRECT
under doctor's car	**under doctor's care**
send you response	**send your response**
sprig into action	**spring into action**
check their backround	**check their background**

To mark omission of spaces, use the space symbol (#).

To mark errors in omitted copy, use the caret symbol (^).

If space is limited, add the caret in the exact spot in the text where the omission occurs and write the insertion in the side margin. If several words must be added, and insufficient space is available in the side margin, write the copy in the top or bottom margin of the page and extend a line from the copy to the caret.

	MARKED COPY	CORRECTED COPY
insert space. #	# mail to/this address	mail to this address
Insert copy. ^	e premium is du^soon	premium is due soon
	the Be sure^coverage is ^extensive.	Be sure the coverage is extensive.
	job Your^application is done very well.	Your job application is done very well.

2-6 PROOFREAD AND MARK

Some of the following phrases have omitted copy errors. Use the appropriate proofreader marks to identify the corrections. If the phrase is correct, write **C** to the left of the number.

1. the eletion results
2. when you message arrives
3. the resulting conseqences
4. soon to be released
5. an interestng person

2-7 PROOFREAD AND MARK

Proofread the keyed copy for omitted copy errors by comparing it with the correct handwritten copy. Use the appropriate insert mark to identify the corrections that should be made. If the sentence is correct, write **C** to the left of the number.

1. Your evaluation has been scheduled for next month.	1. Your evaluation has been schedule for next month.

2. You will be recognized for your achievements on Friday.	2. You will be recognized for you achievements on Friday.
3. The advertisement will appear in Thursday's newspaper.	3. The advertisment will appear in Thusday's newspaper.
4. If you are able to attend, please let me know.	4. If you are able to attend, please let me know.
5. Factory orders will be increasing.	5. Factory ordrs will be incrasing.

NUMERICAL ERRORS

Accuracy of numbers is extremely important because many decisions are based on numerical data. Errors in dates, amounts of money, percentages, telephone numbers, social security numbers, and statistical copy can be very costly as well as embarrassing. Transposition of numbers is a very common numerical error. Similarly, errors within listed items occur frequently, particularly as items are added to or omitted from a list.

Never assume that a number is correct. In fact, check all numbers twice. If a number has been copied from another source, check to be sure that it has been copied correctly. Verify all extensions and totals. Proofread numbers digit by digit. For example, read the number *1994* as "one-nine-nine-four" instead of "nineteen ninety-four." If numbers are to be spelled out and also written in figures, as required in many legal documents, check to be sure that both numbers are the same; for example, six months (6 months). Finally, check your calendar to make sure the day agrees with the date listed. Is the correct date Friday, May 5 or Thursday, May 5?

2-8

PROOFREAD AND MARK

Proofread the keyed copy for numerical errors by comparing it with the correct handwritten copy. Use the appropriate proofreader marks to show corrections. If the sentence is correct, write **C** to the left of the number.

1. The exam will have 35 questions.	1. The exam will have 53 questions.
2. Send a check for $139.52 with your order.	2. Send a check for $39.52 with your order.

3. His office telephone number is 555-7089.	3. His office telephone number is 555-7098.
4. only 9 percent volunteered immediately.	4. Only 29 percent volunteered immediately.
5. Her address is P.O. Box 1327.	5. Her address is P.O. Box 1327.

2-9

PROOFREAD AND MARK

Mark any errors in the keyed list by comparing it with the correct handwritten list. Use the appropriate proofreader marks to show corrections. If the list is correct, write **C** to the left of the number.

1. Carrie C. Wilson, No. 53118	1. Carriee C. Wilson, No. 531188
2. Doug E. Johnsson, No. 873241	2. Doug E. Johnsson, No. 873241
3. Michael Watermann, No. 318661	3. Michail Waterman, No. 381661
4. Kris R. Braun, No. 9733332	4. Kriss R. Braun, No. 973332
5. Roger C. Everyman, No. 35826	5. Rogre C. Everyman, No. 358362

SPELLING AND WORD USAGE

Misspellings are a distraction to the reader. They are embarrassing to the writer and reflect negatively on the company. Learning to recognize these errors is critical to being a good proofreader. Develop the habit of checking a dictionary or spelling guide whenever you are unsure of a word. If you are using word processing software, use the spell checker provided with your software. Remember, the spell check program will miss words that are spelled correctly but used improperly. To find these errors, you will need to use the spell checker in addition to carefully reading your document.

The Appendix of this text contains a list of frequently misspelled words and another list of commonly confused words. To strengthen your ability to spell these words correctly, twelve spelling words and three groups of confusing words will be included in the Spelling and Word Usage Check section of each chapter. In addition, these words will be applied in Proofreading Applications, Part A, at the end of each chapter.

✣ Check short words, such as *of*, *on*, *or*, *an*, and *at*, for possible misstrokes.

✣ Proofread numbers carefully for transposition errors.

✣ Check for repetition of words and/or repetition of numbers in a list.

✣ Check separately for errors in numbers, dates, technical information, and names of people.

✣ When using any word processing software, always use the spell checker. Remember, using your spell checker is only one step in proofreading. You must also read each word carefully to make sure you intended to use that specific word.

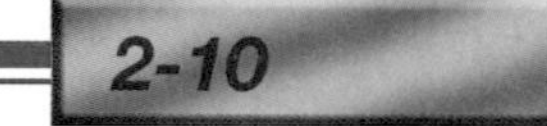

2-10

SPELLING AND WORD USAGE CHECK

Compare the words in Column A with the corresponding words in Column B. One of the words is spelled or used incorrectly. Use the appropriate proofreader marks to correct the misspelled or misused words. If both words are correct, write **C** to the left of the number.

	Column A	Column B
Ex.	adn	and
1.	writing	writting
2.	potencial	potential
3.	addressed	adressed
4.	participate	participate
5.	oppertunity	opportunity
6.	electrical	electricle
7.	participants	particpants
8.	confrence	conference
9.	appreciate	apperciate
10.	guarantee	quarantee
11.	institutoin	institution
12.	responsibel	responsible
13.	Further discussion is needed.	It is further than I thought.
14.	You're contract is ready to be signed.	You're the only one qualified.
15.	See their test scores.	Place it over their.

PROOFREADING APPLICATIONS PART A

2-11

PARAGRAPHS

Proofread the following paragraphs to locate spelling and word usage errors. Use the appropriate proofreader marks to show the corrections.

Among the many profesional organizations is the Associated Writers of America. This is ann organization for persons who are keenly interested in writing as a profession and as a hobby. Two major events for the AAW are its annual national convention and its special fall conference, whih features presentations of information for both current and potenttial writers.

The confrence is held in a different city each year with arrangements worked out by the AWA conference mamager. He or she will work out details to quarantee that all persons attending the conference will have the oppotrunity to participate in a number of meetings.

At the last conference, the particpants were addressed by a writer whose major occupation is serving as president of an electricle company. His talk on the struggled to perfect his writing style helped many in the audience apppreciate the challenge of good writing.

If you are intrested in becoming a part of this group and in attending any of its regional or national conferences, simply watch your newspaper for infomration on where to join.

PROOFREADING APPLICATIONS PART B

2-12

BUSINESS LETTER

Proofread the letter for spelling errors. Correct the errors using the appropriate proofreader marks.

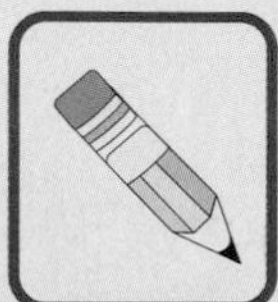

Writers Supplies, Inc.
Suite 47—Hibbard Building
349 West Grandview Drive
Des Moines, Iowa 50313-1298
Phone: 515/555-3883 • Fax: 515/555-3885

Septebmer 23, 20—

Ms. Janet R. Jameson, Chair
National Convention Commitee
Assocaited Writers of America
3462 West Grant Avenue
Omaha, NE 68111-1742

Dear Ms. Jameson:

Yes, we except your invitation to particpate as an exhibitor at your June convention. We have been a strong beleiver in the work of the AAW and its many proffessional activities.

Thank you for sending a copy if the layout for the exhhibits area. We prefer to have the two booths numbered 32 and and 34 by the north entrance to teh hall with one double electricle outlet.

Would you send us a price list of boothe supplies so that we can place our order as soon as possible. The list should be sent to the ofifce adress given above by fax or by regular mail. Also, would you let us know to whom our payment should be snet. An adressed envelope is enclosed for your convienience.

Sincerely,

Connie Brown, Manger
Sales and Marketing

tbe
Enclosure

2-13

MEMO

Proofread and mark the spelling errors in the following memo.

Writers Supplies, Inc., Memorandum

DATE: September 23, 20--

TO: Department Heads

FROM: Connie Brown, Sales and Mraketing

SUBJECT: Booth Exhibit at AWA Convention

Janet Jameson, chair of the AWA Convention Committee, has invited us to display some of our porducts next summer at there national convention. It will be held on June 21-22-23 in the Civic Center. Attendance is expected to exceed 1,000 participants.

Please prepare a breif e-mail outlining what items you would like to see on display. It will be a grate oppertunity to meet potencial customers and to display the items we have abailable.

Let us plan to meet on Otcober 8 at 10 a.m. in Confrence Room Room 32 to talke over our plans.

tbe

2-14

E-MAIL

Proofread and mark the spelling erros in the following e-mail.

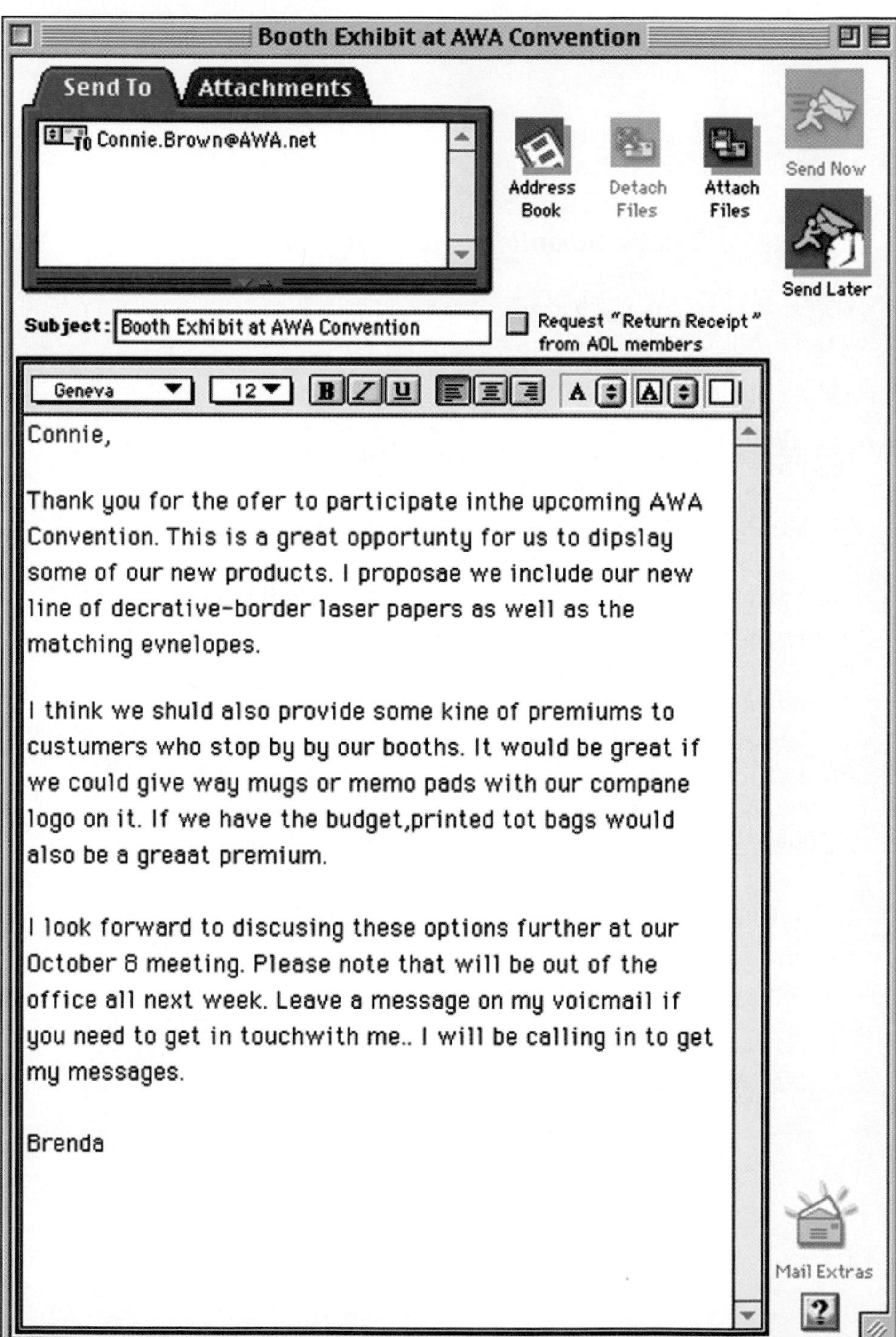

Booth Exhibit at AWA Convention
Send To
Attachments
Connie.Brown@AWA.net
Address Book
Detach Files
Attach Files
Send Now
Send Later
Subject: Booth Exhibit at AWA Convention
Request "Return Receipt" from AOL members
Geneva
12
Connie,
Thank you for the ofer to participate inthe upcoming AWA Convention. This is a great opportunty for us to dipslay some of our new products. I proposae we include our new line of decrative-border laser papers as well as the matching evnelopes.
I think we shuld also provide some kine of premiums to custumers who stop by by our booths. It would be great if we could give way mugs or memo pads with our compane logo on it. If we have the budget,printed tot bags would also be a greaat premium.
I look forward to discusing these options further at our October 8 meeting. Please note that will be out of the office all next week. Leave a message on my voicmail if you need to get in touchwith me.. I will be calling in to get my messages.
Brenda
Mail Extras

COMPUTERIZED PROOFREADING APPLICATIONS

2-15

BUSINESS LETTER

1. Load file CPA2-15 from the TMPL02 subdirectory on your template CD. (This is a computer copy of Application 2-12.)
2. Proofread the letter on the screen (use a proofreader card). Correct all errors on the screen copy that you have indicated with proofreader marks in Application 2-12.
3. Format the letter with 1-inch side margins and the date on line 15.
4. Save the letter to your hard drive or to a separate diskette using the same file name.
5. Print the letter.
6. Proofread the printed document. If you find any additional mistakes, correct the errors on both the hard copy and the screen.
7. Save the revised document and print it.

2-16

BUSINESS LETTER

1. Load file CPA2-16 from the TMPL02 subdirectory on your template CD.
2. Proofread the letter on the screen by comparing it with the correct handwritten letter that follows.
3. Correct all mistakes.
4. Put the date on line 15.
5. Save the letter using the same file name.
6. Print the letter with 1-inch side margins.
7. Proofread the hard copy. If you find any additional mistakes, correct the errors on both the hard copy and the screen.
8. Save the revised document and print it.

November 8, 20--

Mr. Alfred Price, Sales
Acme Computers, Inc.
372 North Washington Road
St. Louis, MO 63102-4772

Dear Mr. Price:

Associated Writers of America has asked us to have an exhibit at its national convention next summer. We have accepted the invitation and now are putting together a list of items that we will be using for the booth.

Because of the popularity and increasingly widespread use of the new version of Grammaretics 4U, we would like your assistance with part of the display. We want to have information about that software program available for those who might stop at our booth.

Would you send me a list of what you can have for us. An addressed envelope is enclosed for your speedy reply.

Sincerely,
Connie Brown, Manager
Sales and Marketing

tbe
Enclosure

CHAPTER 3

WORD DIVISION ERRORS

The following headlines were reported in *The Working Communicator* under "Humorous headlines and other laughing matters." How would you rewrite these headlines to make them more readable?

- Police begin campaign to run down jaywalkers (reported on the Internet, source unknown)
- Study: Doctors keep dying alive against their wishes (from *The Des Moines Register*)
- Cold wave linked to temperatures (reported on the Internet, source unknown)

Source: *The Working Communicator* is published by Lawrence Ragan Communications, Inc., 212 West Superior, Chicago, IL 60610.

Objectives

- Apply word division rules.
- Recognize hyphenation errors.
- Use appropriate proofreader marks to correct hyphenation errors.
- Spell correctly 12 frequently misspelled words.
- Use correctly 3 pairs of commonly misused words.

CHAPTER 3 WORD DIVISION ERRORS

THE NATURE OF WORD DIVISION

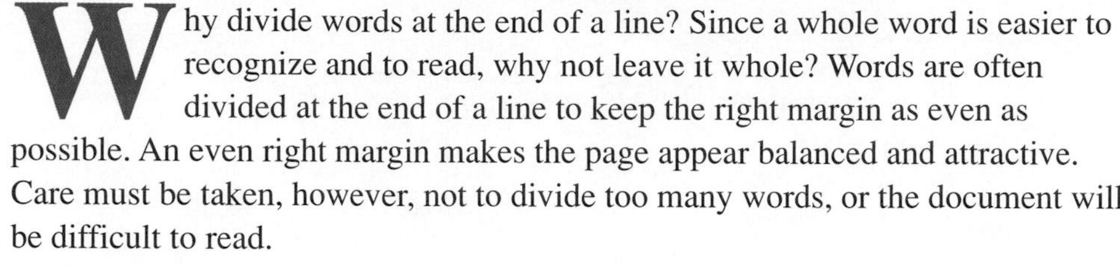

Why divide words at the end of a line? Since a whole word is easier to recognize and to read, why not leave it whole? Words are often divided at the end of a line to keep the right margin as even as possible. An even right margin makes the page appear balanced and attractive. Care must be taken, however, not to divide too many words, or the document will be difficult to read.

The use of word processing software has made the task of word division easier and faster. Most word processing software has a special feature called **automatic hyphenation**. This feature automatically finds words that break at the end of a line and hyphenates them between syllables. However, automatic hyphenation may result in undesirable breaks. Thus, even when using this feature, word divisions must be checked carefully to ensure accuracy.

If text has been entered with the automatic hyphenation feature turned off, words that do not fit completely on one line are **wrapped** or moved to the next line. But, the **wraparound mode** may result in an extremely ragged and unattractive right margin. To fix this, the operator may manually divide end-words in the appropriate places or use the justification method, which adjusts each line to meet the right margin. Regardless of the software used, an efficient proofreader should carefully check each document for the following:

- **Errors in word division.**
- **Excessive word division.**
- **Extremely ragged right margin (indicating insufficient word division).**

GUIDELINES FOR WORD DIVISION

Every office worker (the originator, document specialist, word processor, administrative specialist, proofreader, or anyone else who is responsible for producing business documents) should know and apply the basic rules of word division. While studying the specific word division rules, keep in mind these simple guidelines:

1. **Use a hyphen to show where a word should be divided.**
2. **Always divide words between syllables.**
3. **If necessary, use a dictionary to determine the correct syllabication.**
4. **Leave as much of the word as possible at the end of a line before dividing. This makes the word easier to identify.**
5. **Do not divide words at the end of more than two consecutive lines.**
6. **Never divide the last word of a paragraph or the last word of a page.**

As you review the word division rules in this chapter, you will note that some rules state "avoid dividing." This means that though it may be permissible to divide a word at a certain point, it is not recommended. Such words have both acceptable and preferred division points. For example, it is acceptable to divide *external* after *ex-*; however, the preferred division point is *exter-*, which allows the reader to more easily identify the word.

While proofreading, use the insert hyphen symbol to indicate the division of a word. If a word has been incorrectly divided, use the delete and close-up symbols as shown here.

	MARKED WORD	HYPHENATED WORD
=/ Insert hyphen. /=	pro/duc/tion	pro- duc- tion
	crit/i-cal	crit- ical
	quar/t-er	quar- ter

Note: The examples given in each of the rules in this chapter appear in three columns. In the first column, the correct syllabication of the word is given. The appropriate proofreader mark(s) is used to divide the word in the second column. The third column shows the correct division according to the rule being applied.

Rule 1 Divide a word only between syllables. A one-syllable word cannot be divided.

SYLLABICATION	MARKED WORD	HYPHENATED WORD
mem o ry	mem/o/ry	mem- o- ry
pho to graph	pho/to/graph	pho- to- graph
called	—	called
thought	—	thought

Rule 2 Do not divide a word with five or fewer letters. Avoid dividing a word with six letters.

SYLLABICATION	MARKED WORD	HYPHENATED WORD
pow er	—	power
cit y	—	city
lo cate	—	locate
of fice	—	office

WORD DIVISION ERRORS

3-1

PROOFREAD AND MARK

If a word is divided correctly, write **C** to the left of the number. If a word is divided incorrectly or in a manner that is not preferred, use the appropriate proofreader marks to correct the division.

1. inspec- tion
2. pro- mise
3. de- vice
4. fly- ing
5. con- struct- ion
6. laugh
7. fer- ry
8. fam- i- liar
9. pro- minent
10. later

Rule 3 At least two letters must appear at the *end* of a line (*in-* crease) and at least three letters must appear at the *beginning* of the next line (larg- *est*, but not larg-*er*).

Note: Although it is acceptable to divide after a two-letter syllable at the beginning of a word (*re-* pairing), it is better to avoid doing so (*repair-* ing).

SYLLABICATION	MARKED WORD	HYPHENATED WORD
in ter cept	inter/cept	inter- cept
sym pho ny	sym/phony	sym- phony
a bided	—	abided
cen ter	—	center

Rule 4 Generally, divide between double consonants. However, when the root word ends in double consonants and a suffix is added to the word, divide between the root word and the suffix.

Note: A **consonant** is any letter of the alphabet other than a vowel. A **root word** is the base word. A **suffix**, usually of one syllable, is the ending that is added to the base word.

SYLLABICATION	MARKED WORD	HYPHENATED WORD
har ass ment	harass/ment	harass- ment
suc cess ful	success/ful	success- ful
call ing	call/ing	call- ing
con fess ing	confess/ing	confess- ing

Rule 5 Divide between double consonants when the final consonant of the root word is doubled before adding a suffix.

SYLLABICATION	MARKED WORD	HYPHENATED WORD
ad mit tance	**admit/tance**	**admit- tance**
pro gram ming	**program/ming**	**program- ming**
con trol ling	**control/ling**	**control- ling**

3-2

PROOFREAD AND MARK

If a word is divided correctly, write **C** to the left of the number. If a word is divided incorrectly or in a manner that is not preferred, use the appropriate proofreader marks to correct the division.

1. ambi- tious
2. en- forcement
3. en- during
4. garden- er
5. guard- ed
6. i- magine
7. dres- sing
8. profes- sional
9. suppres- sing
10. ball- oon

Rule 6 Divide after a single-vowel syllable except when the single-vowel syllable is followed by the ending *ble*, *bly*, *cle*, or *cal*.

SYLLABICATION	MARKED WORD	HYPHENATED WORD
pos i tive	**posi/tive**	**posi- tive**
res o nance	**reso/nance**	**reso- nance**
log i cal	**log/ical**	**log- ical**
lov a ble	**lov/able**	**lov- able**

Rule 7 Divide between two single-vowel syllables when each of the two vowels is pronounced separately.

SYLLABICATION	MARKED WORD	HYPHENATED WORD
sit u a tion	**situ/ation**	**situ- ation**
e val u a tion	**evalu/ation**	**evalu- ation**
hu mil i a tion	**humili/ation**	**humili- ation**

WORD DIVISION ERRORS

Rule 8 Divide compound words between the words. If the compound word is hyphenated, the only acceptable point of division is *after* the hyphen. In such cases, use the diagonal mark without the hyphen symbol.

	MARKED WORD	HYPHENATED WORD
Insert diagonal mark. /	self-/control	self- control
Insert diagonal mark & hyphen. /=	tax/=free	tax- free
	senator/=elect	senator- elect

Note: A **compound word** is made up of at least two words and may be written as one word (*somewhere*) or as a hyphenated word (*self-concept*). Check a dictionary if you are unsure about the correct spelling.

COMPOUND WORD	MARKED WORD	HYPHENATED WORD
side line	side/= line	side- line
steam roll er	steam/= roller	steam- roller
chair per son	chair/= person	chair- person

The Word command for a nonbreaking space is as follows: **Control + Shift + Spacebar = Nonbreaking space.** The WordPerfect command for a hard space is as follows: **Control + Spacebar = Hard Space.**

3-3

PROOFREAD AND MARK

If a word is divided correctly, write **C** to the left of the number. If a word is divided incorrectly or in a manner that is not preferred, use the appropriate proofreader marks to correct the division.

1. grad- uate
2. ad- amant
3. legit- imate
4. exten- uating
5. criti- cal
6. remark- able
7. hand- icap
8. horserad- ish
9. self- rule
10. affilia- tion

Rule 9 Do not divide abbreviations, numbers, contractions, acronymns (initials that represent words), times, or units of measure (a number with a descriptive word). Units of measure must always be written together.

mdse.	UNICEF	15-ft. board
9.25 percent	7 1/2 lb.	6 min.
couldn't	8 kg	C.A.R.E.
Flight 12	10:15 a.m.	No. 10

Rule 10 Avoid dividing proper names, titles, addresses, or dates. If it is necessary to divide these elements, choose a logical point that will give the best readability.

RULE	EXAMPLE
Divide before a surname (or after the middle initial if it is used).	**Carl T. Santos**
Divide between the city and state, not between the state and the ZIP Code.	**Green Bay, Wisconsin**
	San Diego, CA 92110-2134
Divide dates between the day and the year.	**April 15, 20--**
Divide between parts of a city name.	**Santa Barbara**

3-4

PROOFREAD AND MARK

Divide each of the following elements at the most logical point. Use only the diagonal mark to show the divisions. If an element cannot be divided, write **C** to the left of the number.

1. Dr. Carmen R. Delgado
2. hasn't
3. 18 lb.
4. Michiko Yoshikawa
5. SADD
6. September 19, 20--
7. Whitewater, Wisconsin
8. $379,390.92
9. Carbondale, IL 62901-2464
10. Colin DeLoye

✤ As a final step in proofreading a page, read down the right margin to check the hyphenation of all divided words

✤ Use word division sparingly. Some companies and individuals prefer that certain business documents not be hyphenated.

✤ Unless a hard space is used to keep certain words, phrases, numbers or abbreviations together, they may separate when text is added or deleted. Double-check that these words are not separated.

✤ It may be appropriate to use the team method of proofreading when proofreading highly technical or complicated documents. See chapter 1 for proofreading methods.

3-5

SPELLING AND WORD USAGE CHECK

Compare the words in Column A with the corresponding words in Column B. Use the appropriate proofreader marks to correct the misspelled or misused words. If both columns are correct, write **C** to the left of the number.

	Column A	Column B
Ex.	calendar	calender (e marked out, a written above)
1.	substancial	substantial
2.	desirable	desireable
3.	hesatate	hesitate
4.	received	recieved
5.	offerred	offered
6.	design	designe
7.	separate	separate
8.	enclosed	inclosed
9.	maintanance	maintenance
10.	mortgage	moregage
11.	industriel	industrial
12.	transportation	transportacion
13.	Ask Tai to advise us.	I was advized not to go.
14.	It is too expensive.	I want too go too.
15.	This movie effected me.	The call affected her.

3-6

INTERNATIONAL VOCABULARY

Compare the Spanish words in Column A with the corresponding words in Column B. If the word or phrase in Column B is different from the word or phrase in Column A, use the appropriate proofreader marks to correct Column B. If the words in both columns are the same, write **C** to the left of the number.

Column A	Column B
1. desocupado	desocpado
2. inquilino	inquilano
3. financiamiento	financiamiento
4. pedir prestado	pedur prestado
5. domicilio	domisilio
6. alfombra	alfobbra
7. propiedad	propidad
8. terrateniente	teranteniente
9. mercar	mercir
10. desventaja	desvintija

CHAPTER 3

WORD DIVISION ERRORS

PROOFREADING APPLICATIONS — PART A

3-7

WORD DIVISION LIST

*Proofread the words in each line. If one or more words are divided incorrectly, correct the word(s) using the appropriate proofreader marks. Then write the word(s) on the blank line using hyphen(s) to show **all preferred points of division**. If all three words in a line are correct, write **C** on the blank line.*

Ex.	lit- tle	repre- sent	admis- sible	little
1.	stop- ping	corp- oration	worth- while	______
2.	reached	compari- son	deve- lopment	______
3.	mort- gage	collect- ible	infat- uation	______
4.	sep- arate	protec- tion	they'll	______
5.	pho- tograph	touched	for- gotten	______
6.	prefer- ence	curric- ulum	cooper- ated	______
7.	posses- sing	prepa- ration	gas- oline	______
8.	bro-therhood	immedi- ately	pros- ecute	______
9.	compari- son	sister- in-law	mainten- ance	______
10.	suf- ficient	assim- ilate	cons- cious	______
11.	bright- ly	embarrass- ing	tech- nical	______
12.	commit- tee	elec- trical	pharm- acy	______
13.	sche- dule	favor- ably	hasn't	______
14.	practi- cal	trespas- sed	typ- ical	______
15.	height	referr- ed	bull- etin	______
16.	desira- ble	bene- factor	cler- ical	______
17.	bil- lion	im- itation	custo- mary	______
18.	extenu- ating	clarif- ication	reason- able	______
19.	cross- filing	pass- ing	chron- icle	______
20.	brit- tle	human- power	subs- tantial	______

PROOFREADING APPLICATIONS PART B

3-8

NEWSPAPER ADVERTISEMENT

Using the appropriate proofreader marks, proofread and correct all errors in spelling and word division.

ONCE UPON A TIME ...
THEY LIVED HAPPILY EVERY AFTER.

Make your dream come true.

You have a change to own your dream house at Paradise Valley with sensational close-out prices offerred.

So . . . let us help you make your dream come true. And we'll guarantee you'll live happily ever after. Come see these custom-desinged homes today!

Buy one of the last availa-
ble homes now, and we'll give you a $5,000 SPECIAL BONUS for you to use in any way you cho-
ose, like upgrades in flooring, appliances, decorative options, or closeing costs.

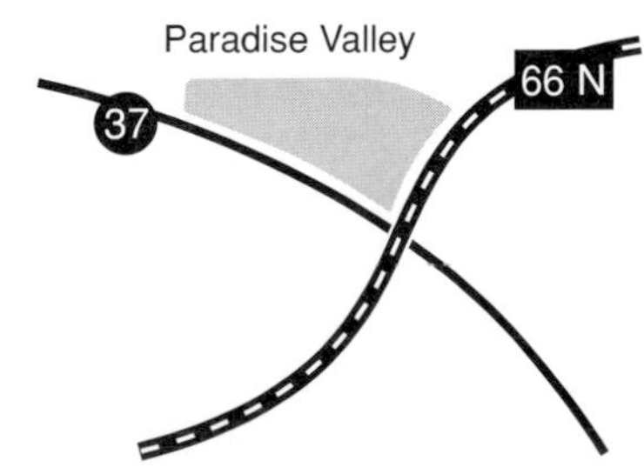

3-9

BUSINESS FLYER

Using the appropriate proofreader marks, proofread and correct all errors in spelling and word division.

ADVISE TO TENANTS . . . DON'T BE SHY.

If you are looking for an apartment to rent, don't be afraid too
appraoch the property managers or landlords and ask some hard
questions. Their answers may effect not only your pocketbook but
also your happiness. In other words, if you want to be happy where
you live, demand what you want. You'll be pleasantly surp-
rised how much you can recieve. After all, you have everything
to gain and nothing to loose. Right?

Here are a few tips that property managers advice today's renter.

⁜ Ask how long the unit has been vacant. If the unit has been
vacant longer than 30 days, you might lower the rent if you barg-
ain with your landlord.

⁜ Ask how long the former tenants were their and how much they
paid in rent. If they rented for more than a year, you may be
able to negotiate and recieve a reduction in rent.

⁜ Don't hesatate to ask for upgrades such as new carpet, new
drapes, or blinds. Offer to paint if is it provided.

⁜ If your'e already renting and would like to stay where you
are, ask for a price cut or some upgrades. It's much more pro-
fitable for your landlord to lower your rent then two look for a
new tennant.

⁜ Be sure that whoever is giving away the most is offerring you
the best deal.

COMPUTERIZED PROOFREADING APPLICATIONS

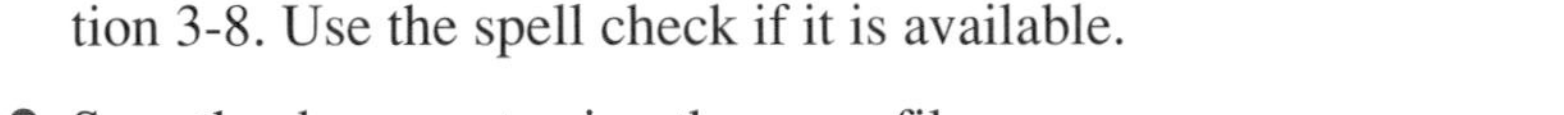

3-10

BUSINESS FLYER

1. Load file CPA3-10 from the TMPL03 subdirectory on your template CD. (This is a computer copy of Application 3-9.)
2. Proofread the flyer on the screen (use a proofreader card). Correct all errors on the screen copy that you have indicated with proofreader marks in Application 3-8. Use the spell check if it is available.
3. Save the document using the same file name.
4. Print the flyer with 1-inch side margins.
5. Proofread the printed document. If you find any additional mistakes, correct the errors on both the hard copy and the screen.
6. Save the revised document and print it.

3-11

BUSINESS LETTER WITH TABLE

1. Load file CPA3-11 from the TMPL03 subdirectory on your template CD.
2. Proofread the letter and make all necessary corrections using the appropriate proofreader marks.
3. Put the date on line 15.
4. Save the document using the same file name.
5. Print the letter with 1-inch side margins.
6. Proofread the hard copy and mark all additional errors.
7. Correct the errors on the screen copy.
8. Save the revised document and print it.

3-12

E-MAIL MESSAGE

1. Load file CPA3-12 from the TMPL03 subdirectory on your template CD.
2. Proofread the e-mail message on screen and make all necessary corrections.
3. Save the document using the same file name.
4. Print the e-mail message.
5. Proofread the printed document. Did you find errors on the printout that you did not find when you proofread the e-mail on screen? Correct any additional errors you found in file CPA3-12.
6. Save the revised document and print it.

CRA1-1

BUSINESS LETTER

Proofread and correct all errors using the appropriate proofreader marks.

HJ Properties
101 North Fountain Parkway
Davison, MI 48858-1015
(313) 555-0028 Fax (313) 555-4661

July 17, 20––

Mr. & Mrs. Bradley Foster III
6593 Rosebud Aveneu
Davison, MI 48423-0039

Dear Mr. & Mrs. Forster

Thank you for stopping at HJ Properties and giving us the opportunity to show you of some of the available properties in Paradise
Valley.

I have contacted the owners of the property you are interested
in purchasing and have offerred them your price quotation of
$242,500. They were pleased and will call tommorrow to let me
know whether or not they will accept your price or make a coun-
teroffer. If they do not call me, I will call them for a defanite
committment.

In the meantime, you may be interested in looking at other attractive properties listed on the inclosed flyer. Call me if you
wish to see some of these homes. We can set up appointments to
veiw them.

Sincerely

Clayton R. Sierra
Residencial Properties Specialist

kj
Encolsure

CRA1-2

FOUR-PAGE MANUSCRIPT

TEAM WORK

Proofread and correct all errors using the appropriate proofreader marks.

CHECKLISTS FOR FIRST-TIME HOME BUYERS:

WISE PLANNING PAYS!

Your first home will very likely be the single most important and largest dollar investment you will ever maek in your lifetime. Therefore, it is wise to do your "homework" before you seen your bank loan officer to obtain home financing.

Buying your first home is especially exciting and satisfying. But it can also be stressful, confusing, overwhelming, and frust–rating; that is, if your are not ready and prepared with rel–evant and important information. You must have all the necessary documents and records at your finger tips when you see the loan officer at the bank. All banks are sincerely interested in prov–iding home loans to potencial borrowers, but only if you are qualified, responsable, and most important of all, prepared!

Preparing for first-time home purchase is a financial challenge. Do you spend more than you make? Increase your savings plan at every oppertunity. Get rid of most of your credit cards. All you need is one—perhaps too at the most. Pay cash when you buy, and avoid paying interest on the installment plan. Pay off ba–lances in full each time you recieve a statement. To spend more as you see your savings grow can be tempting. So can a new car, television, clothing, or jewelery. Resist the temptation to buy more.

Here is one useful checklist that covers things that are most important to first-time home buyers. Your bank will, in all pro–bability, ask you questions pertainting to these items.

CHECKLIST FOR FIRST-TIME FINANCING

1. *Income Sourses* — Include regular pay, overtime, bonuses, commissions, tips, and any other sources of income.
2. *Liabilities* — Make a list of all money you owe—outstan–ding personnal and business loans and credit card account balances.
3. *Pay Records* — Keep all of your recent pay stubs and other kinds of records to show salary and wages recieved.
4. *Tax Returns* — Keep W-2 forms and tax return papers for the past three years.
5. *Down Payment* — Be ready to answer the big question in home purchase: How much down payment do you have too apply toward the purchase of your new home? Obviously, the larger the down payment, the smaller the monthly moregage payments.
6. *Other Assets* — Prepare a summery of liquid assets—things you own—free and clear of outstanding balances—that can quick–ly bring cash. Keep at least three months of bank statements for savings and checking accounts. Keep documents for stocks and bonds, life insurrance policies with cash surrender values, real estate holdings, and reciepts for personnal properties such as cars, furniture, jewelery, antiques, and other items of monetary value.

Heed the advise of real estate experts. Take along the follo–wing checklist when you tour new homes. The list contains those things that are most important to first-time home buyers.

CHECKLIST OF HOME FEATURES

1. *Price* — The most important feature for a first-time buyer is the price of a new home. If the price of a home is high–er than what you can afford, it will not matter what a house looks like or where is it located—you're not ready to buy.
2. *Location* — The home must be in a community that offers all the kinds of services and conveniences that will fill your every–day needs—most importantly how far you will have to to drive and how much time it will take to get to and from your place of employment.
3. *Quality* — Appearrance can be decieving. Examine careful–ly how the house is constructed. Check the walls, doorways, closets, cabinets, floors, trims, painting and finishes, etc. Check the appliances and fixtures. Ask the sales representitive about any or all of these features.
4. Home Features — Keep an open mind. "Specials" and "extras" offerred can be enticing. You may be buying some substancial faetures that you may not need or want, so don't be swayed by them.
5. *Live in It!* — Do you think you'll be happy living in this house? Picture yourself in it. Does it fit your lifestyle?

6. *Builder's Reputation* — Do'nt hesatate to ask about current owners of similiar homes constructed by the same builder. There answers will give you clues about a builder's committment to do business—honestly and positively—that will leave a good image in the community and with you.

A little planning goes a long way in obtaining your first mortgage. Keep your finances and approppriate papers in order. Have a wonderful time finding—and buying—your first home!

Clayton R. Sierra

CHAPTER 4

CAPITALIZATION ERRORS

Word power, the ability to use the correct word, is critical in business writing. Note these differences on the use and abuse of language from wordsmith Scott K. Andersen:

- ***Men do not have blonde hair.*** Men have *blond* hair. And, though the reference is seldom used today, men have *brunet* hair, women have *brunette* hair.
- ***Differ does not mean disagree***. *Differ* refers to things that are unlike others. His hat *differs* from mine. *Disagree* refers to people who have different opinions. She *disagreed* with me about the saltiness of the fries.

Compiled from material in *A Dictionary of Distinctions* by Scott K. Andersen, Tox Publications, 5524-B West Market Street, Greensboro, NC 27409

Objectives

- Understand the basic rules for capitalization.
- Recognize and mark errors in capitalization using the appropriate proofreader marks.
- Spell correctly 12 frequently misspelled words.
- Use correctly 3 pairs of commonly misused words.

CAPITALIZATION

Capital letters show the importance of words. For example, the first word in a sentence, proper nouns, names, and the pronoun *I* are always capitalized. Although the trend is to use fewer capital letters, several basic rules must be followed.

The proofreader marks that indicate the corrections for capitalization errors are shown here:

	MARKED COPY	CORRECTED COPY
Capitalize ≡	**to san Diego**	**to San Diego**
Lowercase /	**the new Member**	**the new member**

Rule 1 Capitalize the first word of every sentence and the first word after a colon if that word begins a complete sentence.

Example: The new semester will begin next week.

Example: The memorandum to parents included the following notation: the new bus schedule will begin the first Monday in October.

Rule 2 Capitalize the first word of every complete quotation. Do not capitalize the first word of an interrupted quote.

Example: "The team," said the coach, "will practice this afternoon."

Example: Miss Wakui announced, "all assignments are due Thursday afternoon."

Rule 3 Capitalize the first word of each item in a list, if each item is a complete sentence. Capitalize the first word of each item in an outline.

Example:

At the end of the class period, follow these steps:

1. Print and turn in a final copy of your assignment.
2. Turn off your computer.
3. Put away your textbook.

Example:

I. Varieties of vegetation
   A. Western hill country
   B. northern plains area

4-1 PROOFREAD AND MARK

Mark all capitalization errors using the correct proofreader marks. If the sentence is correct, write **C** to the left of the number.

1. "We will have lunch," she said, "at the central high school cafeteria."
2. ms. Johnson said, "check your locker in the south hallway."
3. "When the team is on stage," the advisor said, "all of us should stand and cheer."
4. Each person should have the following items in a bag:
   1. sport Shirt
   2. Clean socks
   3. black tie
5. The special meeting is for the following students: freshmen, sophomores, and Juniors.

Rule 4 Capitalize all proper nouns (the names of specific persons, places, and things) and any adjective derived from a proper noun.

CATEGORY	PROPER NOUNS
Brand names	Ford, Kellogg's, Tide, Ore-Ida, Bic
Buildings	The Sears Tower, Trump Tower
Clubs	Boys and Girls Club
Company names	Midwest Express, Mobile, General Electric
Specific courses	English I, Advanced Chemistry (*but not* geometry)
Geographic regions and places	Africa, Mideast, Wales, Frankfurt, the Missouri River, the Smoky Mountains, Lake Superior, Washington Avenue, Sixth Street
Governmental terms	Department of Health and Human Services, Federal Reserve Board, United Nations, Supreme Court, Detroit City Council (*but not "federal" or "state" unless part of an official agency name*)
Historic events	VE Day, Battle of Gettysburg, the Great Depression
Organizations	National Honor Society, Business Professionals of America, Future Business Leaders of America
Organizational terms within one's own firm	the Economics Department, the Education Division, the Board of Trustees, the Arrangements Committee
Religious groups	Lutheran, Jewish, Catholic, Protestant
References to the deity	God, Allah, Yahweh, Holy Spirit

The Word command for changing case is as follows: **Format + Change Case.**

The WordPerfect command for changing case is as follows: **Edit + Convert Case.**

CAPITALIZATION ERRORS

Rule 5 Capitalize days of the week, months of the year, and holidays. Do not capitalize seasons of the year.

Example: The exam is scheduled for November 29, the first Monday after Thanksgiving.

Example: We will have a new schedule for the Winter season by november 1.

Example: There will be a special program in our school on president's day.

Rule 6 Capitalize both parts of hyphenated words if they are proper nouns or proper adjectives. Do not capitalize prefixes or suffixes added to proper nouns.

Example: The name of the new student is Esteban Perez-Vadillo.

Example: The special film is for German-speaking students.

Example: The Central High School-north High School rivalry can be quite intense.

Example: The retirement party was for ex-principal Jefferson.

Rule 7 Capitalize words that show a family relationship when they appear alone or are followed by a personal name. Do not capitalize family relations preceded by a possessive pronoun.

Example: The class reunion was for Uncle George and Dad.

Example: The team manager is cousin Susan.

Example: My Brother got me the interview.

4-2

PROOFREAD AND MARK

Mark all capitalization errors using the correct proofreader marks. If the sentence is correct, write **C** to the left of the number.

1. The textbook was sold to Aunt Phyllis.
2. The leader of the field trip is Judith A. Sutton-smith.
3. The first car in the homecoming parade will be a chevrolet.
4. Classes will Begin on the wednesday after labor day.
5. The federal Reserve Board will meet in the State of Washington.

Rule 8 Capitalize a title that comes before a name. However, you should not capitalize a title that follows a name or is used in place of a name unless it is the title of a high-ranking national, state, or international official (such as the President, Secretary of State, the Queen of England, or the Governor).

Example: Dairy Princess Sherry Maki

Example: Ellery Preston, the president of Beacon Inc.

Example: Cameron Schmidt, Artist in Residence

Example: He was elected president of the United States.

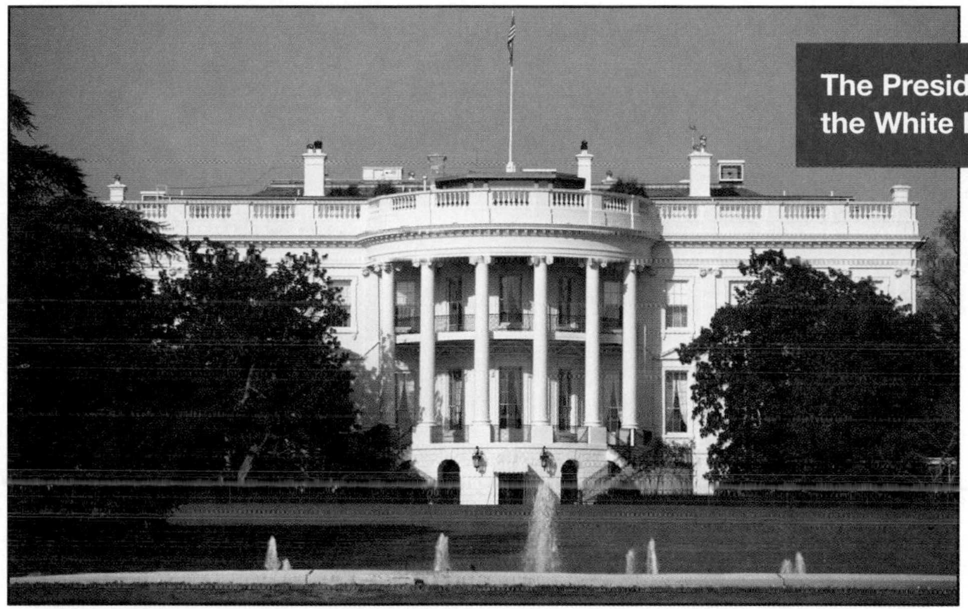

The President lives in the White House.

Rule 9 Capitalize titles in letter addresses and closings. Capitalize the first word, all nouns, and titles in a salutation of a letter, but capitalize only the first word of a complimentary closing. Capitalize both letters of official state abbreviations.

Example:

Ms. Clara Mendez, Head
Counseling Center
Northwest High School
321 North Lincoln Way
Chicago, IL 60614-4321

Dear Ms. Mendez:

Yours truly,

Bruce Karlstad
Department Head

Example:

Mr. Philip Leron
Student senate president
Southwest College
337 East College Street
Albuquerque, NM 87109-3233

Dear Mr. Leron:

Sincerely Yours,

Marian Thomas
Assistant principal

Rule 10 Capitalize the titles of officers in constitutions, bylaws, and minutes of a meeting. Titles of company officials are not capitalized when they follow or replace a personal name.

Example: The constitution states that "the President shall appoint a three-person Credentials Committee."

Example: The minutes were taken by Bryan Victorson, Secretary.

Capitalize academic titles that precede or follow a name. However, do not capitalize academic degrees used as general classifications.

Example: She announced that Dean Antonio Gomez will speak on February 26.

Example: Each of the teachers has a Master's degree.

4-3

PROOFREAD AND MARK

Mark all capitalization errors using the correct proofreader marks. If the sentence is correct, write **C** to the left of the number.

1. The constitution states that "the treasurer shall be responsible for an annual report."
2. Two teachers have received doctor's degrees.
3. The win was coach Neil's 150th victory.
4. The English IV class will be taught by professor Karjala.
5. The title in the closing of the letter should be "high school principal."

Rule 11 Capitalize points of the compass if they refer to specific regions or are used as proper nouns. Do not capitalize points of the compass to indicate directions or general locations.

Example: Next month the choir will tour the West.

Example: All 18 teams will compete in the Southern Region tournament.

Example: The summer school course includes visits to the midwest.

Example: The team will travel East on the first day of the trip.

Rule 12 Capitalize the first word and all important words in titles of literary and artistic works and in displayed headings. Do not capitalize articles (*a, an, the*), conjunctions (*and, as, but, or, nor*), and prepositions containing four or fewer letters (*at, by, for, in, of, on, to, with*) unless they are the first word of a title.

Example: The winning theme was entitled "Searching for the Lost Dream."

Example: Please purchase the paperback book *Guide to Correct Punctuation.*

Example: We are to study the chapter "The Era Of The Ethnic Groups."

Example: The library subscribes to *the Daily Mirror.*

Rule 13 Capitalize a noun that precedes a figure or letter except for common nouns such as line, page, sentence, and size.

Example: Place the instructions in Appendix G.

Example: The assignment begins on page 37.

Example: The sweatshirts should be Size 14.

4-4

PROOFREAD AND MARK

Mark all capitalization errors using the correct proofreader marks. If the sentence is correct, write **C** to the left of the number.

1. The choir will sing "The Sweet Song of Spring" in the concert.
2. All saturday classes are scheduled for towns East of here.
3. Proofread the material starting on Line 8.
4. The new headline should read "Bond Issue Is defeated."
5. the new chapter begins on page 42.

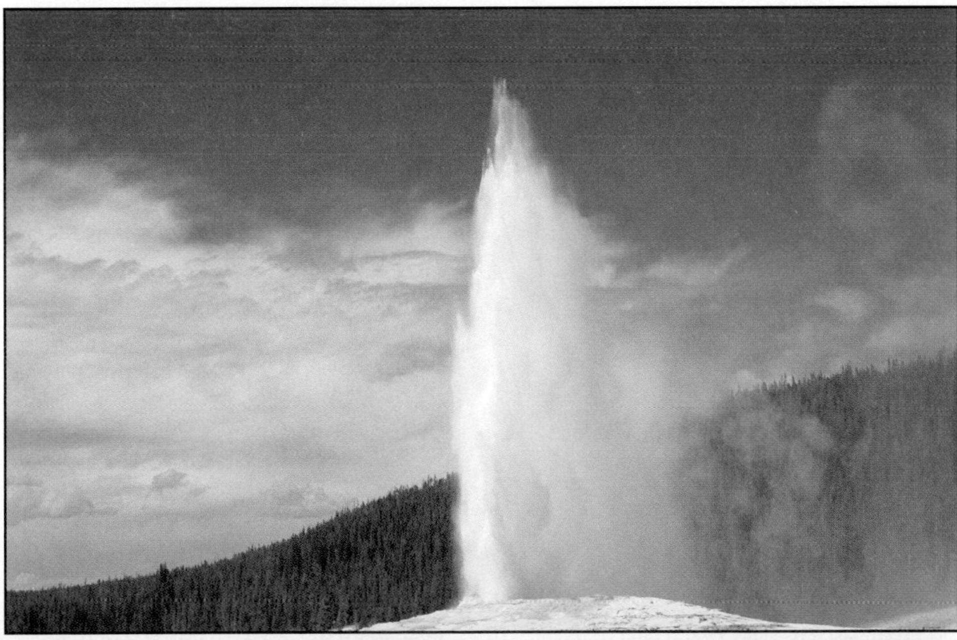

On our tour of the West, we stopped to see Old Faithful at Yellowstone National Park.

✤ When checking for capitalization errors, skim the material to locate words with capital letters and decide if they are capitalized correctly.

✤ Check to ensure that each sentence begins with a capital letter.

✤ Review the word processing function that changes letters from upper to lower case or from lower to upper case.

4-5 SPELLING AND WORD USAGE CHECK

Compare the words in Column A with the corresponding words in Column B. Use the appropriate proofreader marks to correct the misspelled or misused words. If both columns are correct, write **C** to the left of the number.

Column A	Column B
1. access	acess
2. resently	recently
3. schedual	schedule
4. committee	committtee
5. matterial	material
6. audet	audit
7. situation	sitaution
8. appropriate	apporpriate
9. analysis	analysis
10. communication	communiction
11. maxinum	maximum
12. spescial	special
13. offices of the coorperation	We visited the corporation.
14. Apply at the personal office.	Department of Personnel
15. the book's second eddition	the new edition is here

PROOFREADING APPLICATIONS PART A

4-6

PARAGRAPHS

Proofread the following material and mark all errors using the appropriate proofreader marks.

Plans for the publication of the pamphlet entitled *Schools and the future of our City* are complete. The draft copy was approved by the Citizens Committee for future Plans. The Chairperson was principal Roosevelt-Grant. A meeting has been scheduled to discuss the pamphlet in the northeast Part of the district on Tuesday, october 1. Questions to be discussed include the following:

1. what plans are there for new school buildings?
2. should school activities be curtailed?
3. Do taxes have to be increased?

The meeting will be in Room 102 of east High School. Arrangements for additional meetings will be made by Dr. Andrew glivem. The meetings must be concluded in November because voting on the school bond issue will take place a week after thanksgiving.

PROOFREADING APPLICATIONS PART B

4.7

LETTER

Proofread the following letter and mark all capitalization and other mechanical errors using the appropriate proofreader marks.

Central Community High School
372 North Street, St. Louis, MO 63122-2731
(314) 555-9669 • Fax (314) 555-9667

october 1, 20—

Ms. Carlota Silva, President
Northern Fences Corporation
327 Witherspoon Drive
St. Louis, Mo 63138-4422

Dear Ms. Brown:

The Citizens Commitee for Future Plans recently published a booklet about planning for our future schools. This was done to help the Citizens of our community better understand the effect that our schools have on the life of our community.
As a member of the committee, I would be pleased to meet with your westside Business Culb to reveiw the contents of the pamphlet and to help the members understand the importance of the facts that the commitee has assembled. Would there be time during your October 15 meeting for such a presention? An ddressed envelope is enclosed for your reply.

Sincerely,

Marilyn Roosevelt-Grant
Principal

tcm
Enlcosure

4-8

MEMORANDUM

Proofread the following memo and mark all errors using the appropriate proofreader marks.

Central Community High School
Memorandum

DATE: October 25, 20--

TO: Citizens Committee for Future Plans

FROM: Marilyn Roosevelt-Grant, Principal

SUBJECT: Schedule for Community Meetings

The final printed copies of our report, *Schools and the Future of our City*, were delivered to my office late yeterday afternoon. A copy is enclosed for you. Your assistance in preparing this verry comprehensive document is appreciated.

As we discussed in our last meeting, the next step is to distribute coppies throughout the community and to have meetings with various clubs and organizations. Based upon our discussions, I have perpared the following schedule for several committee members to meet with six comunity groups:

Group	Committee Members
Westside business Club	Marilyn Roosevelt-Grant and Carleton Rivera
Northenders	George Olson And Diane Porozny
Central City founders	Ila Mary Jackson and Fred Flanery
Area 12 Council	Jose Velez and Elsa Greenberg
Suburban Grants Committee	Dorothy Williams-Evans and Jim Pugh
Southland commercial Club	Earl Just and Kathryn Ann Soo

Would the first pesron listed contact the preisdent of the group and request the oppertunity to meet with them at their Next meeting. Be sure to let me know when you will be meeting with with your grup. My phone number is 555-1877.

Enclosure

COMPUTERIZED PROOFREADING APPLICATIONS

4-9

LETTER

1. Load file CPA4-9 from the TMPL04 subdirectory on your template CD. (This is a computer copy of Application 4-7.)
2. Proofread the letter on the screen (use a proofreader card). Correct all errors on the screen copy that you have marked with proofreader marks in Application 4-7.
3. Format the letter with 1-inch side margins and the date on line 15.
4. Save the letter using the same file name.
5. Print the letter.
6. Proofread the printed document. If you find any additional mistakes, correct the errors on both the hard copy and the screen.
7. Save the revised document and print it.

4-10

MINUTES

1. Load file CPA4-10 from the TMPL04 subdirectory on your template CD.
2. Proofread the copy on the screen by comparing it with the correct handwritten copy that follows on pages 55 and 56.
3. Correct all mistakes.
4. Save the minutes using the same file name.
5. Put the date on line 15, and print the minutes with 1-inch side margins.
6. Proofread the printed document. If you find any additional mistakes, correct the errors on both the hard copy and the screen.
7. Save the revised document and print it.

4-11

E-MAIL MESSAGE

1. Load file CPA4-11 from the TMPL04 subdirectory on your template CD.
2. Proofread the e-mail message and make all necessary corrections.
3 Save the document using the same file name.
4. Proofread the printed document. If you find any additional errors, correct the errors on both the hard copy and the screen.
5. Save the revised document and print it.

Central High School Student Council
St. Louis, Missouri
Minutes for October 25, 20--

The regular meeting of the Central High School Student Council was held on Thursday, October 25, 20--, in Room 205. Members present:

Eric Anthony, Grade 10	Haru Tokuda, Treasurer
Mary Staloch, Grade 10	Carol Goudge, Secretary
Tony Tiese, Grade 11	Ken Baertsch, Vice President
Chih Liang, Grade 12	Colleen Seifer, President
Janice Ludwig, Grade 12	Ms. Adrian, Advisor
Steve Hovland, Grade 11	Mr. LuCuyen, Advisor

Members absent: none

1. Call to Order and Roll Call. The meeting was called to order at 1:45 p.m. by President Seifer. All members were present for roll call.
2. Minutes. The October 18 minutes were read by Secretary Goudge and approved as read.
3. Treasurer's Report. Treasurer Tokuda reported that the balance in the treasury was $405.12.
4. Unfinished Business.

   4.1 Homecoming Buttons. The homecoming buttons have arrived and can be sold starting October 28. Each council member is to sell at least 25 buttons.

4.2 Homecoming Parade. Janice Ludwig reported that seven floats plus the marching band have already signed up for the Homecoming Parade.

5. New Business.

5.1 Student Guide. Mr. LuCuyen asked if the Student Council wanted to participate in the preparation of a booklet entitled Student Guide for New Students. After discussion, it was agreed that we did.

5.2 Fall Cleanup. Chih Liang moved that the Student Council assist with fall Cleanup activities on November 12. The motion was seconded and adopted.

6. Announcements. Vice President Bartsch announced that the Homecoming Parade Planning Committee would meet during fourth period on Tuesday.

7. Adjournment. Tony Tiese moved to adjourn. The motion was seconded and adopted. The meeting was adjourned at 2:35 p.m.

Carol Goudge, Secretary

CHAPTER 5

ABBREVIATION ERRORS AND ROUGH DRAFTS

To be effective, an abbreviation must have the same meaning for both the writer and the reader. If confusion results, the wrong message may be conveyed. Which word or phrase is correct for the following abbreviations?

- **AA** (administrative assistant, Alcoholics Anonymous, associate in arts)
- **ABA** (Amateur Boxing Association, American Bankers Association, American Bar Association)
- **RR** (railroad, rural route)

Objectives

- Apply common abbreviation rules.
- Proofread revisions made from rough drafts.
- Spell correctly 12 frequently misspelled words.
- Use correctly 3 pairs of commonly misused words.

ABBREVIATIONS

An **abbreviation** is a shortened form of a word or phrase. Only standard abbreviations should be used. Consult a dictionary if you are in doubt about the correctness of an abbreviation.

Abbreviations may be important space savers in business writing, especially in short documents. Because the reader may not be familiar with an abbreviation, spell it out the first time and place the abbreviation in parentheses; for example, *Certified Professional Secretary* (*CPS*). Thereafter, use only the abbreviation. **Note:** Only use an abbreviation when you know the reader will understand it as you intended.

Some abbreviations are acceptable with or without periods (for example, *ft.* or *ft*; *mi.* or *mi*). Use one style consistently within a document. One space follows a period used after an abbreviation (*Mr. Luft*), and no space follows a period within an abbreviation (*p.m.*).

Use the following proofreader marks to make corrections in abbreviations.

	MARKED COPY	CORRECTED COPY
Spell out. sp	Send by Dec. 20	Send by December 20.
Insert period.	Mrs Pahl will be	Mrs. Pahl will be
Close up space.	U. S. Post Office	U.S. Post Office
Delete period.	Radio Station K. V. G. N.	Radio Station KVGN

GENERAL STYLE

Some abbreviations may be used with any formal and informal writing. The following guidelines are appropriate for most business communication (letters, memos, reports, and electronic communications) as well as for general usage. Consult a good reference manual for more detailed rules.

Personal and Professional Titles

Personal titles are used as a mark of courtesy. Generally, they include *Mr.*, *Mrs.*, *Miss*, *Ms.*, or *Dr*. Professional titles may also indicate one's military, religious, or educational status. Apply these rules for abbreviating titles:

Rule 1 Abbreviate personal and courtesy titles that come before personal names.

Examples:

Mr. Zehnder	Messrs. Zehnder and Hanson (plural of *Mr.*)
Mrs. Vogelsberg	Mmes. Vogelsberg and Connor (plural of *Mrs.*)
Ms. Hackbart	Dr. Whitney Wieland

Note: *Ms.* is appropriate when the marital status of a woman is unknown, when the woman prefers this title, or when the marital status of the woman is unimportant. *Miss* is not an abbreviation.

Rule 2 Abbreviate personal titles following names. Titles such as *Jr.*, *Sr.*, *2d.* or *III* are generally not set off by commas; however, academic and professional titles are.

Examples:

Jackie Ellison Jr.	Randall Markum 2d
Elizabeth Arnneski, CPS	Bradley Pearson III
Paul Altman, Esq.	Emily Stinson, Ph.D.

Rule 3 Do not abbreviate titles appearing with surnames.

Example:

Doctor Karjala	*but*	Dr. Betty Karjala

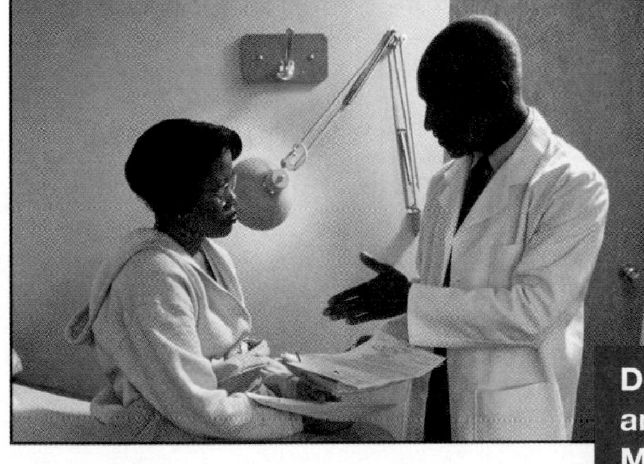

Doctor Mann answered Mrs. Morgan's questions.

Rule 4 Write out professional titles whenever possible.

Examples:

Professor Kris Thoms	the Reverend Carlos Cruz

CHAPTER 5

ABBREVIATION ERRORS AND ROUGH DRAFTS

Company Names

Words such as *Bros.* (Brothers), *Co.* (Company), *Inc.* (Incorporated), *Ltd.* (Limited), and *Mfg.* (Manufacturing) are often abbreviated in official company names. Check the company letterhead for the appropriate style.

Examples:

Rounded Seeds, Inc.

Canadian Coins, Ltd.

Rangers Mfg.

5-1

PROOFREAD AND MARK

Use the appropriate proofreader marks to identify the corrections that should be made. If the sentence is correct, write **C** to the left of the number.

1. The defendant is Mister Jones.
2. All we know is that some one named Dr. Huston answered.
3. Tell Miss. Jennings that her company is the first respondent.
4. Norman Howard, Ph.D., will forward the signed contract.
5. Prof. Houdeck will be in charge of the session.

Organizations

Abbreviate names of government and private agencies, organizations and associations, radio and television broadcasting stations, and other groups when appropriate. These abbreviations are generally written in all capital letters without periods.

Examples:

FBI	Federal Bureau of Investigation
NBC	National Broadcasting Company
KRBI	(Call letters for a radio station)
KMSP-TV	(Call letters for a television station)

Note: Government organizations often include the abbreviation *U.S.* No space follows the period within the abbreviation.

Addresses

Rule 1 Words and directions within addresses should not be abbreviated. However, compound compass point directions, such as *NW, NE, SW,* and *SE, are* abbreviated when used after street addresses.

Examples:

Avenue	Drive	Road
Boulevard	Lane	Square
Building	Parkway	Street
Court	Place	

469 Broadway Square West

2639 Foshay Place SE

Rule 2 Two-letter state abbreviations are appropriate only when they appear with a ZIP Code in an address. The Appendix lists the traditional and two-letter state abbreviations.

Examples:

800 College Avenue Saint Peter, MN 56082-1498	She lives in Saint Peter, Minnesota.

Rule 3 Do not abbreviate the name of a city, state, or country, or prefixes to most geographic names except when space is a problem. Periods are used with these abbreviations.

Examples:

Saint Clair *or* St. Clair

Fort Madison *or* Ft. Madison

Mount Saint Helens *or* Mt. St. Helens

United States *or* U.S. (no space after the internal period)

South Africa *or* S. Africa

California *not* Calif.

5-2

PROOFREAD AND MARK

Use the appropriate proofreader marks to identify the corrections that should be made. If the sentence is correct, write **C** to the left of the number.

1. We cannot send the report to the U. S. Department of the Treasury.
2. The road crosses the corner of the state of ND.
3. The ABC Radio Network was able to achieve its goal.
4. Omaha, Neb., will eliminate the surcharge.
5. Send the list of addresses to 4903 E. Alberta St.

Mount Saint Helens erupted on May 18, 1980.

Time

Abbreviate the standard time zones and expressions of time. Note the use of periods in the following examples.

Examples:

CDT (Central Daylight Time)

PST (Pacific Standard Time)

a.m. and p.m. (no space after the internal period)

Note: The abbreviation *a.m.* stands for *ante meridiem* (before noon), while *p.m.* stands for *post meridiem* (after noon).

INFORMAL OR TECHNICAL STYLE

Some abbreviations are appropriate for use in technical documents such as lists, business forms, or informal documents or when space is a problem. Such abbreviations are not appropriate in formal reports or business correspondence.

Days and Months:

Sun.	Thurs.	Jan.	May	Sept.
Mon.	Fri.	Feb.	June	Oct.
Tues.	Sat.	Mar.	July	Nov.
Wed.		Apr.	Aug.	Dec.

Measurements:

in *or* in.	yd *or* yd.	oz *or* oz.
ft *or* ft.	sq *or* sq.	lb *or* lb.

Expressions:

acct.	*for*	account
bal.	*for*	balance
dept.	*for*	department
ea.	*for*	each
EOM	*for*	end of month
PO	*for*	purchase order
P.O.	*for*	post office
No.	*for*	number (used when a number follows the abbreviation; e.g., The stock number is No. 4406.)
vs.	*for*	versus

PROOFREAD AND MARK

5-3

Use the appropriate proofreader marks to identify the corrections that should be made. If the sentence is correct, write **C** to the left of the number. Use the "general style" (not the "informal" or "technical style") in proofreading this exercise and all exercises that follow.

1. The hockey game will begin at 8 p. m.
2. This decision will benefit the persons who register on Sat.
3. The enthusiasm of persons in the Acctg. Dept. is appreciated.
4. You should arrive at 8:05 a. m. E.D.T. on Wed.
5. Please notify KXLM-TV that the reception on Feb. 28 will be held at the U. S. Department of the Interior.
6. Saint George, Ut., is where our consultant lives
7. The lawsuit in general court will be titled *Grant vs. Erickson.*
8. Gloves, Inc. has opened a branch store near the K.X.T.Y. transmitter.
9. Have Prof. Stoney forward the results to the Ind. graduate school.
10. Will Ms. Anderson have the current schedule ready by Jan. 18?

ROUGH DRAFTS

Newly composed documents are usually not in final form. They may contain keying and formatting errors. Sometimes word originators simply "jot down" ideas and instruct a copyeditor to finish composing, keying, formatting, and printing the document.

The copyeditor, using a pen and proofreader marks, makes corrections or revisions to the printed document. The result is a rough draft. On the basis of this rough draft, the copyeditor completes the final editing, formatting, and printing of the document. Both the word originator and the copyeditor need to use proofreader marks correctly. Then revisions will be marked consistently, and fewer errors will result.

When revising text, originators may move copy, change spacing or return copy to its original form. Proofreaders must learn to recognize and apply the following proofreader marks when revising text.

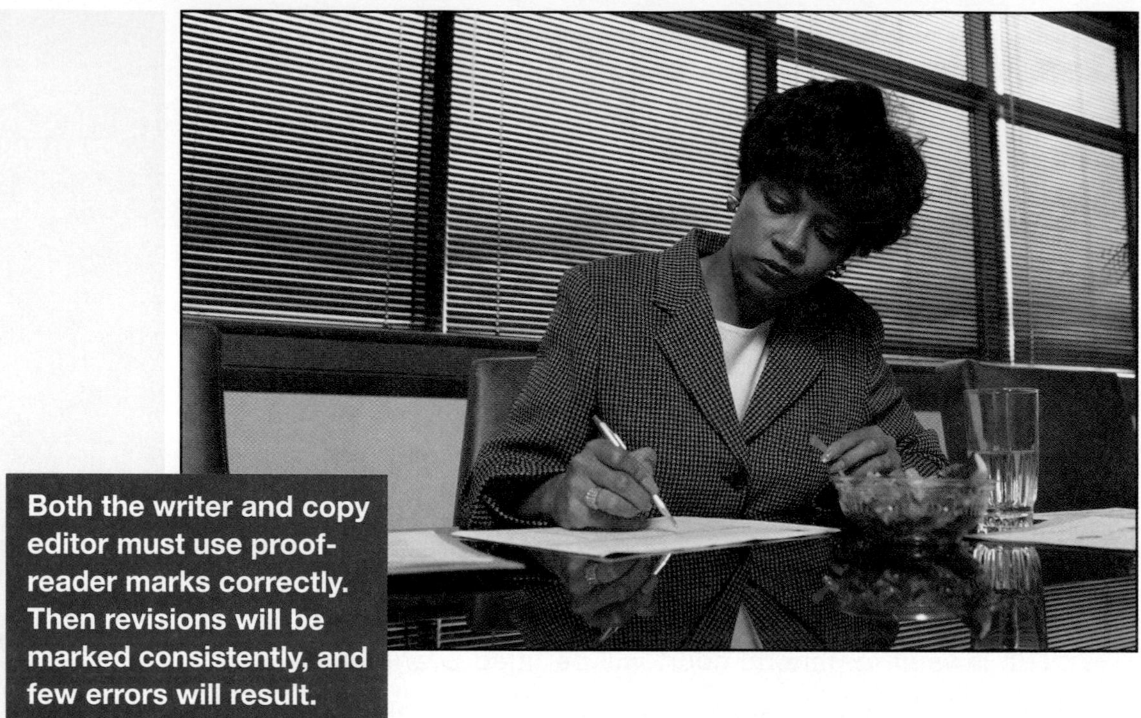

Both the writer and copy editor must use proofreader marks correctly. Then revisions will be marked consistently, and few errors will result.

	MARKED COPY	CORRECTED COPY
Move. (circle with arrow)	your letter ~~of~~ May 1	your May 1 letter
Stet (keep "as is"). stet	the ~~spacious~~ room	the spacious room
Single-space. SS	SS products were ready to be sold through the	products were ready to to be sold through the
Double space. DS	\$12,087 3,724 DS \$15,811	\$12,087 3,724 \$15,811

5-4

PROOFREAD AND MARK

In the following sentences, mark the corrections according to the information given in the "Changes" line.

1. The benefits cannot be changed before the is approved.

   Changes: Add "contract" between "the" and "is."

2. The bush should be planted by May 15.

   Changes: Move "by May 15" to the beginning of the sentence; capitalize "by"; lowercase "The"; add "currant" between "the" and "bush."

3. Three youths the Council meeting on October 12.

   Changes: Move "on October 12" to the beginning of the sentence; capitalize "on"; lowercase "Three"; add "spoke at" between "youths" and "the."

4. By working extra hours and putting in more time, we will be able to achieve the goals set at teh beginning of the year.

   Changes: Move "By working extra hours and putting in more time," to the end of the sentence; delete the comma after the word "time"; lowercase "By"; capitalize "we"; spell "the" correctly.

5. the motion was seconded after a long discussion

   Changes: Capitalize "the"; insert "and approved" between "seconded" and "after"; insert a period at the end of the sentence.

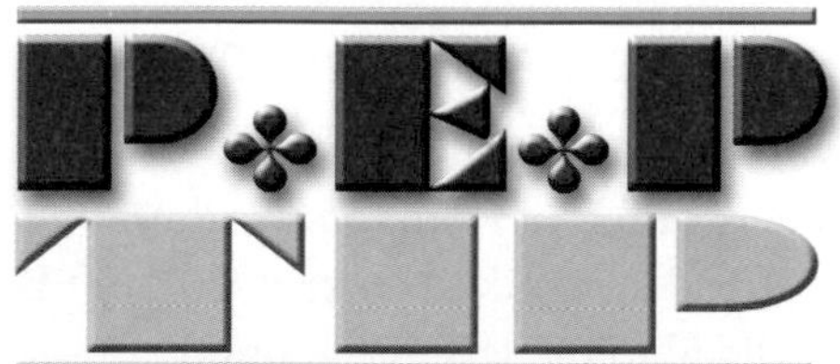

✣ Use only abbreviations which will be understood by your audience.

✣ Be selective in using abbreviations in business letters, memos, reports, and electronic communications.

✣ Depending on the software program you use, your spell checker may recognize abbreviations differently. However, you can add commonly-used abbreviations to your word processing dictionary so those abbreviations are not flagged as possible errors.

5-5

SPELLING AND WORD USAGE CHECK

Compare the words in Column A with the corresponding words in Column B. Use the appropriate proofreader marks to correct the misspelled or misused words. If both columns are correct, write **C** to the left of the number.

Column A	Column B
1. benefit	benefit
2. particular	particlar
3. committment	commitment
4. enthusiasm	enthusiasam
5. consultent	consultant
6. defendent	defendant
7. achieve	achieve
8. can not	cannot
9. believe	beleive
10. eliminate	elimanate
11. congratulations	congradulations
12. corporate	corporite
13. he was elected to the council	the counsel meeting
14. the currant year	the current administration
15. the line moved forward	a foreward-looking friend

5-6

INTERNATIONAL VOCABULARY

Compare the Spanish words in Column A with the corresponding words in Column B. If the word or phrase in Column B is different from the word or phrase in Column A, use the appropriate proofreader marks to correct Column B. If the words in both columns are the same, write **C** to the left of the number.

Column A	Column B
1. logro	logra
2. sentencia	sentensia
3. empleado	enpleado
4. vigilancia	vigilancai
5. obsequio	obsequio

PROOFREADING APPLICATIONS PART A

5-7

MEMORANDUM

Proofread the following memo and mark all errors using the appropriate proof-reader marks

Acme Insurance Company, Inc., Memorandum

DATE: Sep. 5, 20--

TO: Jason Realstad, Editor
ACME NOTES

FROM: Mary Lorenz, Chairperson
Awards Committee

SUBJECT: Items for Newsletter

Here are two items for the Dec. issue of the ACME NOTES. Please modify them to fit the available space.

Item 1. Year End Awards Program Scheduled. The annual Awards Program will be held in the Swift Auditorium on Jan. 11. The auditorium is located at 9550 Prince Blvd. here in Manhattan.

An important part of the program will be the presentation of special awards for outstanding achievement during this currant year. In addition, recognition will be given to company employees who have been with the company for 25 years, 30 years, 35 years, or 40 years.

The speaker for the program will be Antonio Perez, corporate consultant for Maxon Industries, Chicago, Ill. His enthusiasm in working with companies like ours will be of particular benefit to us as we embarck upon next year's sales compaign. Mr Perez has shown a tremendously large no. of people how to achieve the goals they have set. His message will be currant and direct. He will give us many usable suggestions.

Please attend the annual Awards Program and extend your personal congradulations to the award winners. More information will be distributed in Dec.

Item 2. Manager's Meeting Scheduled. Janice Keltgen, legal council, has asked to meet with supervisorson Thurs., Jan 10. The company was a defendant in a recent court case that we won. Ms. Keltgen feels that a meeting is needed to summarize the result of the case and to help eliminate midunderstandings in the company's hiring process. We believe you will find this meeting well worth your time to attend.

PROOFREADING APPLICATIONS PART B

5-8

LETTER

Proofread the following letter and mark all errors using the appropriate proofreader marks.

ACME INSURANCE COMPANY, INC.
3842 West Grand Avenue • St. Paul, MN 55110-2910
612/555/4886 • Fax: 612/555/4888

Dec. 3, 20—

Ms. Floragene Adams, President
Southern Armstrong, Ltd.
728 Imperial Drive So.
Nashville, Tn 37210-4217

Dear Ms. Adams:

It is a pleasure to confirm our invitation to you to be the speaker at our Apr. 22 Seminar here in Wichita. You were recommend to us by Candace Okano, president of Midwest Travel Comp. in Kanas City, Kans.

The in-service meteing will be held in Suite 332 in the Grand Central Ins. Bldg. The Semminar will start at 10 a. m.

Two other speakers who will also be meeting with our managers will be Josefina Ramos, chairperson, board of directors, Grant Grinders, Inc., and Arthur Proehl, legal council for Jackson County. We had also invited Bill Symthe, president, Toledo Consulting. Unfortunately, he can not be with us for this meeting.

Additional information will be sent to you under separate cover concerning travel and housing arrangements for you while you are are here with us. If you have any questions, be sure to let me kno. We are looking forward to your being with us.

Sincerely,

Louis Roe
Seminar Coordinator

tfd

EDITORIAL

5-9

Proofread the following editorial and mark all errors using the appropriate proofreader marks.

EDITORIAL FOR ACME NOTES

As we approach the end of the year, it appropriate in the spirit of the holiday season that we estend appreciation to the many persons who have made this a successfful year. We sincerely appreciate your strong commitment to our company

First, to the memb. of the Sales department, we salute you for your tremendous effort and responde during the fall Slaes Campaign. Even though there has been an economic recession, yhou ahve been able to help our customers meet ther needs in a very positive way.

Second, to allemployees, we salute your for your escellent community service activities. Because we have been a longtime member of the Central City community, it is important that we show our suport as a company for the many areawide activities and projects. Improvemments in community result in improvements for us.

Third and finally, to our customers, we salute them for their loyalty and partidularly their response to our request for assitance in the product improement program. Preliminary results from the midyear survey show that over 50 percent of our cutomers provided reactions to our line of prodducts, with many of them offering suggestions for expanding the products and service thatw have available.

Have a happy holiday season! Thanks again!

COMPUTERIZED PROOFREADING APPLICATIONS

5-10

LETTER

1. Load file CPA5-10 from the TMPL05 subdirectory on your template CD. (This is a computer copy of Application 5-8.)
2. Proofread the letter on the screen (use a proofreader card). Correct all errors on the screen copy that you have indicated with proofreader marks in Application 5-8.
3. Format the letter with 1-inch side margins and the date on line 15.
4. Save the letter using the same file name and print the letter.
5. Proofread the printed document. If you find any additional mistakes, correct the errors on both the hard copy and the screen.
6. Save the revised document and print it.

5-11

MEMORANDUM

TEAM WORK

1. On the handwritten memo on pages 71 and 72, mark the changes requested (shown in the box on page 72) using the appropriate proofreader marks.
2. Load file CPA5-11 from the TMPL05 subdirectory on your template CD.
3. Proofread the copy on the screen by comparing it with the corrected handwritten rough draft.
4. Correct all mistakes.
5. Save the memo using the same file name.
6. Put the date on line 15, and print the memo with 1-inch side margins.
7. Proofread the printed document. If you find any additional mistakes, correct the errors on both the hard copy and the screen.
8. Save the revised document and print it.

5-12

E-MAIL MESSAGE

1. Load file CPA5-12 from the TMPL05 subdirectory on your template CD.
2. Proofread the e-mail message and make all necessary corrections.
3. Save the document using the same file name and print the message.
4. Proofread the printed document. If you find any additional errors, correct the errors on both the hard copy and the screen.
5. Save the revised document and print it.

Memo

DATE: November 23, 20-
TO: Ramona Schroader, Head
Human Resources Department
FROM: Marie Lorenz, Awards Committee
SUBJECT: Preliminary List for Awards

As you know, our annual Awards Program will be held on February 3 with the dinner starting at 6 p.m. We anticipate that the program will last from 6:45 p.m. to 8:15 p.m.

A major part of the program will be the presentation of awards to various individuals and several departments. One category of individual awards is for those who have worked at the company for 25 or more years.

Would you review the records of all employees and prepare a list according to the following categories:

1. employed for 25 years
2. employed for 30 years
3. employed for 35 or more years

It is our plan to give those with 25 years a wristwatch. Those with 30 years will receive a piece of crystal glass, and those with 35 years will receive a miniature sculpture. In addition to identifying each person, we will need a brief biographical sketch for each one that can be printed in the program. Would you contact each awardee to help prepare a brief paragraph or two about their years here at ACME.

Finally, will you arrange for the number of awards to be given in each category. Each watch should be engraved with a suitable inscription.

Could we have a preliminary report on the number of awards and the names of the awardees by December 15.

PARAGRAPH	CHANGES TO BE MADE IN MEMO
Paragraph 1	Delete "As you know." Capitalize "our."
Paragraph 2	Insert "major" between "one" and "category."
Paragraph 3	In Item No. 3, delete "or more."
Numbered items should be double-spaced.	
Paragraph 4	Replace "piece" with the word "vase."
Paragraph 5	Delete "that can be printed."
Paragraph 5	Move "in the program" to appear after "person."
Paragraph 6	Replace "watch" with "award."
Paragraph 7	Change date to December 1.

CHAPTER 6

NUMBER EXPRESSION ERRORS

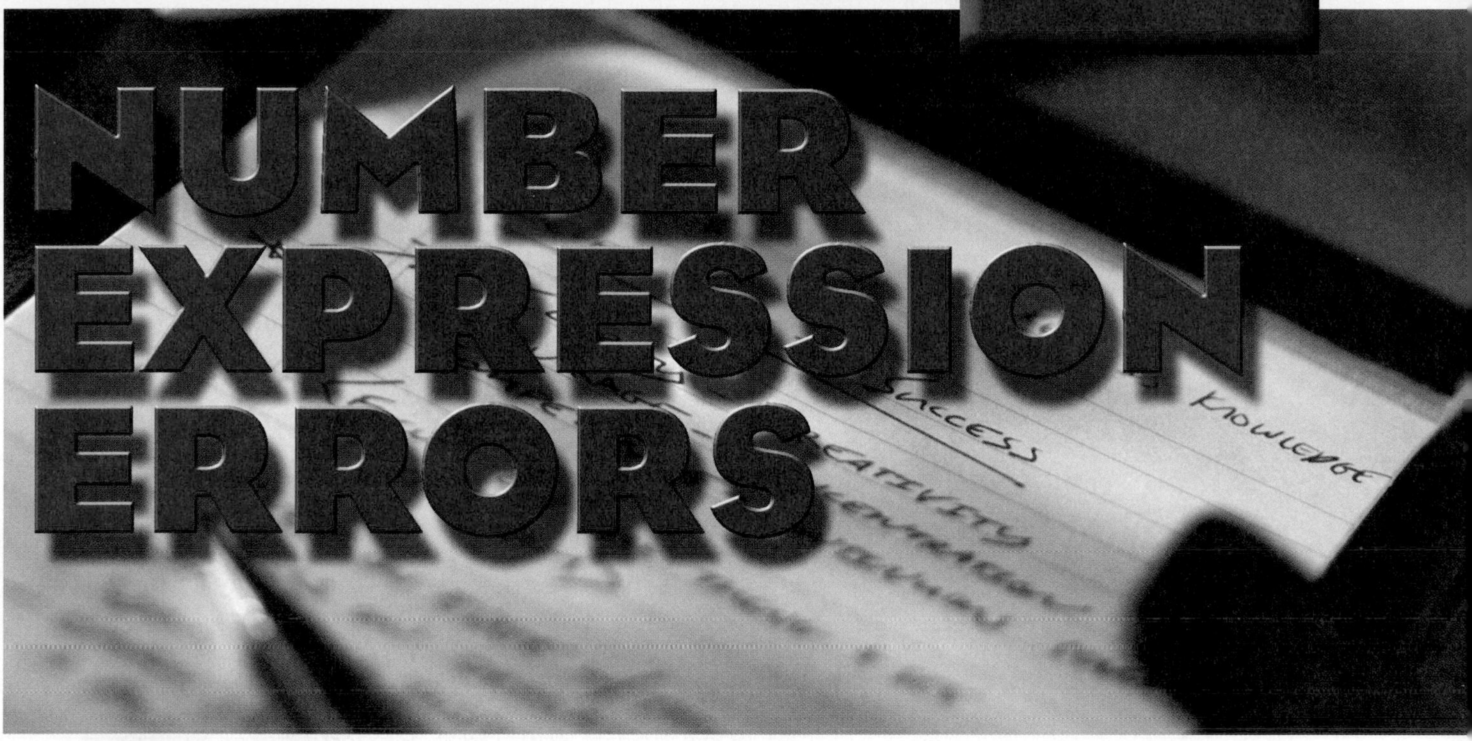

It should be obvious why the use of exact numbers is critical when working with business documents. Documents with incorrect numbers could cost your company thousands, even millions, of dollars. Imagine ordering 10,000 widgets with the specifications of 2" x 12". When the widgets arrive, you realize that each widget should have been 2" x 21" (not 2" x 12"). These widgets are of no value to your company because they are not long enough for the product you make. If each widget cost your company $10, your company has just paid $100,000 for 10,000 items it cannot use. Not only are you out that much money, you do not have the exact item needed to begin construction.

Objectives

- Recognize errors in the expression of numbers.
- Spell correctly 12 frequently misspelled words.
- Use correctly 3 pairs of commonly misused words.

CHAPTER 6

NUMBER EXPRESSION ERRORS

The frequent use of numbers in business correspondence has created an increased need for accurate proofreading. Financial reports, telephone numbers, longer ZIP Codes, and credit card identifications are just a few of the ways in which more and more numbers are being used.

Often, numbers must be checked against a source document for accuracy. For example, amounts listed on an expense summary are checked against receipts. Many of the decisions you will make regarding numbers, however, will be related to whether the numbers should be expressed as figures or as words. The guidelines presented here will apply to most of the situations you will encounter.

When you locate an incorrectly expressed number, use the same proofreader marks that you have already learned for identifying the errors.

	MARKED COPY	CORRECTED COPY
Spell out. sp ◯	There were (3) cars in the holiday race. [sp]	There were three cars in the holiday race.
Express as figures. ~~fifteen~~ 15	Invite ~~eighteen~~ 18 persons to dinner.	Invite 18 persons to dinner.

NUMBERS EXPRESSED AS WORDS

Follow these general guidelines for expressing numbers as words.

Rule 1 Spell out numbers from one to ten. Express numbers above ten in figures. When a sentence contains a series of numbers, some of which are over ten and some of which are under ten, use figures for consistency.

Example: Our agent will describe the terms of five different policies.

Example: The teacher brought 6 tablets, 20 diskettes, and 4 textbooks.

Example: This group insurance policy will cover all ~~fifteen~~ 15 employees.

Example: Please include 5 apples, 18 oranges, and ~~eight~~ 8 lemons on the list.

If numbers can be grouped into different categories within a sentence, examine each category separately. Use the same style for all numbers within a related category.

Example: From the new book list for the seven library branches, we have ordered 21 hard copy versions, 33 paperback copies, 5 cassette recordings, and 9 CDs.

Example: The Sports Complex, which is open eight hours on Sundays, has 8 tennis courts, ~~four~~ 4 weight rooms, and 16 racquetball courts.

Rule 2 Spell out numbers that begin a sentence even if figures are used later in the sentence. When numbers from twenty-one to ninety-nine are spelled out, key them with a hyphen.

Example: Twenty-seven children went on the trip 11 months ago.

Example: (14) [sp] people were selected for the jury, even though only eight were needed.

When a large number begins a sentence, rewrite the sentence so that it does not begin with a number.

Example: Twenty-one thousand one hundred fifty-two people live in that town.

Rewritten: There are 21,152 people living in that town.

Twenty-seven children went on the field trip 11 months ago.

Rule 3 Spell out approximate amounts and isolated fractions. Mixed numbers (a figure and a fraction) are expressed as figures. (Use a hyphen to join the numerator and denominator of a fraction written in words, unless either element already contains a hyphen.)

Example: The group drank almost fifteen gallons of lemonade at the picnic.

Example: The builder will need pipe that is 2 1/8" in diameter.

Example: The gasoline gauge showed the tank to be (3/4) [three-fourths] full.

Example: His shoe size is ~~nine and one-half.~~ [9 1/2]

Rule 4 Spell out street numbers through ten as ordinals (first, second, etc.). Use figures for house and building numbers. An exception is house or building number One, which is written as a word.

Example: The business has moved to 297 Sixth Street.

Example: The tennis courts are located near the corner of Trent Avenue and [Seventh] (7th) Street.

Example: MFC National Bank is located at One Gateway Drive.

Rule 5 Spell out ages ten and under unless stated specifically in years, months, and days. Use figures for ages 11 and over.

Example: His daughter is six years old.

Example: On April 16, he will be ~~seven~~ [7] years, ~~five~~ [5] months, and ~~eight~~ [8] days old.

Rule 6 When two numbers are used together, spell out one of the two—preferably the one that is the shortest word.

Example: At the sale, he found 6 ten-gallon cans.

Example: The inventory includes ~~twenty-four~~ [24] (2) [sp]-roll packs of paper towels.

NUMBER EXPRESSION ERRORS

6-1

PROOFREAD AND MARK

Use the appropriate proofreader marks to correct the errors in number expression. If the sentence is correct, write **C** to the left of the number.

1. The colors of the copies in the 3 categories should be 30 red, ten white, and 36 blue.
2. 16 new windows will be sent to your address at 9054 6th Avenue.
3. In order for the program booklet to fit into the six and three-fourths envelope, the booklet must be one-eighth inch shorter.
4. We received five hundred eight-page brochures.
5. The previous instructor distributed almost fifty copies.

NUMBERS EXPRESSED AS FIGURES

Follow these general guidelines for expressing numbers as figures.

Rule 7 Use figures to express time except when used alone or with the contraction *o'clock*. Use *a.m.* or *p.m.* with figures. Zeros are not required for on-the-hour times of day.

Example: The appointment has been scheduled for 5 p.m.

Example: The bus will depart at (5) [sp] o'clock.

Rule 8 Use figures *without* adding *d*, *st*, or *th* after a month to express the day and the year. (Set the year off by commas when it follows the month and day.)

Example: The Declaration of Independence was signed on July 4, 1776.

Example: His retirement will be on August ~~Ninth,~~ 9 20—.

Express the day in ordinal figures (*1st*, *2d*, *3rd*, *4th*, etc.) when the day precedes the month or when the month is omitted. (The preferred abbreviation of *second* and *third* is *2d* and *3rd*.)

Example: The state conference will start on the 21st of November.

Example: The ~~fifth~~ 5th of May will be a school holiday.

Rule 9 Express in figures dimensions, measurements, and weights.

Example: The rug measures 10 by 12 feet.

Example: The fish weighed ~~five~~ 5 pounds.

Rule 10 Express in figures street numbers over ten and all address numbers except One. Street numbers above ten may be expressed as either cardinal numbers (*22*) or ordinal numbers (*22d*). However, be consistent and use one style.

Example: Please send the order to 607 South 38th Street.

Example: The art gallery will be located at One Park Drive.

Example: The parade will begin at the corner of Main and (9th) [sp] Street.

Rule 11 Express as figures numbers following nouns such as *page*, *chapter*, *room*, *rule*, and *policy*.

Example: Our final statement begins at the bottom of page 41 in Chapter 4.

Example: According to Rule ~~six,~~ 6, the motion is not needed.

Rule 12 Express in figures amounts of money, decimal amounts, percentages, and interest periods that include the year, month, and day.

Example: The cost per person will be $9.97.

Example: Money that is deposited into the account will earn ~~five~~ 5 percent interest.

Spell out the word *cents* for amounts under a dollar (*15 cents*, not *$.15*).

Example: The small souvenirs can be sold for 47 cents each.

Example: Be sure to add ~~six~~ 6 cents to the total for the tax.

Express even amounts of money within a sentence without zeros or decimal points (*$10*).

Example: The special ticket price will be $8 per person through Friday.

Example: The necklace will cost ~~nine dollars~~ $9 when it is on sale.

In legal documents, express amounts of money in both words and figures.

Example: In consideration of One Hundred Sixty Dollars ($160), the contract will be binding on both parties.

Example: Upon payment of Four Hundred Thirty-two Dollars and Twenty-one Cents ($432.21), the loan will be considered paid in full.

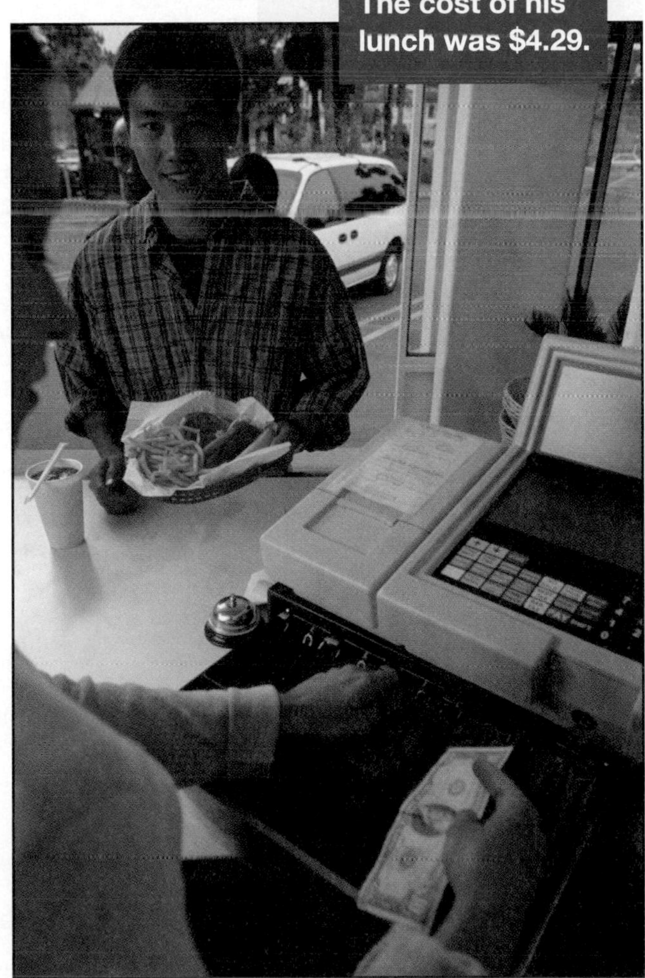

The cost of his lunch was $4.29.

6-2

PROOFREAD AND MARK

Use the appropriate proofreader marks to correct the errors in number expression. If the sentence is correct, write **C** to the left of the number.

1. The candidates' meeting will be held at 876 East 5th Street.
2. She purchased 4 $100,000 policies for her business.
3. The council approved the start of construction of an officebuilding at 976 South Sixteenth Street.
4. On the questionnaire, he stated his son's age as 6 years, 6 months, and 27 days.
5. He purchased thirty-six 9-inch dividers for the file cabinets.

ZIP CODES

To assist the post office, the addresses on all letters and envelopes should include the correct two-letter state abbreviation and ZIP Code. Whenever possible, the ZIP Code should contain nine digits.

The proofreader should be sure the ZIP Code on the envelope is the same as the ZIP Code in the letter address. Accuracy in ZIP Codes is important because errors will cause delays in the delivery of the correspondence. The Appendix contains a list of the two-letter abbreviations for states and U.S. territories. When in doubt about a ZIP Code, check the official ZIP Code directory available from the U.S. Postal Service. You may also find ZIP Code information on the Internet.

Note: The U.S. Postal Service requests that envelope addresses be single-spaced and keyed in all capital letters with no punctuation.

Example: MS DEBBIE GONZALEZ
547 INDIANA AVENUE
CENTER POINT WV 26339-0487

6-3

PROOFREAD AND MARK

Proofread the envelope addresses by comparing them to the correct letter addresses on the left. Correct the envelope addresses using the appropriate proofreader marks. If the envelope address is correct, write **C** to the left of the number.

Letter Address	Envelope Address
1. Ms. Hilda Morales	MS HILDA MORALES
431 Maiden Way	431 MAIDEN WAY
Denver, CO 80233-0499	DENVER CO 80233-0499

2. Mr. Chuck Hansen	MR. CHUCK HANSON
Brown Insurance Company	BROWN INSURANCE COMANY
P.O. Box 1923	P.O. BOX 123
Garland, TX 75046-1623	GARLAND TX 705466-1623
3. Feather Duster, Inc.	FEATHER DUSTER INC.
Attention: Credit Department	ATTENTION CREDIT DEPAARTMENT
807 Second Street South	870 SECOND STREET SOUHT
Kalamazoo, MI 49009-1208	KALAMAZOO MI. 49009-120
4. Professor Andres Sandoval	PROF ANDRES SANOVAL
Marysville State College	MARYSVILLLE STATE COLLEGE
546 South Cleveland Road	564 SOUTH CLEVLAND RAOD
Memphis, TN 38104-3232	MEMPHIS TENN 83104-2332
5. Ms. Laura Johnreit	MS. LAURA JOHNRIET
Vice President for Sales	VICE PRESIDENT FOR SALES
West Fisheries Company	WET FISHERIES COMPAYN
901 Jefferson Boulevard	905 JEFFERSEN BUOLEVARD
Vancouver, WA 98660-3692	Vancouver Wa 98606-6392

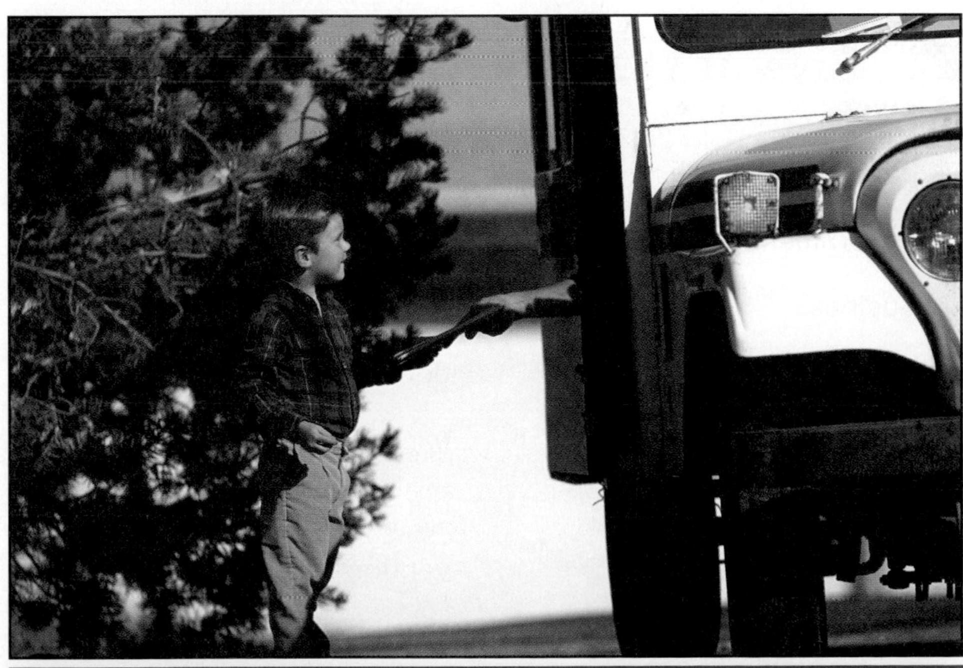

Accuracy in ZIP codes is important because errors will cause delays in the delivery of correspondence.

✤ Check the accuracy of all extensions, calculations, and totals of numbers.

✤ Verify the accuracy of numbers against their source document.

✤ Check the alignment of decimals that appear within a column.

✤ Although the style of expressing numbers as words or figures may vary depending upon the formality of the document, follow one style consistently within a document.

SPELLING AND WORD USAGE CHECK

Compare the words in Column A with the corresponding words in Column B. Use the appropriate proofreader marks to correct the misspelled or misused words. If both words are correct, write **C** to the left of the number.

Column A	Column B
1. secrateries	secretaries
2. complience	compliance
3. emergency	emergency
4. questionaire	questionnaire
5. pryor	prior
6. categories	catagories
7. government	goverment
8. business	buisness
9. correspondance	correspondence
10. excellent	excellent
11. consensus	consensis
12. vendur	vendor
13. It's time to go.	They say its going to rain.
14. This was the cite of a battle.	They excavated the site.
15. Austin is the capital of Texas.	Visit the state capitol

PROOFREADING APPLICATIONS PART A

6-5

MEMORANDUM

Proofread the printed memo that follows by comparing it with the correct handwritten memo on page 82. Mark all errors using the appropriate proofreader marks.

EASTERN COLLEGE MEMORANDUM

DATE: October 9, 20--

TO: Louise Howlett, Assistant Dean
College of Business

FROM: Emilia Sanchez, Registrar
SUBJECT: Enrollment Report for Fal Semester

Registrations for all calsses for the fall semester have been comleted. The final day for late registrations was on October 6th. Class lists have been sct to all of the proffesors in the College of Business.

Here are the registraion numbers for the classes about which you inquired:

		Men	Women	Total
CIS 110	Computer Information Systems	14	18	32
CIS 231	Novell Networks	12	19	32
EC 101	The American Economy	6	7	14
ACT 301	Accounting Principles	16	16	32
ACT 315	Financial Accountng	12	13	25
ACT 441	Auditing	9	11	20
MKT 310	Introdction to Marketing	18	21	40
MGT 221	Business Law	21	22	43
OIS 250	Desktop Publishng	19	29	39
OIS 344	Managerial Communications	15	16	31

The number of students enorlled in the other courses will be sent to you next week.

tbs

Memo

DATE: October 9, 20--
TO: Louise Howlett, Assistant Dean
College of Business
FROM: Emilia Sanchez, Registrar
SUBJECT: Enrollment Report for Fall Semester

Registrations for all classes have now been completed. The final day for late registrations was October 6. Class lists have been sent to all of the professors in the College of Business.

Here are the registration numbers for the classes about which you inquired:

		Men	Women	Total
CIS 110	Computer Information Systems	14	18	32
CIS 237	Novell Networks	12	19	31
EC 101	The American Economy	6	8	14
ACT 301	Accounting Principles	16	16	32
ACT 315	Financial Accounting	12	13	25
ACT 441	Auditing	9	11	20
MKT 315	Introduction to Marketing	19	21	40
MGT 221	Business Law	21	22	43
OIS 250	Desktop Publishing	19	20	39
OIS 344	Managerial Communications	15	16	31

The number of students enrolled in the other courses will be sent to you in a different memo.

tbs

PROOFREADING APPLICATIONS — PART B

6-6

MEMORANDUM

Proofread the printed memo that follows by comparing it with the correct handwritten memo on page 84. Mark all errors using the appropriate proofreader marks.

GREAT ISLAND PUBLISHING CENTER MEMO

DATE: October 10, 20—

TO: Laurine Rantzeed
Budget Office

FROM: Trudy Washington, Head
Communication Center

SUBJECT: Budget Request for Next Year

Enclosed with this note is our completed budget request for next yeaqr. Your attention is called to several items:

29 reams of orange offset paper has been requested because next year we will be pulbishing and distributing the enviromnental prmotion flyer each month.

The postage amt. has been inrceased to $950.00 because of and expected increase in postral rates.

The BHD Company has informed us that the next version of their word proccesing software porgram will be availabel on the 6 of Aug.; therefore, we will need at least $825.00 of the equipment budget to received the appropriate software upgrade.

In additin, the newest model of their computer should be availabe on or shortly after August 31st. Finally, the miscellaneous amount has been increased by seven percent to help in case of an emergency situation.

Memo

DATE: October 10, 20--

TO: Laurine Rantzeed
Budget Office

FROM: Trudy Washington, Head
Communication Center

SUBJECT: Budget Request for Next Year

Enclosed with this note is our completed budget request for next year. Your attention is called to several items:

Twenty-nine reams of orange offset paper have been requested because next year we will be publishing and distributing the environmental promotion flyer each month.

The postage amount has been increased to $950 because of an expected increase in postal rates.

The B+D Company has informed us that the next version of their word processing software program will be available on the 6th of August; therefore, we will need at least $825 of the equipment budget to receive the appropriate software upgrade.

In addition, the newest model of their computer should be available on or shortly after August 31. Finally, the miscellaneous amount has been increased by seven percent to help in case of
an emergency situation.

6-7

LETTER

Proofread the printed letter that follows by comparing it with the correct handwritten letter on page 86. Mark all errors using the appropriate proofreader marks.

NATIONAL ACTIVITIES ASSOCIATION
632 Grandy Building
278 Balsam Avenue, Boise, ID 83701-1609
(208) 555-1178 • Fax (208) 555-1179

Dedember 19, 20--

Mr. Albert Edwin Gater, President
Emerald City Enterprises, Inc.
363 N. Raintree Aven.
Portland, OR 97222-0384

Dear Al:

Thank you for your kind hospitlaity during my recent visit with you you and the planning committee. I have reviewed the notes that Mr. Grant prepared, and I ask that if the following corrections might be made.

1. The business meeting should be schedualed for Rom Seven rather than 17.
2. The four seminars on Friday morning hsould be planed to have room for at least 40 persons per session.
3. The banquat on Friday night will start at 7:00 o'clock p.m. rather than 8:00 p.m.
4. The shuttle buses will need to leave the main control every fifteen minutes
5. The special V.I.P. reception on Saturday should be planned for thirty-one persons.

If you have any quetsions, be sure to let me know.

Sincerely,

Agnes Woo

tis

December 19, 20--

Mr. Albert Edwin Gater, President
Emerald City Enterprises, Inc.
363 North Raintree Avenue
Portland, OR 97222-0348

Dear Mr. Gater:

Thank you for your kind hospitality during my recent visit with you and the planning committee. I have reviewed the notes that Mr. Grant prepared, and I hasten to ask if the following corrections might be made:

1. The business meeting should be scheduled for Room 7 rather than 17.
2. The four seminars on Friday morning should be planned to have room for at least 40 persons per session.
3. The banquet on Friday night will start at 7 p.m. rather than 8 p.m.
4. The shuttle buses will need to leave the main hotel every 15 minutes.
5. The special VIP reception on Saturday should be planned for 31 persons.

If you have any questions, be sure to let me know.

Sincerely,

Agnes Woo

tis

COMPUTERIZED PROOFREADING APPLICATIONS

6-8

MEMORANDUM

1. Load file CPA6-8 from the TMPL06 subdirectory on your template CD. (This is a computer copy of Application 6-6.)
2. Proofread the memo on the screen (use a proofreader card). Correct all errors on the screen copy that you have indicated with proofreader marks in Application 6-6.
3. Format the memo with 1-inch side margins.
4. Save the memo using the same file name and print it.
5. Proofread the printed document. If you find any additional mistakes, correct the errors on both the hard copy and the screen.
6. Save the document and print it.

6-9

NOTICE

1. Mark the necessary changes for the rough draft notice that follows on page 88.
2. Load file CPA6-9 from the TMPL06 subdirectory on your template CD.
3. Proofread the copy on the screen by comparing it with the rough draft memo.
4. Correct all mistakes. The rough draft copy may also have other errors that have not been marked.
5. Save the notice using the same file name.
6. Print the notice with 1-inch side margins.
7. Proofread the printed document. If you find any additional mistakes, correct the errors on both the hard copy and the screen.
8. Save the revised document and print it.

6-10

E-MAIL MESSAGE

1. Load file CPA6-10 from the TMPL06 subdirectory on your template CD.
2. Proofread the e-mail message and make all necessary corrections.
3. Save the document using the same file name and print it.
4. Proofread the printed document. If you find any additional errors, correct the errors on both the hard copy and the screen.
5. Save the revised document and print it.

CLASS RUNION TIME

You are cordially invted to attend the reunions for the Classes of 1980-1985. They will be held on Friday, January 15th, in room fourteen of the Central Confrence Center, 469 Grand Ave. west in Birmingham. Registration and the social hour will begin at 5:30 o'clock p.m. The dinner will begin at 6:30 and the program at 7:30. We anticipate that the program will be over by 9:30. The rest of the evening will be availabal for remembering and listening to the musci of THE ORANGE APPLES, an old-time music pep band from the high school.

A questionaire is enclosed fr you to share with us your "personal history" since the big day in the early eighties. Please complete the questionnaire and return it in the enclosed envelope to the high school secretaries office as soon as possible. We'll include a summary of the responses in the Early Eighties booklet you will get when you register.

Your friends and mine have done lost of things since we left the alma mater. Here's the change to catch up in a ahurry in oen evening! See you there!

CUMULATIVE REVIEW APPLICATIONS NO. 2

CRA2-1

MEMO REPORT

Proofread and correct all errors using the appropriate proofreader marks.

DATE: June 28th, 20––

TO: Julia Delgado, Head of Correspondence Services

FROM: Fuji Nagai, Administratative Support

SUBJECT: Report on Biennial Confrence

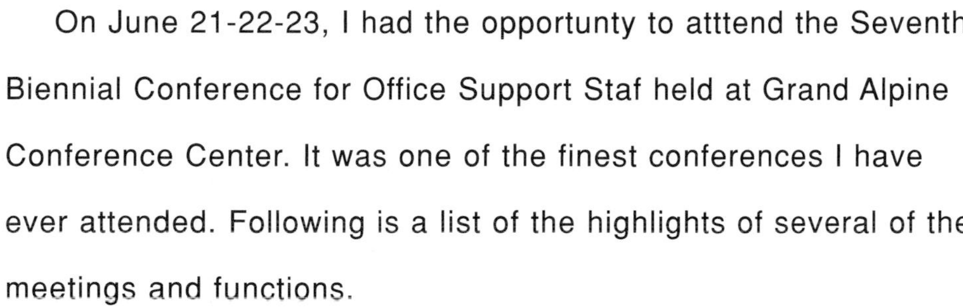

On June 21-22-23, I had the opportunty to atttend the Seventh Biennial Conference for Office Support Staf held at Grand Alpine Conference Center. It was one of the finest conferences I have ever attended. Following is a list of the highlights of several of the meetings and functions.

On Monday, Jun 21, the conference opened with an excellant presentation at 1:00 p.m. by Ralph Stanman. He share with us the idea that all of us have a unique role to play in our workplace. His use of humor helped us understand more fully the points he made.

At 2:45 o'clock Sandra Martin spoke on the topic entitled "Really Listening to our Colleagues." She had some excellant suggestions for dealing with staff coflict.

An interesting idea that was tried this year was to have a barbarshop chorus composed of people attending the conference. Since I sing allto, I attended the rehearsals and sang with them each of the three times they preformed.

The first day concluded with a picnic in the mane cafetria. It was held inside because it became quiet cool and uncomfortable to be outside.

On Tusday the 22d, we started at 9:00 a. m. with a general session where Jerrimae Conger from the U. S. Department of Labor presented the results of a survey about "What is a support person?" Her comments summarized one of the most extensie research studies of this type ever made. A highlight of her talk was the summar of comments made by the respondents to the item asking about professional associatons.

At 10:30 a.m., we divided into 12 small groups to discuss a wide variety of topics. The two that I felt were the most interesting were "Rating Business Software," by Nina Howardson, and "Re-specting Others Through Better Listening." That talak was given by Kay Meier. Ms Meier gave all of us a chance to learn what our "Ear-Q" was. (Mine is very average.)

The talk by Nina Howarsdon includd a lot of infomrtion about various types of administrative and finalcial software. I was able to save several of the handouts that she showed to us. The one that I particularly liked showed the projected uses that can be made of WordWow Version 2.3. Because we are using Version 2.2, it might be apporpriate to considere upgrading our system in the office.

After the second small group sesion, all of us at the confrence heard an exellent presentation by Norman Quiret from the U. S. Post Ofice. He brought all of us up to date on the most recent rules, regulations, and requirements for using the post office. He really emphasized the importance of using all capitol letters when addressing envelopes.

At 3:45 on Tuesday afternon, all of of the persons attending the Confrence were invited to attend an indsutry trade show in the main ballrom.

A major event for the entire conference was the banquet. It started with the giving of door prizes and then followed with one of the funnest speakers we have every had at the confrence. He spoke for almost an hour, but time just seemed to fly by. One of the funniest stores was about a lady who died and on her tombstone was the inscription "I told you I was sick."

At the door prize drawing, I was fortunite enough to win one of the two grand prizes—a 50 percent discounton next year's conference registration fee.

On Wendesday the 23th, we started with an excallent presenation by a police officer, Nabuaki Enami. He gave us suggestions for help our home, business, and personal safety. It was interesting because so many persons should use a little extra causion in their work.

Following a refreshment break, the conference ended with a presentation by the president of Northern Jeremy Steet, Inc. The theme for this final session was "Realizing the Importance of Staff Relationships."

After attending all of the sessoins and talking with people from across the country, I felt very exhilarated about the work of a support person.

A statistical summary of the registrations showed that their were over three hundred and fifty persons from 25 different states attending the conference. 10 different types of support positions were represented at the conference.

Because the Grand Alpine Conference Cnter was over70 miles from the International Airport, transportation was provided by van directly from the Airport to the center. Housing was in the center's housing units with single, double, and trple rooms available. It is my strong recomendation that we consider using the Grand Alpine Conference Center for our annual sales meeting. The center has excellent facilities, superb food, a friendly and conscientious staff, and a real desier to help any organization meets its goals.

If you would like me to draw up a more formal prposal for holding our Sales meeting there, just let me know. Doctor Anderson has agreed to work with me in drawing up the details. Some preliminary informatin regarding costs shows that it would be about twenty five percent cheaper to hold the meeting at the center, even though more travel would be needed. Another factor to consider might be that we limmit the number of sales associates allowed to attend.

If you want us to draw up a plan, we'll include informatin abaout how many culd attend and what the costs would be for groups of various sizes.

CHAPTER 7

SENTENCE CONSTRUCTION ERRORS, PART I

When it comes to business communication, your writing style is important. Your mastery of a clear, concise writing style is essential to success because how you say something may be as important as what you say. A poor writing style can result in confusion, both to your company and to your customers. Think of the confusion that may have resulted from the following sentences written by people completing an accident report:

- The accident happened when the right back door of a car came around the corner without signaling.
- The other car hit my truck without giving warning of its intentions.
- He had been driving 45 years before falling asleep and having an accident.
- No one was to blame for the accident, but it would never have happened if the other person had been alert.

Objectives

- Recognize incomplete sentences (fragments).
- Find and mark errors in subject-verb agreement.
- Find and mark errors in singular/plural nouns.
- Identify intervening modifiers and indefinite pronouns.
- Find and mark errors in compound and collective nouns.
- Spell correctly 12 frequently misspelled words.
- Use correctly 3 pairs of commonly misused words.

CHAPTER 7

SENTENCE CONSTRUCTION ERRORS, PART 1

Your instructor wrote on your term paper, "You done a well job!" What would be your reaction? Are you pleased? Yes, for the complimentary remark and the high grade you earned, but are you impressed with your instructor's use of English grammar? It is not likely. In fact, you may react negatively and lose confidence in your instructor's ability to communicate correctly and effectively.

Business people react the same way. A person is judged on his or her ability to communicate clearly and correctly—when speaking or writing. Your ability to communicate effectively in the business world is extremely important.

Proofreading for correct grammar requires patience and attention to detail. You must be alert and look for errors in grammar usage and sentence construction.

Chapters 7, 8, and 9 will discuss the most important principles of correct grammar. In this chapter, you will review and apply the rules of basic sentence structure. You will learn to recognize complete sentences and sentence fragments. You will learn to identify and use singular, plural, compound, and collective nouns. You will also learn how intervening modifiers and indefinite pronouns affect subject-verb agreement.

If you locate a grammar error when proofreading, draw a line through the error and write the correction above the error. If you are unsure of the correct grammatical structure or the writer's intended message, write a question mark in the right or left margin of the page. The question mark indicates to the writer that the meaning is not clear and that the sentence should be revised or rewritten.

	MARKED COPY	CORRECTED COPY
Change copy as indicated. ——	Ten resumes were ~~was~~ received.	Ten resumes were received.
Question the author. ?/	If I have a question. ?/	If I have a question, I will ask her.

SENTENCE STRUCTURE

A **complete sentence** is a group of words that has a subject and a verb and expresses a complete thought. The **subject** is the person, place, or thing the sentence is about. It may be a noun or a personal pronoun (*I*, *you*, *he*, *she*, *it*, *we*, or *they*) that takes the place of the noun. The **verb** tells what the subject is or does. Verbs express either action or a state of being.

Action verbs often include **helping verbs** that indicate the **tense** (timing) of the verb. The main helping verbs are *is*, *are*, *be*, *am*, *was*, *were*, *has*, *have*, and *had*. Other helping verbs include *may*, *might*, *must*, *ought*, *can*, *could*, *would*, *should*, *shall*, *will*, *do*, *does*, and *did*. Helping verbs are easy to recognize because they help the main verb tell what the subject is doing.

ACTION VERBS	STATE-OF-BEING VERBS
Dexter *drives* a green Jaguar.	**Juana *is* an actuary.**
I *jog* five miles every day.	**The food *looks* delicious.**
The manager *uses* the computer.	**I *am* the chairperson.**

A **verb phrase** consists of the main verb plus any helping verbs. (A **phrase** is a group of words that does not contain both a subject and a verb.) In the following examples, the subjects are underscored once, and the verb phrases are underscored twice.

Example: Bingo (S) will be held (V) in the Sunset Room.

Example: Cruise ships (S) are designed (V) for passenger comfort.

Example: How many cruises have (V) you (S) taken (V)?

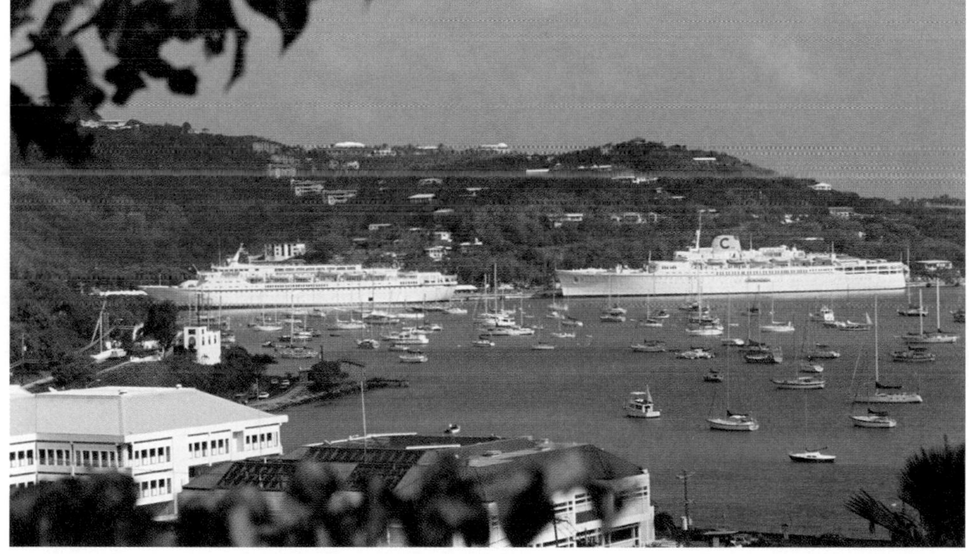

Linking verbs are state-of-being verbs. The most common linking verbs are forms of the verb *be* (*is*, *am*, *are*, *was*, *were*, *being*, *has been*, *have been*, and *had been*). Other linking verbs include *appear*, *become*, *feel*, *look*, *seem*, *taste*, and *sound*. Linking verbs answer the question "What?" and are always followed by nouns, pronouns, or adjectives (called *complements*). **Complements** are words used after linking verbs to describe or rename the subject of the sentence.

The difference between a helping verb and a linking verb is that the helping verb is part of the verb phrase containing an action verb and helps to ask questions, give commands, or make statements. The linking verb "links" the subject of the sentence to the word (noun, pronoun, or adjective) that immediately follows the linking verb and completes the meaning of the subject by describing or renaming it.

In each of the following examples, the subject is underscored once, and the linking verbs (or verb phrases) are underscored twice. Can you find the complements in the sentences?

Example: Gunther (s) looks (v) worried. (Gunther looks what?)

Example: Sarah (s) is (v) the cruise director. (Sarah is what?)

Example: Tuesday's activities (s) were (v) fun. (Activities were what?)

Example: Cruises (s) are becoming (v) favorite vacation choices. (Cruises are becoming what?)

7-1

PROOFREAD AND MARK

In each sentence, underline the subject once and the verb or verb phrase twice.

1. The president of the travel agency is Carole Sandersen.
2. The cruise ship was refurbished two years ago.
3. Santa Barbara seems like a popular port of call.
4. The barge cruise on the River Nile sounds exciting.
5. Luxury cruises have become very competitive.

SENTENCE FRAGMENTS

A group of words that contains a subject and a verb is a complete sentence. If either the subject or the verb is missing, it is an incomplete sentence—more commonly known as a **sentence fragment**. When you locate a sentence fragment, write a question mark in the left or right margin of the page. This will alert the writer to explain the meaning of the sentence or to revise it. If the correction appears obvious, simply correct the fragment by changing it into a complete sentence.

SENTENCE FRAGMENT	COMPLETE SENTENCE
When you talk to travel agents. ?	**When you talk to travel agents, they will explain all the options.**

7-2

PROOFREAD AND MARK

Write a question mark in the margin if the group of words is a fragment. Correct the copy if the error is obvious. If the group of words is a complete sentence, write **C** to the left of the number.

1. The king of vacations.
2. Choosing which cruise to take. One of life's most delectable dilemmas.
3. A wide variety of itineraries from which to choose.
4. The new addition to The Diamond Dining Room. Built by Panthos Contracting in 1999.
5. Accommodations range from inside cabins to penthouse suites.

SINGULAR AND PLURAL NOUNS

The subject and verb must agree in number (singular or plural) and in person (first person: *I*, *we*, *our/ours*; second person: *you*, *your/yours*; third person: *he*, *she*, *it*, *they*, *theirs*). A singular subject requires a singular verb. A plural subject requires a plural verb. Most singular present-tense verbs in the third person end with an *s*. Therefore, an *s* ending on most verbs indicates that the verb is singular. In the examples, the subjects are underscored once, and the verbs are underscored twice.

Example: Cruising (s) offers (v) value that other kinds of travel do not offer.

Example: That agency (s) specializes (v) in cruises and land tours.

Example: Rachel (s) and Celia (s) ~~is~~ are (v) fortunate to be able to travel in Europe.

Example: The cruise director's position (s) require[s] (v) enthusiasm and stamina.

Note: When *there* or *here* introduces a sentence, the subject follows the verb. *There* and *here* are never used as subjects of sentences. In the following examples, the subjects are underscored once, and the verbs are underscored twice.

Example: There are (v) culinary artists (s) preparing food fit for royalty.

Example: Here is (v) an interesting itinerary (s).

Example: Here ~~are~~ is (v) the list (s) of five-star cruise ships.

Example: There are (v) cruise lines (s) that offer~~s~~ special interest programs.

7-3

PROOFREAD AND MARK

In these sentences, correct the verb rather than the subject. Use the appropriate proofreader marks to correct the errors in subject-verb agreement. If the sentence is correct, write **C** to the left of the number.

1. Fantasy Cruise Line offer special group rates.
2. There was many shipboard activities to keep you busy.
3. Some passengers fears becoming seasick on a cruise ship.
4. Here are the list of ports on the Mexican Riviera cruise.
5. We highly recommend cancellation insurance.

INTERVENING MODIFIERS

The subject and verb must always agree in number, even if modifiers of a different number separate them. A **modifier** is a word or a word group that describes and is usually related to the subject of the sentence. Modifiers that occur between subjects and verbs are called **intervening modifiers**. When proofreading for errors in subject-verb agreement, disregard intervening modifiers. The intervening modifiers are italicized in the following examples. The subjects and verbs are also identified. (Remember, the verbs must agree with the subjects, not the modifiers.)

Example: Proper attire (S), *as well as courtesy and civil behavior*, is expected (V) on any cruise ship.

Example: Travel agents (S) *with training and experience* are (V) very helpful.

Example: The ports (S) *of call* ~~is~~ are (V) usually considered in selecting a cruise vacation.

Example: Travel counselors (S) *who assist people in selecting the right tour* agree~~s~~ (V) that satisfaction is based on attitude and flexibility.

7-4

PROOFREAD AND MARK

Use the appropriate proofreader marks to correct the errors in subject-verb agreement. If the sentence is correct, write **C** to the left of the number.

1. *Stardream*, like its partner ship *Stardust*, have a similar deck plan.
2. Active programs, as well as total relaxation, adds to your enjoyment.

3. The attendant who cleans and furnishes your cabin daily are responsible for your ultimate comfort during the cruise.
4. Everyone, from the captain to the assistant waiter, is devoted to treating you like a VIP.
5. Travel videotapes about every type of cruise imaginable is available for your viewing pleasure.

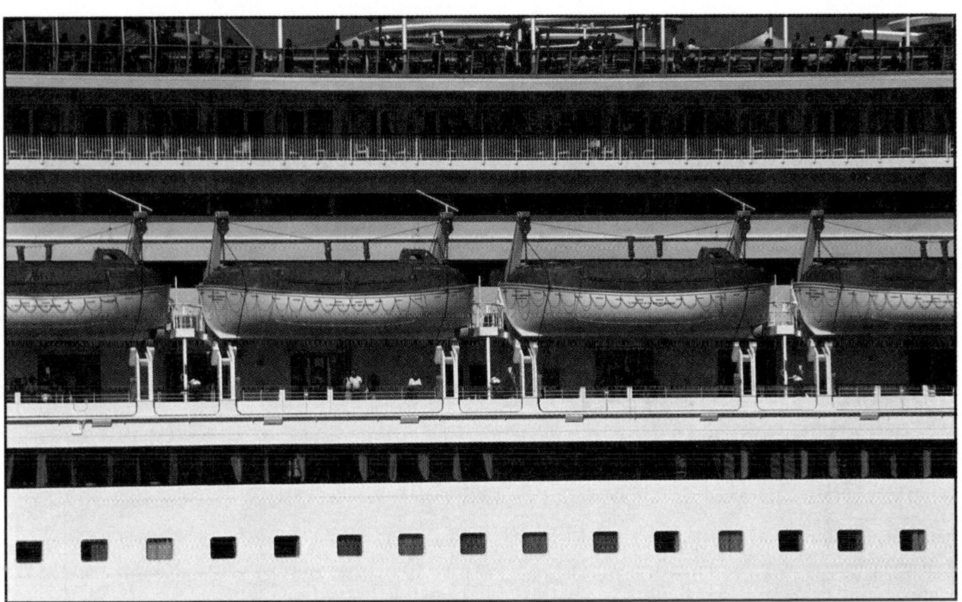

COMPOUND SUBJECTS

Sentences that contain two or more subjects are said to have **compound subjects**. Compound subjects, usually joined by the word *and*, require plural verbs. In the following examples, the compound subjects are underscored once, and the verbs are underscored twice.

Example: Quality food (S) and excellent service (S) are featured (V) on every cruise.

When a compound subject refers to one person or thing, use a singular verb.

Example: My friend (S) and colleague (S) is (V) an experienced world traveler.

When the compound subject is preceded by *each*, *every*, *many a*, or *many an*, use a singular verb.

Example: Many a client (S) and travel agent (S) has wished (V) he or she could communicate more effectively.

Example: Every man (S) and woman (S) who signed up has been entered (V) in the mystery passenger contest.

When a compound subject is joined by *or* or *nor*, the verb may be either singular or plural. Use a singular verb if two or more singular subjects are joined by *or* or *nor*. Use a plural verb if both subjects are plural. If one of the subjects is singular and the other is plural, the verb should agree with the subject closest to the verb. In these examples, the subjects are underscored once, and the verbs are underscored twice.

Example: The chief purser or the assistant is always ready to help.

Example: Neither the main showroom nor the lounges are large enough.

Example: The dining room captains or the restaurant manager accept special requests.

7-5 PROOFREAD AND MARK

Use the appropriate proofreader marks to correct the errors in subject-verb agreement. If the sentence is correct, write **C** to the left of the number.

1. Reading and sunning are two popular deck activities.
2. Destination and ports of call has always been considered important factors in selecting a cruise.
3. My associate and bridge partner, Natalia Suvarov, have decided to join me on the Rhine River cruise.
4. Evening dining or dancing do not always require formal dress.
5. The cruise director and entertainers has excellent voices.

COLLECTIVE NOUNS

A noun that denotes a collection of persons or things regarded as one unit is called a **collective noun**. Examples of collective nouns are *team*, *choir*, *chorus*, *flock*, *herd*, *audience*, *staff*, *crowd*, *faculty*, *orchestra*, *committee*, *company*, *group*, and *people*.

When a collective noun refers to the collection as a whole, use a singular verb. When a collective noun refers to members of the collection as separate persons or things, use a plural verb. In the following examples, the collective nouns are underscored once, and the verbs are underscored twice.

Example: The cruise staff was on duty day and night. (The staff is acting as a single unit.)

Example: The cruise staff were introduced at the welcome party. (Each member of the staff was introduced individually.)

Example: The audience ~~were~~ was pleased with the ship's entertainment.

Example: The group has signed up for three different shore excursions.

Note: Do not treat a collective noun as both singular and plural in the same sentence.

Example: The audience was positive with ~~their~~ its praise.

7-6

PROOFREAD AND MARK

Use the appropriate proofreader marks to correct the errors in subject-verb agreement. If the sentence is correct, write **C** to the left of the number.

1. The ship's entertainers rehearse at 3:15 daily.
2. The committee were undecided about which tour to give.
3. The deck staff has been assigned to different duties.
4. The game team consist of six persons.
5. A flock of sea gulls follow the ship everywhere.

INDEFINITE PRONOUNS

An **indefinite pronoun** does not refer to or specify a particular noun. Some indefinite pronouns are always singular, others are always plural, and still others may be either singular or plural, depending upon their relationship to other words in the sentence. Study the following indefinite pronouns to become familiar with their number.

ALWAYS SINGULAR		ALWAYS PLURAL	SINGULAR OR PLURAL
anybody	everything	both	all
anyone	many a	few	any
anything	many an	many	more
each	neither	several	most
either	nobody	none	
every	somebody	some	
everybody	someone		
everyone	something		

Indefinite pronouns used as the subject of the sentence must agree in number with the verb. When a pronoun may be either singular or plural, check the noun to which the pronoun refers. The noun often occurs in a phrase beginning with *of*, as the following examples show. In the examples, the subjects (in some cases, indefinite pronouns) are underscored once, and the verbs are underscored twice.

Note: Be careful when using the indefinite pronouns *most*, *some*, and *both*. Nouns immediately following these words are used as adjectives—not pronouns. When the phrase "of the" precedes a noun, *most*, *some*, and *both* are used as pronouns.

Example: Either (S) of the two cabins is (V) adequate for two persons. (*Either* is singular and the subject of the sentence.)

Example: Both cabins (S) are (V) adequate for two persons. (*Both* is used as an adjective.)

Example: Both (S) are (V) adequate for two persons. (*Both* is plural and the subject of the sentence.)

Example: Most (S) of the passengers are (V) happy with the cruise. (Most refers to *passengers*, which is plural and the subject of the sentence.)

Example: Most passengers (S) are (V) happy with the cruise. (*Most* is used as an adjective.)

Example: Most (S) are (V) happy with the cruise. (*Most* is plural and the subject of the sentence.)

Example: Most of the events ~~is~~ are designed for group participation.

Example: Everyone seem^s to be enjoying the cruise

Example: Everybody ~~are~~ is in a festive mood tonight.

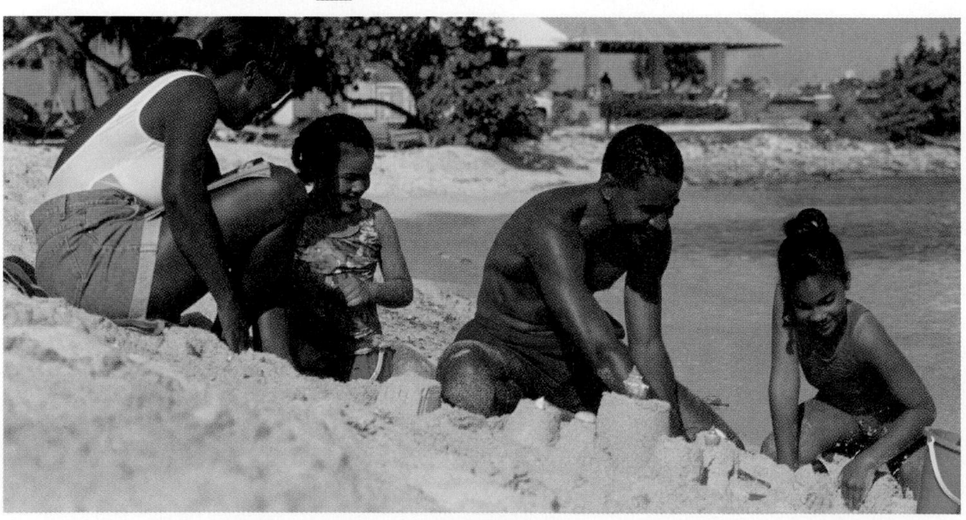

7-7

PROOFREAD AND MARK

Use the appropriate proofreader marks to correct the errors in subject-verb agreement. If the sentence is correct, write **C** to the left of the number.

1. Most of the cruise staff also works as entertainers.
2. Many passengers considers entertainment and food more important than accommodations.
3. Nobody in our group have gained weight on this cruise.
4. Some of the duty-free items in the boutique is being offered at a 40 percent price reduction.
5. Everyone who performs in the passenger talent show receives a souvenir medal.

✤ When proofreading for errors in subject-verb agreement, be alert for nouns whose singular and plural forms are spelled differently.

Singular	Plural
analysis	analyses
basis	bases
criterion	criteria (or criterions)
medium	media

✤ Use the team method of proofreading to improve accuracy, especially for longer documents.

7-8

SPELLING AND WORD USAGE CHECK

Compare the words in Column A with the corresponding words in Column B. Use the appropriate proofreader marks to correct the misspelled or misused words. If both columns are correct, write **C** to the left of the number.

Column A	Column B
1. descriptive	discriptive
2. orientation	oriention
3. planing	planning
4. pursue	pursue
5. brochure	broshure
6. consistant	consistent
7. efficient	efficeint
8. impliment	implement
9. successful	successfull
10. responsibilities	responsabilities
11. arrangements	arrangments
12. internationl	international
13. What a nice complement!	She gave the chef a compliment.
14. I assure you it is okay.	You must ensure me he is safe.
15. We will go wheather it is sunny or not.	Whether he wins or loses is okay.

7-9

INTERNATIONAL VOCABULARY

Compare the Spanish words in Column A with the corresponding words in Column B. If the word or phrase in Column B is different from the word or phrase in Column A, use the appropriate proofreader marks to correct Column B. If both columns are the same, write **C** to the left of the number.

Column A	Column B
1. aventurero	aventureor
2. viaje	viajje
3. coste	cotse
4. fecha	fecha
5. buenas tardes	buenas tardese

PROOFREADING APPLICATIONS PART A

7-10

TRAVEL BROCHURE

Proofread the following brochure and correct all errors using the appropriate proofreader marks.

DISCOVER ALASKA'S INSIDE PASSAGE!

The pristine waters of the Inside Passage leads you to some of the friendliest little towns in the word. Each one of the towns are unique and rich in history and heritage. Totems depicts the Indian spirits of the bald eagle, the whale, and the raven. Russian onion-domed churches gleams with gold icons. The many wonders of Alaska awaits your discovery. Let's visit seven of Alaska's most visited sites.

Ketchikan. The Tongass Tribe of Tlingit call this historic "First City of Alaska" their home. Fishing along the Ketchikan Creek established this town as the "Salmon Capital of the World." Equally impressive are the large collection of totem poles. Fly over or cruise to Misty Fjords National Monument. Waterfalls cascades down sheer granite walls. Abundant wildlife.

Wrangell. The Russians and the British flew there flags here before. The united state purchased Alaska in 1867. The bust of three gold rushes surely made this a flourishing timber industry town. Everything in this small but spirited town are within walking distance—shops, saloons, galleries, and museums.

Sitka

Sitka. One look and you'll agree why lovely Sitka is considered one of Alaska's most beautiful towns. Reminders of its Russian past includes demonstrations of totem caving, lively performances of the New Archangel Dancers, St. Michael's Cathedral with its gleeming dome and priceless icons, the Russian Bishop's House, and the old cematery.

Juneau

Juneau;. Rated among the state's top ten attractions are the mighty Mendenhall Glacier. Daily lectures and film explains the phenomenon of this river of ice. A helicopter take you right on the glacier floor so you can walk on the silent, white sheet of ice. There are plenty ot see and do in this state capital.

Haines

Haines. Every winter the majestic bald eagles congregate, over 3,500 of them, more than all the other states combined. And feed on the late run of chum salmon in the Chilkat River. Equally unforgetable are the visit to the Chilkat Center for the Arts to watch dancers in authentic costumes interpet Tlingit Indian legends. A salmon bake could very well be the final touch to make your day in Haines.

Skagway

Skagway. The stampede of the gold rush in 1896 triggered a frenzied journey by thousands of prospecters. These wild and wooly days have been preserved in history at the Klondike Gold Rush national historical park. Old wooden boardwalks and false-front buildings still stands. An auto or bus tour follow the Trail of '98, which present the ninety five-year history of Skagway.

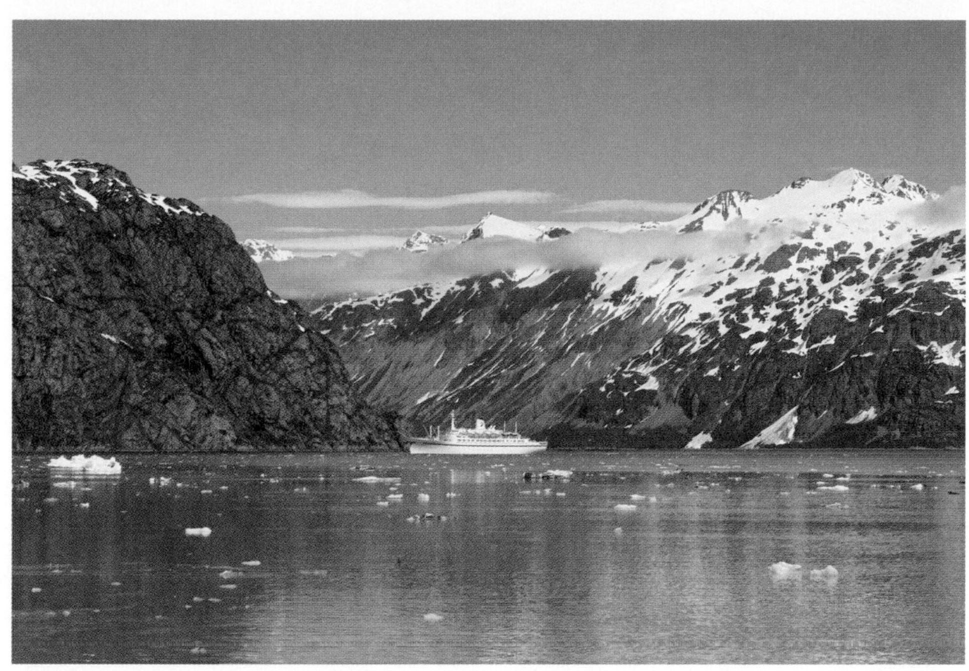

Glacier Bay

Glacier Bay. A whale breaches, seals lolls languidly on floating ice castles, and mountain goats gambols on the rocky terrain nearby. Suddenly, without warning, a mammoth chunk of ice break loose from a glacier and thunder into the blue-green waters of the bay. No trip to Alaska would be completed without a visit to witness 2 hundred years of the Ice Age.

PROOFREADING APPLICATIONS PART B

7-11

BUSINESS LETTER

Proofread the following letter and correct all errors using the appropriate proofreader marks.

January 16, 20—

Diamond Cruise Line
432 North Shore Avenue,
San Francisco, CA 94114-1642
Phone: 415-555-0220
Fax: 415-555-0221

Mr. & Mrs. Hector Romero
9067 Vista Avenue
Albuquerque, NMex. 87108-4631

Dear Mr. & Mrs. Romero

Thank you for your letter of January twenty-seven and your generous comments about your succesful Caribbean cruise abroad the Blue Diamond. We are delighted that you had a plaesant experence.

All of us at Diamond cruise line is looking forward to an exciting year! The descriptive literature we have enclosed includes information on our sheduled voyages for 20––. Please note the high lighted announcements of two new cruise routes—the North Cape and the Mediterranean/Black Sea cruises. Both cruises offers overnight visits to such international cities as the fishing village of Honnisvag, Norway, in the Arctic, and Odessa, Ukraine, the "Pearl of the Black Sea."

You, as a member of our Diamond Society, knows that we take our responsabilities for our clients very seriously. Our cheif concern is to give you consistant, high-quality products and efficeint, friendly service—the best value for your money. So, as a past Diamond cruise passenger, you will be entitled to a special members-only savings of $500 off per person on all staterooms and $1,000 of on penthouse suites for our 13- and 14-day sailings from July through September. Of course, all cruises includes the fly-free bonus from any of our gateway cities. And a $100 on-board credit per person.

Don't wait! Either of our two 5-star jewels, the Blue Diamond or the White Diamond, still have spaces availble. Call your travel agent today to make arrangments for your next cruise!

See you on broard!

Bruce K. Patterson
Manager

rjs

Enclosure

7-12

ANNOUNCEMENT

Proofread the following announcement and correct all errors using the appropriate proofreader marks.

CRUISE REVIEW

Thank you for sailing with Diamond Cruise Line. We apperciate your business, and serving you have been our pleasure.

It is our goal to provide a cruise vacation that you will want to to experience again and again. You can greatly assist us in achieving this objective by completing the inclosed cruise review questionaire.

Your comments is very important to us, and every Cruise Review are read. Your responses are completely confidencial, so please give us your honest opinion. About every aspect of this cruise.

Thank you for taking a few moment of your time to complete this Cruise Reveiw. Those who return the completed questionnaire within three weeks will be invited to attend a complementary reception on their next cruise. We look foreward to welcomming you aboard again soon.

David F. Schilla, Presdent

Diamond Cruise Line

COMPUTERIZED PROOFREADING APPLICATIONS

7-13

BUSINESS LETTER

1. Load file CPA7-13 from the TMPL07 subdirectory on your template CD. (This is a computer copy of Application 7-11.)
2. Proofread the letter on the screen (use a proofreader card). Correct all errors on the screen copy that you have indicated with proofreader marks in Application 7-11. Use the spell check if it is available.
3. Place the date on line 15, and format the letter with 1-inch side margins.
4. Save the letter using the same file name.
5. Print the letter.
6. Proofread the printed document. If you find any additional mistakes, correct the errors on both the hard copy and the screen.
7. Save the revised document and print it.

7-14

MAGAZINE ARTICLE

1. Load file CPA7-14 from the TMPL07 subdirectory on your template CD.
2. Proofread the article and make all necessary corrections.
3. Save the article using the same file name.
4. Print the article with 1-inch side margins
5. Proofread the printed document. If you find any additional mistakes, correct the errors on both the hard copy and the screen.
6. Save the revised document and print it.

7-15

E-MAIL MESSAGE

1. Load file CPA7-15 from the TMPL07 subdirectory on your template CD.
2. Proofread the e-mail message and make all necessary corrections.
3. Save the document using the same file name and print the message.
4. Proofread the printed document. If you find any additional errors, correct the errors on both the hard copy and the screen.
5. Save the revised document and print it.

CHAPTER 8

SENTENCE CONSTRUCTION ERRORS, PART 2

Your writing style provides information about you as a writer. Did you mean what you wrote? Will other people interpret your message in the same way you meant it to be understood? How might a doctor interpret the following items found in patients' medical charts?

- Patient has chest pain when he lies on his right side for over a year.
- On the third day the knee was better, and on the fourth day it had completely disappeared.
- By the time she was admitted in the emergency room, her rapid heart had stopped and she was feeling great.
- Appears mentally alert but forgetful.

Objectives

- Locate and correct errors in pronoun-antecedent agreement.
- Identify and correct errors in pronoun case.
- Spell correctly 12 frequently misspelled words.
- Use correctly 3 pairs of commonly misused words.

CHAPTER 8

SENTENCE CONSTRUCTION ERRORS, PART 2

Like proofreading for other types of grammar errors, identifying errors in the proper use of pronouns requires reading the copy very carefully and having a good understanding of the nature of pronouns. Because a pronoun acts as a substitute for a particular noun, the pronoun must give clear and correct reference to the noun. In addition, pronouns have various forms, depending upon their relationship to other words in the sentence. In this chapter, you will learn to identify and correct misused pronouns.

PRONOUN AND ANTECEDENT AGREEMENT

A **pronoun** is a word used in place of a noun. The noun that the pronoun replaces is called the **antecedent**. In the sentence "Roslyn was complimented for her professional attitude," the pronoun her refers to the antecedent Roslyn. To be correct, pronouns must agree with their antecedents in three ways:

- **Person:** A *first-person* pronoun (*I, we*) refers to the person speaking, a *second-person* pronoun (*you*) refers to the person spoken to, and a *third-person* pronoun (*he, she, it, they*) refers to the person you are speaking about.
- **Number:** A singular pronoun (*I, you, me, he, she, it*) refers to a singular noun. A plural pronoun (*we, you, ours, they, theirs*) refers to a plural noun.
- **Gender:** A feminine pronoun (*she, her*) refers to a feminine noun (*Christina, woman, girl, lady*). A masculine pronoun (*he, him*) refers to a masculine noun (*Robert, man, boy, gentleman*). The neutral pronoun *it* may be used when no gender is designated.

	1ST PERSON	2ND PERSON	3RD PERSON
Singular.	I, me, my, mine	you, your, yours	he, him, his, she, her, hers
Plural.	we, us, our, ours	you, your, yours	they, them, their, theirs

In the following examples, the pronouns and antecedents are italicized.

Example: *Donald* paid *his* dues for the ski club. (The masculine, singular pronoun *his* agrees with the masculine, singular noun *Donald.*)

Example: Ten club *members* qualified for the tour, and *they* were all experienced players. (The plural pronoun *they* agrees with the plural noun *members.*)

Example : The *university* will send ~~their~~ its sports director to the tournament. (The singular pronoun *its* agrees with the singular noun *university*.)

Example: *Lori* was thrilled with ~~their~~ her sports trophy. (The feminine, singular pronoun *her* agrees with the feminine, singular noun *Lori*.)

8-1

PROOFREAD AND MARK

Proofread the sentences and correct the pronouns. If the sentence is correct, write **C** to the left of the number.

1. The motorized cart carrying the softball team's equipment was on their way to the field.
2. After making his speech, the coach was pleased to hear the audience enjoyed their talk.
3. The rookies are habitually leaving their extra bats in the dugout.
4. The fans enjoyed the photo opportunity with its softball team, and she had a good time.
5. Sun Beach, the Heat's winter training camp, is ideal because of their location and weather.

COLLECTIVE NOUNS AS ANTECEDENTS

When proofreading for agreement of pronouns and antecedents, watch for collective nouns used as antecedents. Words such as *committee*, *team*, *audience*, or *jury* are called collective nouns because they refer to a collection of objects, people, or animals. (Refer to Chapter 7, page 100, for other examples of collective nouns.) If the members of the collective noun act as a singular unit, use a singular pronoun. If the members of the collective noun act individually, use a plural pronoun. In the following examples, the pronouns and antecedents are italicized.

Example: The *team* made *its* decision after careful analysis of the alternatives. (The collective noun *team* is acting as one unit and agrees with the singular pronoun *its*.)

Example: The *audience* left ~~its~~ their seats immediately after the rally. (The plural pronoun *their* agrees with the collective noun *audience*. In this instance, the pronoun refers to individuals in the audience acting independently.)

COMPOUND ANTECEDENTS

Just as the verb must agree in number with a compound subject, the pronoun must also agree in number with compound antecedents. A **compound antecedent** consists of two or more nouns. Apply the following rules for compound antecedents. The pronouns and antecedents are italicized in the examples.

Rule 1 Two or more nouns joined by *and* require a plural pronoun.

Example: *Courtney*, *Paul*, and *Tim* received *their* applications a week ago.

Example: The team *captain* and the *players* were honored for their winning season.

Rule 2 Two or more nouns joined by *or/nor* require a singular pronoun when both antecedents are singular.

Example: Neither the *board* of directors nor the *commission* is willing to change *its* position regarding the trading policy.

Rule 3 Two or more nouns joined by *or/nor* require a plural pronoun when both antecedents are plural.

Example: Neither the *coaches* nor the *players* have submitted *their* lists of complaints.

Rule 4 If one antecedent is singular and the other plural, the pronoun must agree with the nearer antecedent.

Example: Neither the *captain* nor the *players* were ready for *their* news interview.

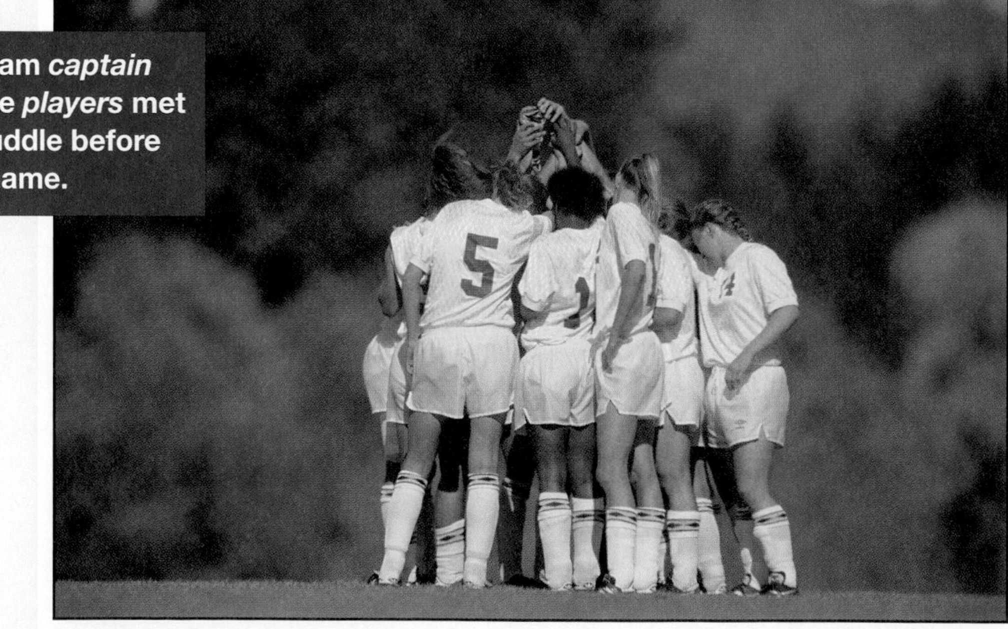

The team *captain* and the *players* met in a huddle before *their* game.

INDEFINITE PRONOUN AGREEMENT

In Chapter 7, you learned that some indefinite pronouns are always singular, others are always plural, and still others may be either singular or plural. When the first pronoun is indefinite and is used as an antecedent, the second pronoun that follows the antecedent must agree in number with the first.

Example: *Each* of the women took *her* turn in demonstrating the techniques. (*Her* agrees with the singular antecedent *each*.)

Example: *Both* of the players were sorry for *their* actions. (*Their* agrees with the plural antecedent *both*.)

8-2

PROOFREAD AND MARK

Proofread the sentences and correct the pronouns. If the sentence is correct, write **C** to the left of the number.

1. The field hockey team's tournament committee made their flight arrangements for the trip.
2. Neither William nor Jonathan has consulted their director regarding the itinerary.
3. Both Coach Thoms and Coach Isobe have made his final selections for the starting players for tonight's game.
4. One of the women has left her golf clubs in the locker room.
5. The boxing team voted to double their effort for the duration of this season.

THE CASE OF THE PRONOUN

Incorrect usage of personal pronouns often occurs because pronouns have different forms known as **cases**. A personal pronoun case changes its form according to its relationship to other words in the sentence. Notice the two masculine pronouns in the sentence, "When John called, he said not to wait for his reply." Even though *he* and *his* both refer to John, the cases are different because the two pronouns have separate functions in the sentence.

The three cases of pronouns are **nominative**, **objective**, and **possessive**. Study the three different pronoun cases and learn to use them correctly. In the examples that follow on page 116, all of the pronouns are italicized.

CHAPTER 8

SENTENCE CONSTRUCTION ERRORS, PART 2

NOMINATIVE CASE

Nominative case pronouns include the singular pronouns *I*, *you*, *he*, *she*, and *it* and the plural pronouns *we*, *you*, and *they*. The nominative case is used in two ways.

Rule 1 Subject pronoun. Use the nominative case when the pronoun acts as the subject of the sentence (subject of the verb). The verb may be the main verb of the sentence or the verb within a clause. (Clauses will be discussed in Chapter 9.)

Example: *He* canceled the game because *we* had to work that week. (Both pronouns are the subjects of verbs—*canceled* and *had*, respectively.)

Example: Two players were hurt during the first quarter, but *they* were not injured seriously. (The pronoun is the subject of the verb phrase *were injured.*)

Example: Bryan and Theresa will officiate while *you* and ~~her~~ she are away.

Example: Michael and ~~me~~ I play well together.

Rule 2 Predicate pronoun. Use the nominative case when the pronoun immediately follows a form of the linking verb be (*am*, *is*, *are*, *was*, *were*, *be*, *has been*, *have been*, *had been*). When a pronoun follows a linking verb, it is called a **predicate pronoun**. A predicate pronoun is used after a verb and refers to the same person or thing as the subject of the verb. A predicate pronoun is always in the nominative case.

Example: It was *I* who called about the schedule. (*I*, a predicate pronoun, follows was, a form of the linking verb *be*.)

Example: The star player for today's game is *she*. (*She*, a predicate pronoun, follows is, a form of the linking verb *be*.)

Example: The only persons who complained were *you* and ~~him.~~ he

Example: The winner of the Satellite News 20-K run was ~~her~~ she.

8-3

PROOFREAD AND MARK

Proofread the sentences and correct the pronoun case errors. If the sentence is correct, write **C** to the left of the number.

1. If the junior players were treated like the varsity players, would they do as well?
2. It was not me who requested that the seats be changed; it was Lee and her.
3. The senior track coach and him can meet with the press today.

4. The person in the photograph is her when she played on the championship team in 1998.
5. The athletics office had a good year because they have an experienced staff.

OBJECTIVE CASE

Objective case pronouns include the singular pronouns *me*, *you*, *him*, *her*, and *it* and the plural pronouns *us*, *you*, and *them*. Because objective case pronouns always function as objects, they are used with action verbs. Objective case pronouns are never used with linking verbs, such as *is*, *are*, *was*, *were*, *seem*, or *become*. The objective case pronoun is used in three ways.

Rule 1 Direct object of the verb. Use the objective case when the pronoun answers the question *what* or *whom* and the pronoun receives the action of the verb (called the object of the verb).

Example: When you call your brother, tell *him* to meet us at Gate 15. (You tell *whom*?)

Example: They selected *him* to be the team captain. (They selected *whom*?)

Rule 2 Indirect object. Use the objective case when the pronoun tells *to whom* or *for whom* something is done.

Example: Mother gave *me* the play-off game tickets for my birthday. (Tells that Mother gave to me the tickets—the preposition *to* is omitted.)

Example: My niece knitted *me* a sports sweater. (Tells that my niece knitted for me a sweater—the preposition *for* is omitted.)

Rule 3 Object of the preposition. Use the objective case when the pronoun is used as the object of the preposition. **Prepositions** are words that relate a noun or a pronoun to other words in the sentence. Some common prepositions are *about*, *after*, *at*, *before*, *between*, *by*, *for*, *from*, *in*, *of*, *on*, *over*, *since*, *to*, *until*, and *with*. A preposition and its object form a **prepositional phrase**. In the following examples, the prepositional phrases with the objective case pronouns are italicized.

Example: Caitlin discussed the gymnastics trials *with her*.

Example: Just *between you and me*, I won't be going to the game today.

Example: Are you saving this seat *for he and I*?

Example: You are assigned to work *with Bryan, Jeff, and she*.

Note: When *to* is followed by a verb, the phrase is called an **infinitive phrase**. No other preposition can be used as an infinitive. Do not confuse the preposition *to* with the infinitive *to*.

Example: Auri mailed *to him* an Olympic souvenir program. (Shown as a prepositional phrase.)

It is a good idea *to stretch* before jogging.

Example: I plan *to take* the bus to Friday's championship game. (Shown as an infinitive phrase.)

8-4

PROOFREAD AND MARK

Proofread the sentences and correct the pronouns. If the sentence is correct, write **C** to the left of the number.

1. The lacrosse coach sent Glenn and he copies of next week's practice schedule.
2. The sports public relations office will arrange interviews for you and I.
3. I decided to go to the game with Judy and her.
4. The tournament director called the team managers and I to confirm the lineups for the game.
5. After the team won, the owner gave a bonus to he.

WHO AND WHOM

The use of the pronouns *who* and *whom* is the most troublesome, even for experienced writers and speakers. Remember, the rules that apply when using nominative and objective pronouns also apply when using *who* and *whom.*

Who is a nominative case pronoun that may be used as the subject of the sentence or clause. *Who* must also follow a form of the linking verb *be* (predicate pronoun).

Whom is an objective case pronoun that is used as the direct object of the verb, indirect object, or the object of the preposition.

To help you decide which pronoun is the correct one to use, mentally rearrange the sentence and substitute another pronoun, such as *he*, *she*, or *they* in place of "who" and *him*, *her*, or *them* in place of "whom."

Example: *Who* signed up for the tour? (*She* signed up for the tour.)

Example: *Whom* did the agent call? (The agent called *her*.)

Example: To *who* did you send your deposit? (You sent the deposit to *him*.)

Example: The woman in the photograph is *whom*? (*She* is the woman in the photograph.)

If *who* or *whom* appears within a clause, determine the pronoun's use within the clause, ignoring the rest of the sentence. Then substitute another pronoun in place of *who* or *whom*. In the following examples, the dependent clauses are italicized.

Example: Jeanette is the spokesperson *who will represent our group*. (*Who* is the subject of the dependent clause. *She* will represent our group.)

Example: The member *whom we elected* is the most qualified for the position. (*Whom* is the direct object of the verb elected. We elected *her*.)

Example: Jenna, *whom* we know is an experienced player, will represent our team in the qualifying match. (*Who* is an experienced player?)

Example: Sorphea is the person *who* the league selected as the sportsmanship award winner. (The league selected *whom*?)

8-5

PROOFREAD AND MARK

Proofread the sentences and correct the pronouns. If the sentence is correct, write **C** to the left of the number.

1. Kelli, who you know well, is a very intense player.
2. Whom is making our travel arrangements?
3. Whom did you ask to take the basketball team's photographs?
4. Is she the person who you wish to interview?
5. Who do you want for a roommate while the team is on the road this year?

POSSESSIVE CASE

The possessive case includes the singular pronouns *my*, *mine*, *your*, *yours*, *his*, *her*, *hers*, and *its* and the plural pronouns *our*, *ours*, *your*, *yours*, *their*, and *theirs*. Possessive pronouns show ownership, and they are always written without the apostrophe.

Note: Don't confuse the contractions *it's* (it is), *they're* (they are), *who's* (who is), and *you're* (you are) with the possessive pronouns *its*, *their*, *whose*, and *your*.

Example: All of the league teams mail *their* subscription season tickets.

Example: *Whose* racket case is this with the blue and red piping?

Example: The time was changed because of *it's* conflict with another game.

Example: *Your's* were the best score predictions.

Possessive pronouns are also used immediately before a **verbal noun** or **gerund** (verbs ending in *ing* that are used as nouns). In the following examples, the gerunds are italicized.

Example: Bill takes his *jogging* very seriously.

Example: Their *complaining* has ruined the game for everyone.

Example: I appreciate your *working* late this week.

She practices her *riding* everyday.

USING PRONOUNS WITH *THAN* OR *AS*

When using pronouns in comparing two persons or things, the pronoun that follows *than* or *as* can be nominative or objective, depending on the use of the pronoun. Because the clause has been deliberately omitted after the pronoun, mentally restate the clause to determine the correct use of the pronoun. Study these examples carefully.

Example: Mick is taller than *I*. (Mick is taller than I am tall.)

Example: Corrine knows him as well as *I*. (Corrine knows him as well as I know him.)

Example: Corrine knows him as well as *me*. (Corrine knows him as well as Corrine knows me)

Example: My sister keys faster than *I*. (My sister keys faster than I key.)

Example: You helped her more than *I*. (You helped her more than I helped her.)

Example: You helped her more than *me*. (You helped her more than you helped me.)

8-6

PROOFREAD AND MARK

Proofread the sentences and correct the pronouns. If the sentence is correct, write **C** to the left of the number.

1. The team's local ticket office offers the best prices for their home games.

2. The NFL announced their football schedule for the season.
3. You insisting on an aisle seat for the game was a good idea.
4. She was allowed more time for practice than I.
5. Ask Joy and Roy if her time will allow for another match.

✤ Double-check the document. Read the copy the first time for content. Read the copy a second time for consistency and correct grammar.

✤ Use available references if you have questions about correct grammar.

SPELLING AND WORD USAGE CHECK

Compare the words in Column A with the corresponding words in Column B. Use the appropriate proofreader marks to correct the misspelled or misused words. If both columns are correct, write **C** to the left of the number.

	Column A	Column B
1.	acknowledge	acknowlege
2.	noticeable	noticable
3.	convenience	convience
4.	facilities	facilities
5.	monitoring	monitering
6.	occasionally	occassionally
7.	reciept	receipt
8.	particpation	participation
9.	paralel	parallel
10.	processing	proccessing
11.	quality	guality
12.	persevarance	perseverance
13.	The assistance was appreciated.	He will offer assistans.
14.	Seal the envelope.	The envelope went in the mail.
15.	Procede to the front line.	The meeting will proceed.

PROOFREADING APPLICATIONS PART A

8-8

LIST OF SENTENCES

*Proofread the following sentences and mark all pronoun, spelling, and word usage errors using the appropriate proofreader marks. If the sentence is correct, write **C** to the left of the number.*

1. Team owner Fay Sonamaran is one of the persons who's winning record was acknowleged at the sports awards banquet.
2. To who did you write about the reciept?
3. It was very noticable that you played better than me during today's match.
4. I enjoy many sports, but particapating actively in it is not always convient.
5. The public relations staff said it's two assistance will not be attending the banquet next week.
6. Federal tax laws require that we send a receept to any contributr who sends a check for $250 for our scholarship program.
7. The U.S. skating team will perform its exhibition program at the facilities in Marina Heights.
8. The star player for the team is her.
9. My sister-in-law is a noticably better tennis player than me, but I occassionally win a game.
10. The Rhinelander Curling Association announced that anyone can attend their meetings.

11. The meeting of the Whitland Athletic Club was disrupted by him arriving late.
12. Mail you're reply in the enclosed, self-addresed envelop before the May 30 deadline.
13. When the members of the International Olympic Commitee meets, it is required to show their identification cards at the gate.
14. It is her whom we want to recommend for membership in the Garfield Spirit Club.
15. Between you and I, the new Milwaukee Sports Arena is the most outstanding facilty of its kind in the country.
16. The paperwork was completed by the manager and I.
17. To who should you address an inquiry about paralell parking at the stadium?
18. Members of the wrestling team has its own ideas of how quality training helps.
19. The marching band, with their bright new uniforms, proceded the float carrying the football players in the parade.
20. Their persevarance paid off because the players won in the second overtime period.

PROOFREADING APPLICATIONS — PART B

8-9

BUSINESS LETTER

Proofread the following letter and correct all errors using the appropriate proofreader marks.

SAN JOSE PANTHERS
Southern City Stadium
48322 Buckingham Avenue • San Jose, CA 95136-2382
(408) 555-1468 • Fax (408) 555-1469

Febuary 28, 20––

Miss Jeanne R. Hudson
400 Lake Street
Seattle, WA 98125-4130

Dear Miss Hudson:

You are among a select group of baseball fans who we beleive will be interested in a once-in-a-lifetime opportunty to meet and socialise with its favorite team. At the same time, you will enjoy a regimen of healthful diet, exercise, and sleep at our quiet, pleasant facilties.

The baseball team is the San Jose Panthers. For the past two years, the team have provided a limited group of its fans the unprecidented opportunity to join them during spring training for two weeks of healthful and enjoyable work and relaxation. You will become a part of the team themself, particpating in not only all planing sessions but also all strategy meetings, practice sessions, etc. You will also have available the full services of our training staff to help you avoid that occassional cramp and to treat them if they do occur.

The enclosed broshure, <u>Guidelines for Training Session</u>, will provide information for the two sessions sheduled. The price for both session include all expenses: lodgeing, food, transportation, and gratuities. We will also provide a broshure discribing the hotel accomodations and the siteseeing tours available in the area.

During the last three days of training, the players will be divided into two teams: Panthers I and Panthers II. These teams will play in a miniseries to determine the champion, and awards will be presented at apporpriate ceremonies.

As we anticapate a considerable responce to this offer, we will apperciate a prompt reply in the conveneint, inclosed self-addresed envelop.

Yours truly,

Chuck T. Underwood
President
rks

Enclosures: List of Do's and Don'ts
Self-Addressed Envelop
Broshure

8-10

SIMPLIFIED MEMORANDUM

Proofread the following memo and correct all errors using the appropriate proofreader marks.

March 30, 20—

All Supervisers

TRAINING SESSION FOR SAN JOSE PANTHERS' FANS

I am attaching a copy of my letter of Febuary 28, 20—, and the broshure entitled Guidelines for training session. These were sent to a select group of baseball fans who have indicated an interest in joining the San Jose Panthers for a limited time during our spring training at our Marina facilties.

You will be contacted individually by Vice President Don Burnside. In connection with logistics and related handeling. However, I would like to take this oportunity to encourage you to extend yourself in making the particpants in this program feel he is joining our family.

Remember, these people are more than guests; they are sincere and dedicated fans of the Panthers whom have cheered us when we were up and encouraged us when we were down. Its easy to acknowlege the applause and wave the pennats when "Lady Luck" is smiling. But it takes a special, dedicated fan to remain devoted to us team.

Please make use of the many convenent and exclusive touches included in this excellant program. Such as the extensive menu that can be tailored to accomodate individual preferences as well as needs. Food is a most important part of this program, and we want to make sure that even those guests who have restricted diets enjoy his meals.

So, I am asking for your assistants in monitering this program to insure that our guests enjoy there stay with us. When they return home, there happy memories will encourage them to join us again next year.

Thank you for you're continued support in making this an outstanding program.

Chuck T. Underwood
President

Attachments 2

COMPUTERIZED PROOFREADING APPLICATIONS

8-11

SIMPLIFIED MEMORANDUM

1. Load file CPA8-11 from the TMPL08 subdirectory on your template CD. (This is a computer copy of Application 8-10.)
2. Proofread the letter on the screen (use a proofreader card). Correct all errors on the screen copy that you have indicated with proofreader marks in Application 8-10.
3. Place the date on line 15, and format the letter with 1-inch side margins.
4. Save the memo using the same file name.
5. Print the memo.
6. Proofread the printed document. If you find any additional mistakes, correct the errors on both the hard copy and the screen.
7. Save the revised document and print it.

8-12

ENUMERATED LIST

1. Load file CPA8-12 from the TMPL08 subdirectory on your template CD.
2. Proofread the list and make all necessary corrections.
3. Save the list using the same file name.
4. Print the list with 1-inch side margins.
5. Proofread the printed document. If you find any additional mistakes, correct the errors on both the hard copy and the screen.
6. Save the revised document and print it.

8-13

E-MAIL MESSAGE

1. Load file CPA8-13 from the TMPL08 subdirectory on your template CD.
2. Proofread the e-mail message and make all necessary corrections.
3. Save the document using the same file name and print the message.
4. Proofread the printed document. If you find any additional errors, correct the errors on both the hard copy and the screen.
5. Save the revised document and print it.

CHAPTER 9

SENTENCE CONSTRUCTION ERRORS, PART 3

Your writing style includes the six "C's" of communication: courtesy, clarity, conciseness, correctness, completeness, and coherence. When you edit your documents, check to ensure that the message will be clear to your audience. How seriously do you think the principal took the following excuses when she received them?

- Please accuse Sam for being absent on February 29, 30, and 31.
- Sandy is under our doctor's care and should not take physical education. Please execute her.
- Ashley could not be in school last week because she has very close veins.

Objectives

- Understand the significance of phrases and clauses.
- Find and mark errors in parallel structure.
- Identify and correct dangling modifiers.
- Use bias-free language.
- Spell correctly 12 frequently misspelled words.
- Use correctly 3 pairs of commonly misused words.

CHAPTER 9 SENTENCE CONSTRUCTION ERRORS, PART 3

In Chapter 7, you learned that a sentence contains a subject and a verb and expresses a complete thought. Generally, sentences contain other elements that help to convey the writer's message. The alert proofreader must check that these elements are positioned correctly to ensure consistency and clarity. The proofreader must also check the language for any bias.

SENTENCE ELEMENTS

In addition to the words that act as subjects and verbs, most sentences also contain phrases and clauses. A **phrase** is a group of two or more related words without a subject and a verb. The entire phrase in a sentence may act as a noun, a verb, an adjective, or an adverb. Phrases may also modify nouns and verbs. Phrases that function as adjectives or adverbs are usually positioned near the words they modify. The phrases are italicized in the following examples.

Example: *The certified public accountant* audited their accounting records. (noun phrase acting as the subject)

Example: Douglas *should work together* with Alice on the assignment. (verb phrase)

Example: The book *lying on the table* belongs to Beatriz. (adjective phrase that modifies the noun *book*)

Example: My first class started *on time*. (adverb phrase that modifies the verb *started*)

Example: *Running late*, I forgot my 3 p.m. appointment. (participial phrase that modifies the subject *I*)

Example: Amelia will return *in the morning*. (prepositional phrase that is used as an adverb and modifies the verb *will return*)

Example: The sweatshirt *with the gold stripes* is mine. (prepositional phrase that is used as an adjective and modifies the noun *sweatshirt*)

Example: Ellis wants *to retire*. (infinitive phrase that is used as a noun and is the direct object of the verb *wants*)

Clauses are groups of words that contain a subject and a verb. If the clause expresses a complete thought, it is a sentence and is called an **independent clause**. If the clause does not express a complete thought, it is called a **dependent clause**. In the following examples, the independent clauses appear in bold and the dependent clauses in italics. The subject and verb of both clauses are identified.

s v
Example: **The representative returned my call.**

s v s v
Example: *If you will leave your number*, **I will call you tomorrow**.

s v s v
Example: *When the package arrives*, **Beau will sign for it.**

9-1

PROOFREAD AND MARK

In each of the sentences, identify the underlined group of words. To the left of the number, write **P** for phrase, **IC** for independent clause, or **DC** for dependent clause.

1. <u>If we are to arrive on time</u>, we must follow their directions.
2. <u>You shouldn't leave the interview</u> without asking when they will contact you with their decision.
3. <u>When you volunteer for the position</u>, consider the work hours and your ability to complete the necessary tasks.
4. <u>The grievance committee has total commitment</u> to further the work.
5. <u>For most people</u>, satisfaction is an important consideration.

PARALLEL STRUCTURE IN SENTENCES

Words, phrases, or clauses within a sentence that are related in meaning should be written in the same grammatical form. Using the same form makes the ideas **parallel**. When adjectives are parallel to adjectives, phrases are parallel to phrases, and clauses are parallel to clauses, the meaning of the sentence is clear and logical. When you find a sentence that sounds awkward, revise it so that related ideas are expressed in the same way.

Example: Michelle's career interests are *advertising* and *modeling*. (parallel noun forms, or gerunds)

Example: We are looking for someone who is *courteous*, *dependable*, and *considerate*. (parallel adjectives)

Example: Roland couldn't decide whether *to buy* a laptop computer or *to spend* the money on a trip to visit his sister. (infinitive phrases used as the objects of the verb *decide*)

Example: We will ski and ~~we will be~~ climb~~ing~~ mountains during our vacation. (unparallel verbs)

Example: Sharon is tall, ~~with~~ has brown eyes, and has a cheerful disposition ~~that is cheerful~~. (unparallel adjectives) *Also correct*: Sharon is tall, brown eyed, and cheerful.

Example: I have limited experience using desktop publishing, but I use word processing ~~is being used~~ extensively in my present job. (unparallel clauses)

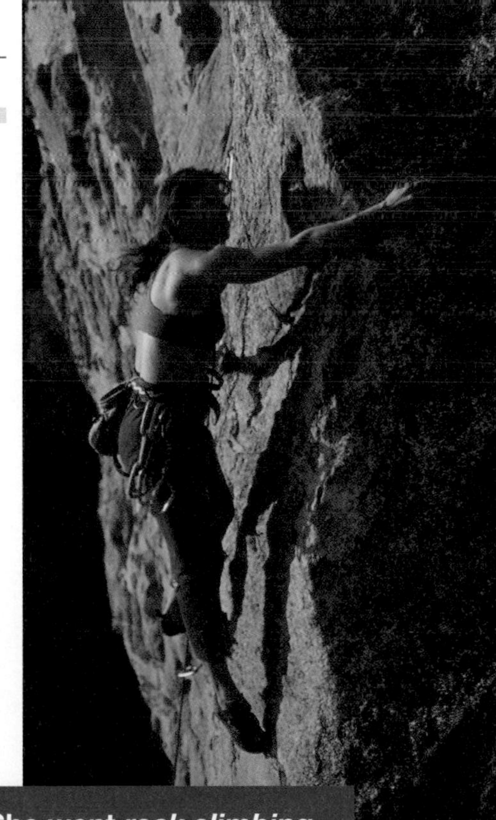

She went *rock climbing* and *camping* in the mountains last week.

CHAPTER 9 SENTENCE CONSTRUCTION ERRORS, PART 3

Errors in parallelism occur frequently within enumerations. All related elements must be stated in the same grammatical structure. Additionally, the same grammatical structure must follow conjunctions that appear in pairs, such as *both ... and*, *either ... or*, *neither ... nor*, *not only ... but also*. These pairs are called **correlative conjunctions**. The parallel elements are italicized in the examples. Note that all the elements end in *ing*.

Example: Past job experience includes the following tasks:

1. *Keying* original copy and *proofreading* first drafts.
2. *Saving* documents.
3. *Printing* and *proofreading* hard copy.
4. *Retrieving* and *revising* documents.

Example: Daniel stated either *that you had changed your mind* or *that you had cancelled your reservation.*

Example: The topics to be covered include the following:

1. Identifying the purpose and audience.
2. To plan the message.
3. Write the message.
4. Editing the message.
5. Direct and indirect messages.

Example: Suzette not only serves on the Personnel Committee but she is also on the Constitution Committee.

9-2

PROOFREAD AND MARK

Correct errors in parallelism using the appropriate proofreader marks. If the sentence is correct, write **C** to the left of the number.

1. We will only hire employees who are hard working, ambitious, and who are trustworthy.
2. The guidelines were written for upgrading all employees, improving the morale, and to augment income.
3. A supervisor was hired to manage the new plant and that he would recommend changes in hiring practices.
4. The equipment now being installed can number the sections, rearrange the margins, and listing the corrections.
5. The editor called me about the manuscript draft and wanted more information about tomorrow's meeting.

DANGLING AND MISPLACED MODIFIERS

A **modifier** is a word, a phrase, or a clause that describes another word in the sentence. To clarify the relationship between the modifier and the word it describes, the modifier must be placed in the correct position. If it does not logically describe any word in the sentence, it is called a **dangling modifier**. If it is not close enough to the word it describes, it is called a **misplaced modifier**. It is best to place the modifier as close as possible to the word it modifies. Study the placement of the modifiers below.

DANGLING MODIFIER	CORRECTED
Keying very rapidly, the report had three errors.	**Keying very rapidly, the operator made three errors in the report.**

MISPLACED MODIFIER	CORRECTED
Mara bought a canary for her friend that sings beautifully.	**Mara bought her friend a canary that sings beautifully.**

Errors frequently occur when introductory phrases and clauses do not modify the subject of the sentence. To correct a dangling or misplaced modifier, revise the sentence so that the subject completes the action described in the introductory phrase. If you are unsure about the subject of the sentence, ask the question "Who?" or "What?" after the introductory phrase. The answer is the sentence's subject, which should immediately follow the introductory phrase. Compare the following sentences.

DANGLING MODIFIER	CORRECTED
Before deciding which van to buy, three agencies were visited by Christopher.	**Before deciding which van to buy, Christopher visited three agencies. (Who visited three agencies?—Christopher)**

MISPLACED MODIFIER	CORRECTED
While jogging on the sidewalk, a cyclist hit Mary Beth.	**While jogging on the sidewalk, Mary Beth was hit by a cyclist. (Who was jogging?—Mary Beth)**

9-3

PROOFREAD AND MARK

Revise the sentences that contain dangling or misplaced modifiers. If the sentence is correct, write **C** to the left of the number.

1. Adept at using software applications, the department decided to hire Tim.
2. The document was accidentally picked up by Myra lying on the desk.
3. Though all the applicants are qualified for the positions, they need improvement in some skills.
4. Alicia showed the supervisor how she used the equipment appearing somewhat doubtful.
5. When leaving for lunch today, a phone message for the supervisor was left by the receptionist.

BIAS-FREE LANGUAGE

A writer or speaker should never send a message that might alienate employees or potential customers. Instead, your message should be unbiased, ethical, and fair to all. **Bias-free language** avoids insensitive language regarding gender, race or ethnic group, age, religion, or disability.

AVOID GENDER BIAS

Traditionally, writers have used *he* or *man* to represent both genders. The practice of gender bias is outdated and no longer acceptable. It is inappropriate to use *he* or *his* to refer to both men and women. Likewise, it is incorrect to assume that certain jobs are "men's work" or "women's work." Today men and women are employed in all occupations, and the *Dictionary of Occupational Titles* was rewritten to reflect job titles and not gender. To classify secretaries, elementary teachers, or nurses as women and pilots, farmers, or police officers as men would be to stereotype occupations.

To treat men and women fairly, follow these general rules:

Rule 1 Use the plural pronouns *they, their, theirs*, or *them* or nouns such as *people* or *persons* when referring to a group that consists of both men and women.

Example: Salespersons must have their weekly reports completed by Monday.

Rule 2 Rewrite the sentence to avoid using pronouns, if it is possible to do so without affecting the meaning.

Example: Sales reports are due on Monday.

Rule 3 Shift the sentence to second person.

Example: As an employee, you are responsible for reporting expenses correctly.

Rule 4 If you must use a singular pronoun, use both he/she and his/her. Do not overuse these expressions, for they can become annoying and sound repetitious.

Example: Each salesperson must have his or her report completed by Monday. (both genders used)

Rule 5 Use parallel phrasing if you must refer to persons by gender. Use "women and men," "females and males," "boys and girls," or "ladies and gentlemen" for parallel structure. You would not say "men and girls" or "women and males."

Example: The boys and girls toured our offices.

Rule 6 Use business terms that do not imply the gender of a person.

OUTDATED (AVOID)	CURRENT (USE)
airline steward or stewardess	flight attendant
businessman	businessperson, executive, entrepreneur, professional
businessmen	businesspeople, people in business
chairman	chair, chairperson, group leader, moderator, president, presiding officer
coed	student
congressmen	members of Congress, congressional representatives, representatives of Congress
foreman	supervisor, manager, executive
housewife	homemaker
mankind	persons, people, humanity, everyone, humankind
man-made	handmade, custom-made, custom-built
manpower	human resources, human power, human energy, workforce, personnel

repairman	repairer, repair person, service technician
salesman	salesperson, sales agent, sales representative
spokesman	speaker, spokesperson, advocate, proponent
statesman	politician, public official, political leader, public servant, government leader
waiter/waitress	server
workmen	workers, employees, personnel

Avoid placing the words *man*, *male*, *lady*, *female*, or *woman* before or after an occupational title. Compare the differences in these examples:

AVOID	USE
lady or female doctor	doctor
male nurse	nurse
policewoman, policeman	police officer
fireman, female fire fighter	fire fighter
male elementary teacher	elementary teacher

The children pay close attention to their elementary teacher.

PROOFREAD AND MARK 9-4

Revise the sentences that contain inappropriate language. If the sentence is correct, write **C** to the left of the number.

1. An elementary teacher must demonstrate that she can teach art in her classes.
2. Brenda Torres is the chairman of the Hospitality Committee.
3. More manpower will be required to complete the installation quickly.
4. Humankind must be aware of the importance of the environment.
5. The sales meeting brought together more than 500 salesmen.

AVOID RACE AND ETHNIC GROUP, AGE, RELIGION, AND DISABILITY BIAS

The principle for writing messages that are sensitive to race and ethnic group, age, religion, or disability is as follows: *Avoid emphasizing race and ethnic group, age, religion, or disability when these categories have no relevance to your message.* Emphasis in business writing should be on competence and relevance, not on categories like race, age, or religion.

Race and Ethnic Group Bias

Mention race or ethnic group only when the race or ethnic group is relevant. Likewise, avoid language that suggests that all members of a certain racial or ethnic group have the same characteristics.

UNACCEPTABLE	ACCEPTABLE
Yens Schmidt is an unusually fast German runner.	**Yens Schmidt is an unusually fast runner. (Being a *German* is not relevant.)**
Celine Casiano, the Spanish clerk, was selected for promotion.	**Celine Casiano was selected for promotion. (Being *Spanish* is not relevant to her promotion.)**

Age Bias

Mention the age of a person only when age is relevant.

UNACCEPTABLE	ACCEPTABLE
Lu Chou, 29, was hired last month.	**Lu Chou was hired last month. (His age, *29*, was not relevant in being hired.)**
Kay Aspen, the 51-year-old president of our company, has resigned.	**Kay Aspen, president of our company, has resigned. (Her age, *51*, was not relevant in her resignation.)**

Religion Bias

Religion usually has no relevance in a business setting and should not be mentioned.

UNACCEPTABLE	ACCEPTABLE
Mavis Mann, the Jewish account executive, gave a presentation on using laptop computers.	**Mavis Mann gave a presentation on using laptop computers. (Being *Jewish* is not relevant.)**

Disability Bias

There is no polite way to label people with a physical, mental, or emotional disability. Eliminate mention of the disability if possible. If you must refer to people in terms of their disabilities, refer to the person first and the disability second. In addition, avoid using terms like *handicapped, crippled, afflicted, retarded,* or *victim.*

UNACCEPTABLE	ACCEPTABLE
A diabetic, Eunice is always the first person to arrive.	**Eunice is always the first person to arrive. (Being a *diabetic* has no bearing on when she arrives.)**
The crippled worker, Kim, faces many barriers on the job.	**Kim, who is disabled, faces many barriers on the job. (Avoid using terms like *crippled*, and refer to Kim by name prior to listing any disability.)**

9-5 PROOFREAD AND MARK

Revise the sentences that contain inappropriate language. If the sentence is correct, write **C** to the left of the number.

1. Mario Cuomo, former Italian-American mayor of New York City, plans to run for U.S. senator.
2. Keith's temper flared when he was questioned.
3. Jason, a member of the ELCA church, took the bus to San Francisco.
4. Arianna, 22, has joined our Accounting Department.
5. As a cancer victim, Janelle is being treated for her disease.

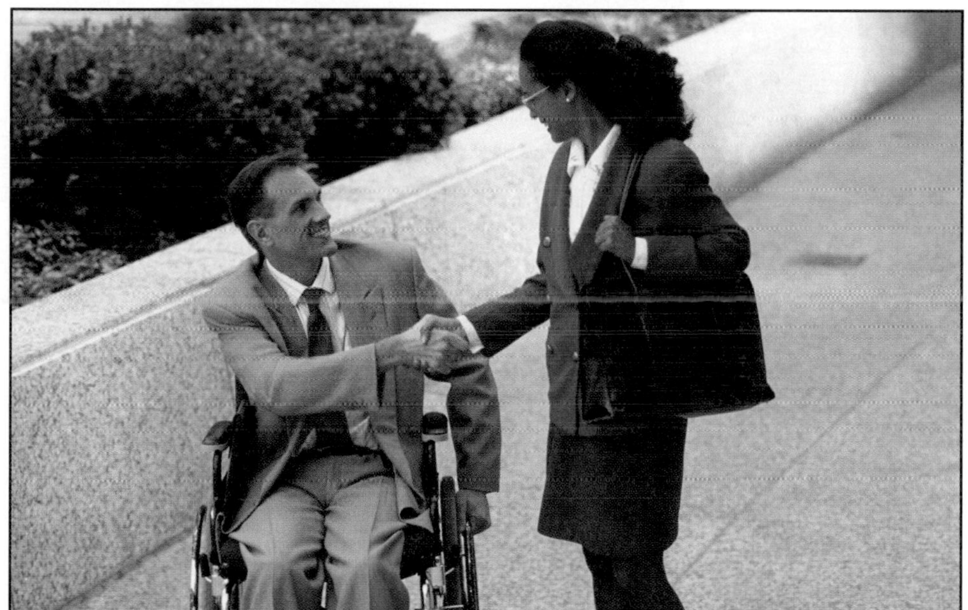

✤ Select words carefully to eliminate insensitivity regarding gender, race or ethnic group, religion, age, or physical condition. Emphasis in business writing should be concerned with competence and relevance, not on categories like gender, religion, or age.

✤ Read one word at a time—the opposite of speed-reading—especially for copy that contains very specialized or highly technical vocabulary. Read unfamiliar words syllable by syllable or letter by letter.

✤ Always check a dictionary to determine whether a compound word is written as one word, as two words, or as a hyphenated word.

9-6

SPELLING AND WORD USAGE CHECK

Compare the words in Column A with the corresponding words in Column B. Use the appropriate proofreader marks to correct the misspelled or misused words. If both columns are correct, write **C** to the left of the number.

Column A	Column B
1. acaddemic	academic
2. applicants	applicants
3. cleint	client
4. decision	decisoin
5. develope	develop
6. eligible	eligable
7. featured	faetured
8. installation	instalation
9. libary	library
10. percent	per cent
11. possibility	possability
12. recommendation	recomendation
13. divide among Jo and me	between the two of us
14. correspondents arrived	The correspondence were
15. Who's letter is it?	Whose sister is coming?

9-7

INTERNATIONAL VOCABULARY

Compare the Spanish words in Column A with the corresponding words in Column B. If the word in Column B is different from the word in Column A, use the appropriate proofreader marks to correct Column B. If the words in both columns are the same, write **C** to the left of the number.

Column A	Column B
1. confite	conffite
2. quesera	quecera
3. compra	comprra
4. limonada	limonade

9-8

BUSINESS LETTER

Proofread the following letter and correct all errors in placement of phrases, parallel structure, misplaced or dangling modifiers, and gender stereotyping. Use the appropriate proofreader marks to make the corrections.

THE GOURMET SOCIETY
143 Grant Plaza • 1621 West Market Avenue
San Francisco, CA 94105-1362
(415) 555-0381 Fax (415) 555-0383

July 24, 20—

Mr. Alton K. Ladene
4090 Strawberry Circle
Denver, CO 80123-4102

Dear Alton

I am excited about your desision to be spokesman at the fall meeting of The Gourmet Society.

This dinner meetting will be held in the San Antonio Room of the Hotel Goldstrike, 9006 Mission Street, San Francisco, CA 94105-3428, at 7 p.m., Tuesday, Sep. 6, 20—. There is a possability that attendance may reach over two hundred. Everyone is elligible to attend, including new aplicants to The Gourmet Soceity and nonmembers. Following dinner, dancing will be featured in the Diamond Room.

I enjoyed your resent article titled "The Many Faces of Pasta" in the June edition of *Cooking Western Style*. Most of our members has read the article and, I'm sure, would be pleased to have you speak on this nonaccademic subject. Topics you may develope in your presentation include the folowing:

1. Selecting the right pasta for the right dish.
2. Pasta calorie count.
3. How to find the stores that offer the largest selection of pasta.
4. Installation of computer softwar to simplify menu development.

You asked if I know any one-liners on the subject of food or dining you can use in your presentation. I don't keep a libary of jokes, but I'm enclosing a list of some I've laughed at in the past—not all one-liners and probably not all funny. Keeping in mind that you will be speaking before a very receptive audience. You can develope an audible appreciation, if not an ocassional belly laugh, should you use them.

Correspondents for meeting arrangements will be handled by this office. Not having completed the logistics for the meeting, the final details will be worked out by me. I will be in touch with you soon.

Again, thank you for agreeing to be our spokesman. As your client, we look forward to your talk. Just among us, I think the meeting is going to be a smash!

Sincerely

THE GOURMET SOCIETY

Friedrich Von Schmidt, Directer

yha

Enclosure

PROOFREADING APPLICATIONS PART B

9-9

NEWSPAPER ARTICLE

Proofread the following article and correct all errors using the appropriate proofreader marks.

THE SMART FOOD SHOPPER

Smart food shopping equal saving money—and their is no better place to save money than the super market. You don't have to go to six different markets just too save 20 cents on a can of vegtables. A little planing is all that are neccessary to make a dent in your food buget.

First, develope the habit of making a list of the food items you need before you leave home. Jott down items before you run out of them, thus elimanating last-minute rushes to the corner conve-nience store where you'll very likly pay much higher prices for the same items.

Planning a food list is elimentary—just like when you balance your budget. Whether or not you need certain items now or latter, if an item is on special sale, buy them anyway—in quantity. A good deal is a good deal, right? But watch out! Five cans for $1 is not a good buy when you can buy one can for 20 cents. Look for the unit price or weight price; that is, how much it cost per ounce, pint, quart, or whatever unit is used in priceing. The larger size isn't always cheaper. If a sale item is out of stock, ask for a rain check so you can buy it at the same reduced price when it is restocked.

Do you clip, save, and used coupons? I do but only for a limited number of national brand. Today, store brands are often as good nationally advertised brands and sell for less. For example, Holiday, the store brand for Truebuy Markets, has kechup and canned tomatos that are just as good as the famous name brands. I use cuopons when items are on sale, which means I get double discounts on those item. On every trip to the supermarket, I save about ten per cent of the total grocery bill when I use coupons.

Be on the lookout for ripe but still quite usable fruits and vegtables. Bannanas are to be eaten when it begins to darken. Specially packages fruits and vegetables are priced much lower than price-per-pound items. Besides, ripe bananas are perfect for making breads, cookies, and cakes; and specially marked vegetables are ideal to make soups, stews, and casserrole dishes.

Then their are wearhouses, discount outlets, and other places where you can shop and save money, such as Buy-4-Less, SaveMore, Wholesale Shopper. You don't always have to buy or in bulk or quantity either. You can buy single items, such as canned or dry goods, juices, diary products, breads and pastries, and fresh produce. In addition, there are specialty stores that always advertises certain items on sale for substancial discounts. These items include baked goods, frozen seafoods, nuts and dreid fruits, canned goods and bottled drinks, coffee and tea, and even candies.

With a list of items and a handful of coupons, the amount you save may surprize you. And remember, make it a habitual of glancing at the cash register to be sure the checkout lady rang up the right price. Scan the register tape before you leave the store. Don't be embarrased to ask for a price check, even for as small an amount of ten cents. After all, who'se mistake was it? Not yours—hers. Be a winner—not a loser!

Happy shopping!

9-10

MAGAZINE ARTICLE

Proofread the following article and correct all errors using the appropriate proofreader marks.

Many of our readers attended the Sep. 6 meeting of the Gourmet Soceity and heard Mr Alton K. Ladene speak on pasta. This is a brief summary of his remarks. The speeech is being printed seprately and will be destributed to all members at our next meeting in Oct.

THE MANY FACES OF PASTA

Pasta in one from or another have been with us for many centuries. No one "invented" it. Rather, pasta have evolved.

The best pasta are made from whole grains. Pasta is conveient, easy to cook, economical, nutritious, and delicious. Pasta is not fattening by itself. Its what you dress it with that makes it fattening.

The day of man-made pasta is declining, but the fresh pastas on the market now is a very good substitute. Even after workign all day, it takes only 30 minute to make a delicius meal.

There are some where in the neighborhood if seven hundred different shapes and sizes of pastas. All are desireable, assuming the flour used is of high quality.

In this calorie-concscious age, the new "light" pastas are dominent in today's market. There not is enough difference in the caleric content to make the "light" pastas worth while. It is, after all, a mater of taste

Don't limit yourself to the Italian varities. Impliment some of the Asian varieties that are comming on the market or that have been on the market for ages. Many supermarkets stocks a variety of dried noodels from Asia. In eddition, the refrigerated section have many freshly made pastas.

There is endless possibilties in preparing pasta dishes. Check your local libary and peruse the many cookbooks available. The amatuer chef will acheive good results if he experment when using pasta. There is really nothing you can do to spoil pasta, accept to overcook it.

Viva la pasta! Enjoy!

COMPUTERIZED PROOFREADING APPLICATIONS

Note to the Student:

- Beginning with this chapter, directions for saving, printing, proofreading the hard copy, and reprinting the document will not be repeated. These functions are standard procedures that you should follow for the applications listed in the Computerized Proofreading Applications at the end of each chapter.
- Also, formatting instructions will not be provided for the documents. If necessary, check the guides in the Appendix, page 275 for assistance.

9-11

NEWSPAPER ARTICLE

1. Load file CPA9-11 from the TMPL09 subdirectory on your template CD. (This is a computer copy of Application 9-9.)
2. Proofread (use a proofreader card) and correct all errors on the screen copy that you have indicated with proofreader marks in Application 9-9. Use the spell check if it is available.
3. Produce the newspaper article in correct format following the standard procedures described in the previous chapters.

9-12

NOTICE

1. Load file CPA9-12 from the TMPL09 subdirectory on your template CD.
2. Proofread the notice and correct all errors using the appropriate proofreader marks.
3. Produce the notice following the standard procedures.

9-13

E-MAIL MESSAGE

1. Load file CPA9-13 from the TMPL09 subdirectory on your template CD.
2. Proofread the e-mail and correct all errors using the appropriate proofreader marks.
3. Produce the e-mail message following the standard procedures.

CUMULATIVE REVIEW APPLICATIONS NO. 3

CRA3-1

BUSINESS LETTER WITH TABLE

Proofread and correct all errors using the appropriate proofreader marks.

Montgomery Community College
3874 Overland Pass Avenue
Mountain View, CA 94040-1928
(510) 555-5688 • Fax (510) 555-5689

Septemeber 3, 20 ––

Mrs. Mary K. Conlon, Chairman
Home Economics Department
Briarwood High School
2404 Briarwood avenue
Sunberg, MN 56289-6925

Dear Mrs. Conlon

Under the guidence of The Gloumet Society, an awareness campagne have been conducted by us for the past month at Montgomery Community College to combat the extensive use of sugar in our student's diets. For your convience, I am catagorizing the nutritional value of variuos soft drinks and juices commonly consumed by students.

We hope to educate our students in the planing of good eating and rinking habits that will reduce the amount of sugar consumned and leads to better health for him and her.

NUTRITIONAL VALUE

Bevrage (4 oz.)	Calories	Carbohydrates	Calcium	Potasium	Iron
Apple Juice	47	11.9	6	101	0.2
Canned	50	10.4	10	110	4.2
Soft Drink	39	10.0	—	—	—
Grape Juice	66	16.6	11	116	0.3
Lemonnade	44	11.4	1	13	—
Orange Juice	45	10.4	11	200	0.2
Canned	48	11.2	10	199	0.4
Concentrate	45	10.7	9	186	0.1
Tomatoe Juice	19	4.3	7	227	0.9
Caned	20	4.0	6	225	0.8

You're help in carrying this campagne over into the after-school activties of students will be apperciated.

Nutritionally yours

Maria Diaz-Kingston, RN

tca

CRA3-2

NOTICE

Proofread and correct all errors using the appropriate proofreader marks.

Crescent City Fire Department—Station 47

NOTICE

TO: ALL FIREMEN ASSIGNED TO STATION 47

EFFECTIVE AUGUST 5, 20--

It is a time-honered tradition in the fire department that all firemen assigned to a given station participate, on a rotation bases, in meal prepartion. Over time, this plan has work well for us. Because of varieous dietary requirements, it is more important than every to watch our intake of salt and other spices.

In an effort to be more aware of different dietary requirments, I have asked The Gourmet society to develope a list of herbs that may be used to prepare our meals.

1. Basil. Sweet flavor with a eromatic oder, used whole or ground. Good with lamb, groun beef, vegitables, dressing, and omlets.
2. Caraway. Has a spicy smell and aromatic taste. Use in cakes, braeds, soups, chese, sauerkraut.
3. Chives. Sweet mild flaver of onion, this herb are excellent in salads, fish, soups, and potatos.
4. Dill. Both seeds and leafs of dill is flaverful. Leaves may be used to garnish or cook with fish, soup, dessings, potatoes, and beans.
5. Fennel. Both seeds and leaves is used. Fennel has a sweet, hot flavor. Use in small quantitys in pies and baked goods.
6. Ginger. A pungent root, this aromatic spice is sold fresh, dried, or gruond. Used in pickles, preserves, cakes, cokies, soups, and meat dishes.
7. Paprika. A bright read pepper, this spice are used in meat, vegetables, and soups. Can be use as a garnish for potatoes, salads, or eggs.
8. Sage. Use fresh or dried. The flowers are some time used in salads. May be used in tomatoe juice, fish, omelets, beef, poultry, and stuffing.

Use these herbs and spicess in small amounts, and taste before adding moer. Our firemen are guaranteed to enjoy these refreshing tastes!

Jon Magnuson, Captain
Station 47

CHAPTER 10

COMMA ERRORS

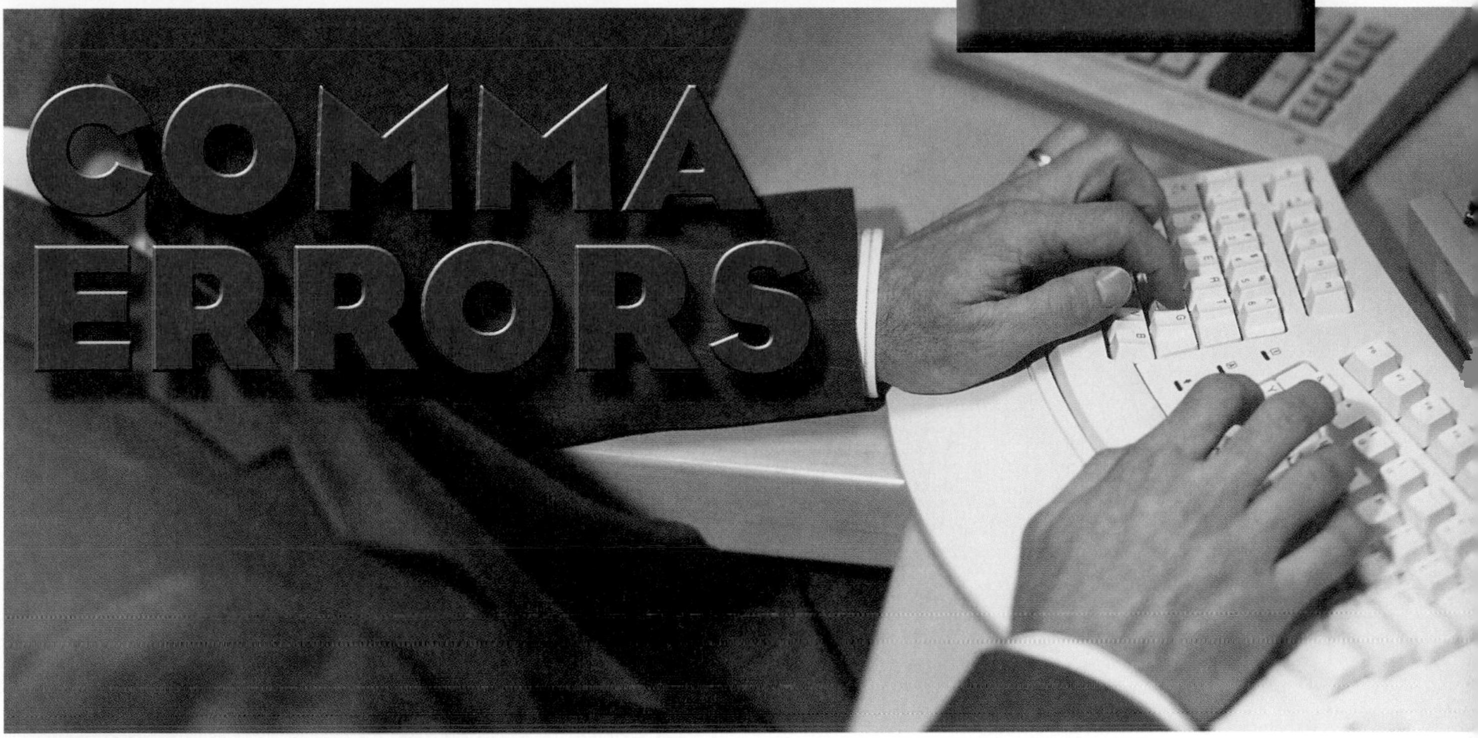

Punctuation has always caused problems for some people. It appears that some people punctuate whenever they pause; others rarely punctuate. But when is punctuation necessary? The purpose of any punctuation mark should be to help the audience correctly interpret a written message. How does punctuation change your interpretation of the following sentences?

- We are going to eat Jack before we take another step.
  We are going to eat, Jack, before we take another step.
- The meeting ended, happily.
  The meeting ended happily.
- The Democrats, say the Republicans, are sure to lose.
  The Democrats say the Republicans are sure to lose.

Objectives

- Identify and correct errors in the use of commas as they apply to compound sentences, introductory elements, and series.
- Identify and correct errors in comma usage as it applies to nonessential elements, consecutive adjectives, direct quotations, dates, addresses, and titles.
- Spell correctly 12 frequently misspelled words.
- Use correctly 3 pairs of commonly misused words.

CHAPTER 10

COMMA ERRORS

THE IMPORTANCE OF PUNCTUATION MARKS

Why are punctuation marks so important in written communication? Why do you need to proofread for punctuation errors? If punctuation marks are used incorrectly or omitted, the meaning of the text may be unclear to the reader.

Punctuation marks are like traffic signals—they tell the reader when to stop, slow down, or proceed. *Terminal* (ending) punctuation marks appear at the end of a sentence and tell the reader to stop. *Internal* (within or inside) punctuation marks tell the reader when to pause, and help the reader to interpret the sentence as the writer intended.

Terminal punctuation marks will be discussed in Chapter 11. In Chapter 10, you will review the rules pertaining to the use of the comma. Because the comma is the most frequently used punctuation mark, this entire chapter will be devoted to comma usage. Use the following proofreader marks to show comma corrections.

	MARKED COPY	CORRECTED COPY
Insert a comma. (mark: ^ with comma)	**The class had already started^, but I walked in anyway.**	**The class had already started, but I walked in anyway.**
Delete a comma. (mark: circled comma with delete sign)	**Rob, and Jennifer will graduate in May.**	**Rob and Jennifer will graduate in May.**

THE COMMA

The comma is an important internal punctuation mark. When used correctly, commas make the relationship between elements (words, phrases, and clauses) in the sentence clear. You learned in Chapter 9 that a clause is a group of related words that contains a subject and a verb. They may be either a dependent clause, which does not express a complete thought, or an independent clause, which does.

INDEPENDENT CLAUSES

A sentence may contain a combination of independent and dependent clauses separated by commas. A sentence that consists of two or more *independent* clauses is called a **compound sentence**. When the independent clauses are joined by the conjunction *and, but, or, nor, for*, or *yet*, separate the clauses with a comma. The word independent means "able to stand alone"; thus, independent clauses in a compound sentence may also be written as two separate sentences. The two clauses are joined with a conjunction simply because they are closely related in meaning. If the two independent clauses are very short, the comma can be omitted.

Example: I called and she answered.

In all of the following examples, the subject and the verb of each independent clause are identified. The conjunctions are italicized.

Example: Alicia's strength (S) is (V) her work ethic, *but* her weakness (S) is (V) her lack of time management skills.

Example: Secretaries (S) are called (V) administrative assistants, *and* they (S) are (V) knowledgeable in office management and computer technology.

Example: George (S) may work (V) in the garden, *or* he (S) may attend (V) the concert.

Note: When "you" is understood to be the subject in both clauses, a comma is still required.

Example: (You) Attend the annual meeting in person, or (you) vote by proxy.

Note: The following sentence contains a compound verb (three verbs). It is still a simple sentence—not a compound sentence. Therefore, a comma is not required.

Example: He will hire a taxi or rent a car and drive to the meeting site.

10-1

PROOFREAD AND MARK

Use the appropriate proofreader marks to correct the errors in comma usage. If the sentence is correct, write **C** to the left of the number.

1. Briana attended the meeting but no new business was introduced.
2. Dianne sent the edited minutes to Jackie and Arlene sent the treasurer's report to Jim.
3. Renee wrote a poem entitled "I Can Do It!" and sent it to the local newspaper for publication in Friday's edition.
4. She is responsible for editing the monthly newsletter and she takes minutes at weekly meetings.
5. *Robert's Rules of Order Newly Revised* shows the correct format for minutes and it also includes a list of motions.

INTRODUCTORY ELEMENTS

Insert a comma after most introductory words, phrases, or clauses that come before the independent clause.

Example: *Therefore*, I have decided to enroll in the computer class. (introductory word)

Jogging long distances is one of her favorite weekend activities.

Example: *In other words*, the course is designed to develop basic skills on three application programs. (introductory phrase)

Example: *When you are ready to print*, enter the correct print code. (introductory clause)

Example: No, you were not late for the first session.

Example: As a rule, it is the chairperson's responsibility to keep the meeting moving.

Example: When the package arrives, check to make sure we received the right order.

Commas are generally not required after introductory words or restrictive, short phrases that answer the questions *when, how often, where*, or *why*.

Example: Tomorrow I will begin my diet. (I will begin my diet *when*?)

Example: In the margin you will find a short definition of new terms. (*Where* will you find a short definition of new terms?)

Commas do not set off noun phrases or noun clauses that function as the subjects of sentences (not introductory). The italicized phrases or clauses in the following examples function as subjects of the sentences and, therefore, are not set off by commas. Note that all the italicized phrases in the following examples answer the question *what*.

Example: *Learning a new video game* can be both fun and frustrating.

Example: *To win this game* will require real team effort.

Example: *Whether we win or lose* will make no difference in our standing.

10-2

PROOFREAD AND MARK

Use the appropriate proofreader marks to correct the errors in comma usage. If the sentence is correct, write **C** to the left of the number.

1. When the delegates arrive they must register at the desk and receive name tags.
2. Using recycled paper to publish our company newsletter, has significantly decreased our supplies and printing costs.
3. Incidentally has the agenda for the October meeting been completed?
4. Completing my assignments on time is at the top of my agenda for things to accomplish next semester.

5. Regardless of what the outcome might be, Felicita is determined to bring the matter, before the Academic Board.

SERIES

Insert a comma after each item in a series (words, phrases, or clauses) except the last item.

Example: I invited Concepcion, Myrna, Wakako, and Billie Jo to the beach party. (series of words)

Example: Martha did not tell us where she would meet us, whom she would be with, or when her flight is due to arrive. (series of clauses)

Example: I scored 76, 94 and 85 on the last three science quizzes.

Example: Please read the chapter, complete the review and study for the test.

Example: Paul and Mary will be the game organizers, Teresita and Darwin will be the race timers, Noriko and Bernardo will be the scorekeepers and I will be the official starter.

Note: Do not use commas when each item in the series is connected by *and, but, or*, or *nor*.

Example: We need Virginia and Jorge and Sarit to watch the monitors.

Example: Neither Jack nor Sue nor Betsy were available.

10-3

PROOFREAD AND MARK

Use the appropriate proofreader marks to correct the errors in comma usage. If the sentence is correct, write **C** to the left of the number.

1. Worth County's top five cities are Grafton, Manly, Kensett, Bolan and Lake Mills.
2. This home unit CD player features full programmability, direct access, shuffle-repeat play functions and remote control.
3. You must have an education degree to teach courses in computers, math, science, and languages.
4. If you buy, sell, develop, manufacture or use RightWord software, you can't afford to miss the RightWord training session this weekend.
5. Her new checking account provides free checks, a Visa credit card, free credit consolidation and a $5000 credit line.

COMMA ERRORS

NONESSENTIAL ELEMENTS

Nonessential elements consist of information that is not necessary to the meaning of the sentence. They include appositives, interrupting expressions, and nonrestrictive phrases or clauses. Set off nonessential elements with commas.

Appositives are words or phrases that rename a preceding noun or pronoun. Commas are used to set off appositives because they are not essential to the meaning of the sentence but provide further identification of the noun or pronoun. The appositives are in italics in the following examples.

Example: Suzanne Russo, *the president*, will preside at the meeting.

Example: San Francisco, *the "City by the Bay*," is a popular vacation and convention site.

Example: Bruce Canton, *a local real estate broker*, will respond to your question.

Example: Their first song, *written while they were teenagers*, was a tremendous success.

Interrupting (also called *parenthetical*) **expressions** include such nonessential words or phrases as *furthermore, however, in addition*, and *of course*. Such expressions often indicate the writer's feelings.

Example: Ruth will, *of course*, accept your dinner invitation.

Example: Annalisa, *however*, is an exceptionally talented pianist.

Example: Saturday's ballgame, *on the other hand*, may attract a larger crowd.

Example: We are determined, *nevertheless*, to finish today.

Nonrestrictive elements include phrases or clauses that further explain or describe the noun or pronoun they modify. However, the information is considered to be nonessential because it is not necessary in understanding the meaning of the sentence. Nonrestrictive clauses often begin with *which, who*, or *whom*. Analyze the following two examples. The nonrestrictive elements are italicized.

Example: Ms. Kline, *who works in the president's office*, will address the March meeting. (The nonrestrictive element does not affect the principal message in this sentence, which is that Ms. Kline will address the meeting in March.)

Example: We have been unable to complete the Johnson contract, *which you had negotiated so successfully*. (The nonrestrictive element has no bearing on the completion of the Johnson contract.)

Do not set off **restrictive** phrases or clauses, those which are essential to the meaning of the sentence. The restrictive clauses appear in italics in these examples:

Example: Those people *who are registered to vote* will be eligible to vote in the school board election. (The restrictive clause identifies the people who are eligible to vote and is essential to the meaning of the sentence.)

Example: We have been unable to complete the contract *that you had just negotiated.* (The restrictive clause identifies which contract is not yet completed.)

Example: The Lundgren bid arrived *after we had made our decision.* (The restrictive clause tells when the bid arrived.)

Example: The shops *that are located in Westwood Mall* are open on the Fourth of July. (The restrictive clause tells which shops are open.)

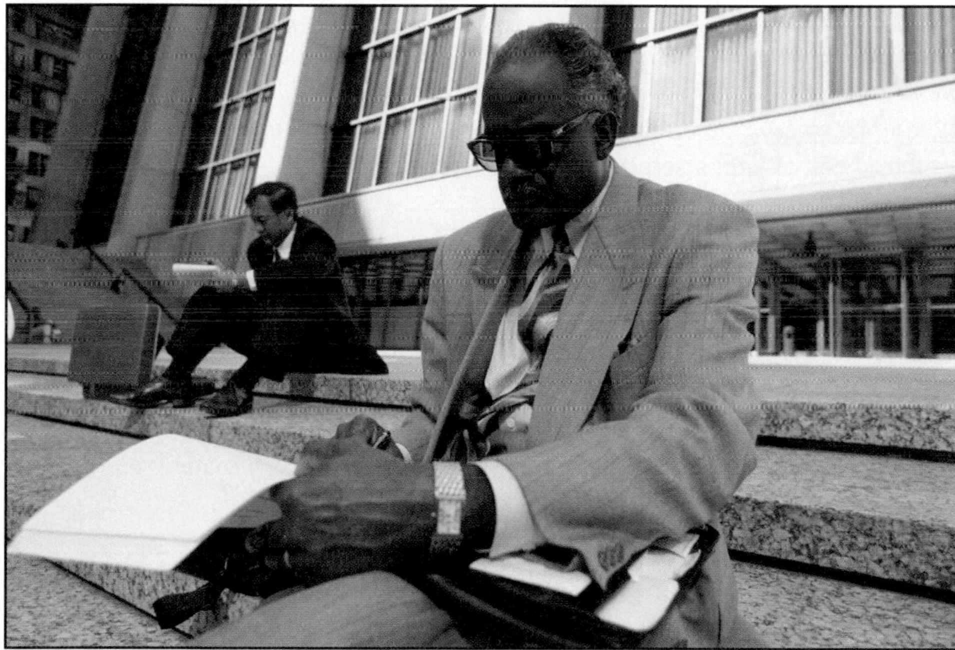

Mr. Patterson, who is a prosecuting attorney, is always working.

PROOFREAD AND MARK

10-4

Use the appropriate proofreader marks to correct the errors in comma usage. If the sentence is correct, write **C** to the left of the number.

1. Corporal Lance Mitchell left the army, as a computer programmer, and started his own software company.
2. Everyone, listed on the attached sheet, will receive a copy of the workshop report.

3. Lake Superior, on the other hand, is the largest of the lakes.
4. Ricardo Santiago, general manager of the Corvallis store has been with the company for 14 years.
5. A photograph and a position statement which each candidate running for office is required to submit will be published with the election ballot.

OTHER COMMA USES

In addition to their very important role of setting off sentence elements, commas perform a variety of other roles.

CONSECUTIVE ADJECTIVES

Use commas to separate consecutive adjectives that are parallel and not joined by a conjunction. Parallel adjectives describe the same noun to the same degree. To determine whether adjectives should be separated by commas, reverse the order of the adjectives and insert the word *and* between them.

Example: Joyce is a sincere, delightful person. (Joyce is a delightful *and* sincere person.)

Example: The student is faced with a difficult, frustrating decision. (The student is faced with a frustrating *and* difficult decision.)

Example: The tall^,^handsome fellow in the photograph is my husband.

Example: They are looking for an intelligent^,^enterprising young person.

10-5

PROOFREAD AND MARK

Use the appropriate proofreader marks to correct the errors in comma usage. If the sentence is correct, write **C** to the left of the number.

1. They enjoyed the sleek simple design.
2. Gentleness, and sincerity, are two personal traits that I look for in people I meet.
3. Carl read the informative, entertaining articles.
4. Listening to soft soothing classical music is my favorite pastime.
5. She is looking for tough dependable tools to purchase for her house.

DIRECT QUOTATIONS

Use commas to set off the exact words of a speaker. Do not set off an indirect quotation. An indirect quotation is a rewording of the person's exact words and is usually introduced by *that* or *whether*.

Example: The director said, "Your music should be returned after the concert." (Direct quotation—a comma and quotation marks are required.)

Example: Jane asked the director whether our music should be returned after the concert. (Indirect quotation—no comma or quotation marks are needed.)

When a direct quotation is broken up into two parts, such as in the next example, place a comma *after* the first part of the quotation (inside the quotation mark) and another comma *before* the second part.

Example: "The class colors," said Chuong, "are pink and green."

Example: Andrei stated "I believe you made the right decision."

Example: He said that "the mail will be picked up at 3:10 p.m."

Example: "On the other hand" Savath remarked "I may surprise you."

Note: Commas and periods at the end of a quotation are *always* placed inside the quotation marks. Other punctuation marks used with quotation marks will be discussed in Chapter 11.

PROOFREAD AND MARK

10-6

Use the appropriate proofreader marks to correct errors in comma usage. If the sentence is correct, write **C** to the left of the number.

1. "Furthermore" Keith said "you must finish painting before you quit for the day."
2. I thought you said that "you would cancel your appointment with your accountant."
3. Van Loc Ho asked me yesterday whether you plan to go skiing this weekend.
4. "I never think about age" Marvin said "because age is only attitude."
5. "Entertaining, uplifting, and funny" wrote the movie critic "and fiendishly clever too".

CHAPTER 10

COMMA ERRORS

DATES AND ADDRESSES

Use commas to set off the year when it follows the month and the day or to separate the weekday from the calendar date. Commas are not required when only the month and the year are given or when military style is used in expressing dates.

Example: August 31, 20––, is the deadline for filing applications.

Example: Our school received its first electronic camera in May 20––.

Example: The letter from General Kraft dated 11 May 20–– was misplaced.

Example: The supplies were sent by air freight on Thursday June 30 20––.

Example: Clarissa graduated in June, 20––.

Use commas to separate address parts when the address appears in text format. Do not use a comma to separate two-letter state abbreviations and ZIP Codes.

Example: The address is Majestic Records, 3090 Brookline Boulevard, Suite 254, Newark, NJ 07110-3201.

DIRECT ADDRESS AND TITLES

Use commas to set off a person's name or title when addressing the person directly.

Example: Please reserve a conference room, Noel, for October 14.

Example: Thanks for helping me with my homework Dad.

Use commas after names of persons when academic and professional titles are used. Do not separate personal titles, such as *Jr.*, *Sr.*, *II*, or *III*, unless you know that the individual prefers to do so.

Example: Professor Navara, Ph.D., is also a certified professional planner.

Example: Melissa Evans, CPA, will lead the panel discussion.

Example: Duane Simpson, Jr. will arrive tomorrow morning.

Example: Brenda Brostrom Ed.D. is the coordinator of the seminars.

Professor Avery, Ph.D., teaches art history.

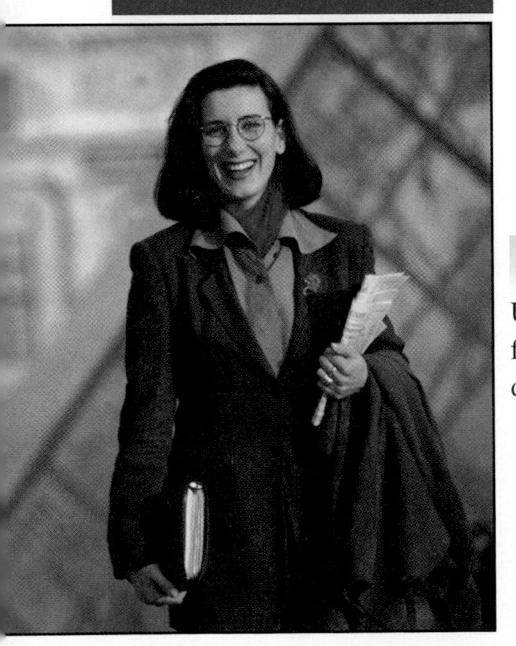

SETTING OFF "INC." OR "LTD."

Use commas to set off the abbreviations or words for "Inc." or "Ltd." when they follow the name of the company, unless you know the official company name does not use a comma.

Example: We will notify United Movers, Inc., of the change of address.

Example: Braniff Limited has been awarded the contract for next year.

10-7

PROOFREAD AND MARK

Use the appropriate proofreader marks to correct errors in comma usage. If the sentence is correct, write **C** to the left of the number.

1. My driver's license expires on Friday, December 28.
2. The return address on the envelope shows 218 South Front Avenue Liberty PA 12981-4825.
3. Can you help me Micha, in solving this difficult problem?
4. Janelle be sure to call the airline if you have to cancel the flight.
5. Afton Companies Inc. is located at 9770 Grandview Street Omaha NE 67115-0893.

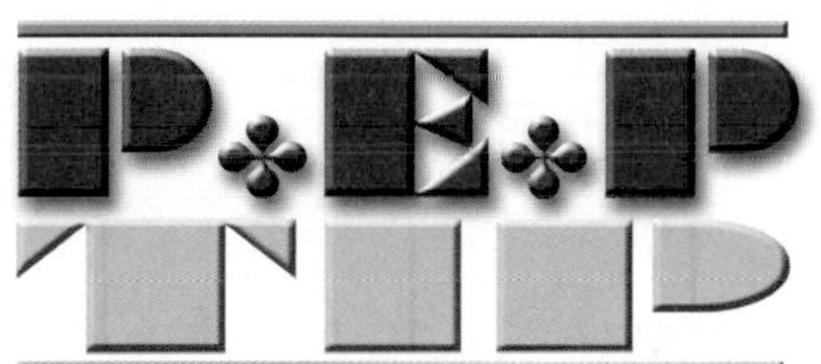

✤ Punctuation marks are designed to add clarity. Check for errors in punctuation that may cause confusion or misunderstanding.

✤ When debating the placement of a comma, identify the rule or rules that apply.

✤ Keep a reference manual handy when proofreading; use it as needed.

✤ Proofread in a quiet place; noise can be distracting.

✤ Pay attention to important information, such as dates, names, addresses, and amounts. Do not assume they are correct.

10-8

SPELLING AND WORD USAGE CHECK

Compare the words in Column A with the corresponding words in Column B. Use the appropriate proofreader marks to correct the misspelled or misused words. If both columns are correct, write **C** to the left of the number.

Column A	Column B
1. article	artical
2. assessment	assesment
3. custermer	customer
4. environment	enviroment
5. equipment	equipement
6. interupt	interrupt
7. maneger	manager
8. orientation	orientation
9. perposal	proposal
10. recognise	recognize
11. representative	representitive
12. session	session
13. All right, you can go.	Everything is alright.
14. corperation from the staff	Cooperation is needed.
15. The latter option is better.	I prefer the later plan.

PROOFREADING APPLICATIONS PART A

10-9

LETTER TO THE EDITOR

Proofread the following editorial letter, and correct all errors using the appropriate proofreader marks.

LETTER TO THE EDITOR, June 6, 20––

The Examiner, Loma Linda, California

Dear Editor:

I would like to offer an assesment of the latest trend in TV programming: reality-based television. On Friday May 13 20––, I arrived home early and interupted my six-year-old son who was watching television. I said "Randy what are you watching?" He replied "Justice Agents." I asked what it was about and he said that it was representitive of the current reality-based series. He also said that "this program depicted the dispensing of justice by agents of a metropolitan swat-team-type organization." Yes six-year-olds do talk like that today. I reconize that young children live in a fantasy world when they watch TV but I also know that they often imitate what they see and hear.

Sitting with Randy for a few minutes I was startled to see that the last part of the show was an uninterupted violent gun battle between the good guys and the bad guys.

My assesment is that it is not alright for a child to see this kind of realism on television. As a responsible parent and custermer of commercial television, I asked myself, "Is this a reality-based show and if so whose reality is it?" More importantly is this a proper environment for a child?

I latter asked myself whether such programs should be available at a time when impressionable children can view them and the answer is that they shouldn't. We must recognise that a show of this kind has the potential for disaster.

Is it really necessary to show such extreme negative enviroment in such detail? To a six-year-old, the actor is not just practicing a craft. The child even an adult is watching someone being brutualized or killed.

I have a perposal to make. Perhaps it would be a good idea for the corperation network to air an oriention sesion demonstrating the art of artifice and makeup so that the young inexperienced and naive viewer can tell the difference between make-believe and reality.

If any reader of this newspaper shares my views voice your opinion by writing to the network, Station KVRT 408 South Bascom Avenue Loma Linda CA 90097-4213.

Clayton Morris Jr.

PROOFREADING APPLICATIONS PART B

10-10

BUSINESS LETTER

Proofread the following business letter, and correct all errors using the appropriate proofreader marks.

STATION KVRT
408 South Bascom Avenue
Loma Linda, CA 90097-4213
Phone 626•555•5593
Fax 626•555•5597

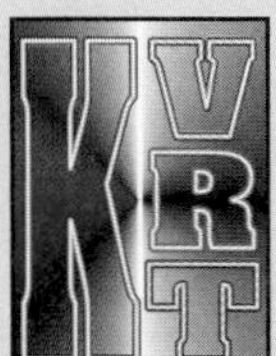

June 10, 20--

Mr. Clayton Morris Jr.
14009 Van Ness Avenue
Loma Linda, CA 90405-0332

Dear Mrs. Morris:

I apprecaited you letter to the editer of <u>The Examiner</u> dated June 6, 20-- concerning reality-based television.

Having a son who is seven I agree that this program is not suitable for viewing by primary school-age children. Since we are concerned with children viewing programs that may be inapropriate for him scheduling is closely audeted by Station KVRT. this program was scheduled for a time period during which we anticapated that young children would not be in the veiwing audience.

Reality-based television leaves much to be desired and should not be used as a means of catagorizing programs. We live in an age when people strongly believe in personal rights, and the want to make their own decisions about which programs to watch.

I like your idea, for a program to educate the young to be aware, that what they see on their television screen is play acting and have no application to real-life situations. Therefore we invite your son and his class mates to be our guest for an oriention tour of Station KVRT. The tour will include sesions with variuos departments, such as costume, makeup and editing, and end with lunch at our new cafeteria. Please limit the number of people in you group to no more than thirty, including teacher moniters.

Please call Mrs. Loretta Harold, a representitive of our Public Relations Dept. to discuss final arrangments.

Sincerly

Alfred P. McRay President

pc: Mrs. Loretta Harold Manger
Public Relations Department

MEMORANDUM

10-11

Proofread the following memorandum, and correct all errors using the appropriate proofreader marks.

STATION KVRT MEMORANDUM

DATE: July 14, 20--
TO: All Department Heads
FROM: Patrick E. James, Vice president Marketing
SUBJECT: Letter to the Editor

On June 6, The Examiner published a letter to the editer from Mr. Clayton Morris, Jr. concerning reality-based television. Mr. Morris expressd his concern for the need for caution in scheduling programs because of the possible negative affects some programs might have on primary school-age children. As a result our president Mr. Alfred P. McRay invited the classmates of Mr. Morris's son to visit our studio. In subsequent correspondants this is how Mr. Morris described the tour.

> Like Dorothy in The Wizard of Oz, we had a feeling that we were no longer in Kansas when we past through the magic portals of Station KVRT. We walked through a maze of camera equipement, sets, backdrops, miniature cities and skyscrappers that appeared to be twenty stories tall.
>
> The makeup department was everyone's favorite. Many of the children had her pictures taken while make up as their favorite movie star, or as Frankenstein, Roger Rabit or King Kong.
>
> Latter we were treated to a delicious lunch at the studio cafteria. This was especially enjoyable to the enthusiastic young visiters because all the teenage stars was having lunch at the same time and all were gracious enough to allow interuptions for autographs.
>
> There was a serious side to our tour. We wanted to show the children that they what view on television is all make-believe. They learned never to try the jumps, falls or other stunts that the see on television; these actions are performed by proffessional actors. A special film was shown demonstrating how these special affects are developd.
>
> We think Station KVRT President McRay, his staff and all the studio personnal for an educational and enjoyable sesion. I hope that other groups will be allowed to benifit from touring your excellant facilties.

We appreciate you coporation in making this visit a memorable one for Mr. Morris and his son's classmates.

rkt

COMPUTERIZED PROOFREADING APPLICATIONS

10-12

MEMORANDUM

1. Load file CPA10-12 from the TMPL10 subdirectory on your template CD. (This is a computer copy of Application 10-11.)
2. Proofread (use a proofreader card) and correct all errors on the screen copy that you have indicated with proofreader marks in Application 10-11. Use the spell check if it is available.
3. Produce the memo in correct format following the standard procedures described in the previous chapters.

10-13

MAGAZINE ARTICLE

1. Load file CPA10-13 from the TMPL10 subdirectory on your template CD.
2. Proofread the letter and correct all errors using the appropriate proofreader marks.
3. Produce the article following the standard procedures.

10-14

E-MAIL MESSAGE

1. Load file CPA10-14 from the TMPL10 subdirectory on your template CD.
2. Proofread the e-mail message and correct all errors using the appropriate proofreader marks.
3. Produce the e-mail message following the standard procedures.

CHAPTER 11

OTHER PUNCTUATION ERRORS

An incorrectly placed comma in a sales contract recently cost an American company $70 million. In Europe, commas are used instead of periods to mark decimal points. This American company misplaced a comma by one decimal point in an international contract. According to a company spokesperson, the customer held them to the price quoted, resulting in a loss of $70 million!

Objectives

- Identify and correct errors in end-of-sentence punctuation.
- Identify and correct errors in the use of semicolons and colons.
- Identify and correct errors in the use of apostrophes, underscores, and quotation marks.
- Identify and correct errors when using quotation marks with other punctuation marks.
- Spell correctly 12 frequently misspelled words.
- Use correctly 3 pairs of commonly misused words.

CHAPTER 11

OTHER PUNCTUATION ERRORS

In addition to the comma, other punctuation marks appear in written material. In this chapter, you will review the use of end-of-sentence punctuation marks—the period, the question mark, and the exclamation mark. You will also learn to use semicolons, colons, apostrophes, underscores, and quotation marks correctly. Finally, you will learn to recognize errors when other punctuation marks are used with quotation marks.

When correcting errors for these punctuation marks, use the following proofreader marks.

	MARKED COPY	CORRECTED COPY
Insert a period. ⊙	Please send me your check⊙	Please send me your check.
Insert a question mark.	How did you do on the test.	How did you do on the test?
Insert an exclamation mark.	Don't touch it.	Don't touch it!
Insert a semicolon.	Tuesday, May 2, Wednesday, May 3, and Thursday, May 4.	Tuesday, May 2; Wednesday, May 3; and Thursday, May 4.
Insert a colon.	Follow these steps 1. Revise copy. 2. Save copy.	Follow these steps: 1. Revise copy. 2. Save copy.
Insert an apostrophe.	the bikers helmet	the biker's helmet
Underscore or italicize. ___ or Ital.	Never write on a diskette.	Never write on a diskette. *Never* write on a diskette.
Insert quotation marks.	She was called Miss Dimples.	She was called "Miss Dimples."

THE PERIOD, THE QUESTION MARK, AND THE EXCLAMATION MARK

There are three **terminal punctuation marks**: the period, the question mark and the exclamation mark. They are used at the ends of sentences and tell the reader when to stop.

Rule 1 Use a period after (1) a statement of fact, (2) an indirect question, or (3) a courteous request. A **statement of fact** is something declared or stated. An **indirect question** is a reworded question or another person's statement. A **courteous request** is not a question, but it is sometimes incorrectly punctuated as a question because it sounds like one. When deciding to use a period or a question mark, remember this tip: If the person is expected to answer in words, use a question mark. If the person is expected to respond with action, use a period.

STATEMENT	INDIRECT QUESTION	COURTEOUS REQUEST
The new furniture was delivered on Wednesday.	**Bea asked if you were available to help.**	**Would you please send this order today.**

Rule 2 Use a question mark after a **direct question**—it requires an answer. When a sentence contains a series of short questions related to one idea, place a question mark at the end of each question in the series. (See example.) Within the series, only the first part is a full question; the rest are not. Therefore, capitalize only the first word of the first part; **do not** capitalize the first word of each remaining part.

QUESTION	INDIRECT QUESTION	SERIES OF QUESTIONS
Did you receive the report?	**He asked if you received the report.**	**Do you wish to look better? feel healthy? lose weight? trim inches?**

Example: Do you remember when the report was sent.

Example: I asked what the features on Model 72K15J were?

Example: After graduation, are you planning to do anything? to travel. to enter college to work Have you considered joining a military service

Rule 3 Use an exclamation mark after a sentence that expresses strong emotion, excitement, surprise, or urgency.

Example: Wow! What a game! But we lost!

Example: Mom! I got the job

Example: Fantastic, Billy

Traditionally, two spaces follow a colon and a mark of punctuation at the end of a sentence. However, proportionally-spaced fonts in many of today's word processing and desktop publishing programs have eliminated the need for two spaces.

Readability and ease of retention are critical factors in your written communications, and not all fonts handle spacing the same way. Therefore, you should evaluate your word-processed documents to determine if one or two spaces are needed after colons and terminal punctuation.

11-1

PROOFREAD AND MARK

Use the appropriate proofreader marks to correct the errors in the use of the period, question mark, and exclamation mark. If the sentence is correct, write **C** to the left of the number.

1. She asked when she could expect the delivery?
2. Did you remember to send a card for his birthday.
3. Ouch. That really hurt.
4. Will you please send us a copy when it is reprinted.
5. How will the trip be continued? by car. by ferry. by air?

THE SEMICOLON

The semicolon provides a stronger break within a sentence than a comma, but a weaker break than a period.

Rule 4 Use a semicolon—not a comma—between two independent clauses of a compound sentence when the clauses are not joined by a coordinating conjunction (*and, but, or, nor, for, yet*).

Example: Wisdom is in knowing what to do next; virtue is in doing it.

Example: The package arrived; it was slightly damaged.

Example: The truths of life are not inborn, each generation must learn them through experience.

Example: I will accept the job if it is offered, I would enjoy working for the firm.

Gina got a puppy for her birthday; it was what she had always wanted.

Rule 5 Use a semicolon between two independent clauses when they are joined by transitional expressions, such as *however, moreover, consequently, namely, nevertheless, therefore, in addition, likewise, on the other hand, besides,* and *accordingly*. A comma is used after a transitional expression of more than one syllable or when a strong pause is needed after one-syllable words like *hence, yet, thus,* and *then*. Remember, a semicolon comes *before* and a comma usually *follows* such expressions.

Example: The workshop will be held July 12-15; in addition, a second workshop is scheduled for August 9-12.

Example: I studied five months for this test; consequently, I was confident that I would pass.

Example: We will meet five hours on Monday; then we are free to work on other projects.

Example: The presentation was scheduled for 9:30 a.m., unfortunately, the speaker missed her flight.

Example: The computer parts arrived this morning, therefore, we can proceed with the repairs.

Rule 6 Use a semicolon—not a comma—between two or more independent clauses of a compound sentence when the clauses are joined by a coordinating conjunction *and* when either or both of the independent clauses already contain commas.

Example: Hiking, boating, and camping are within easy driving distance from the city; but all these activities require special permits.

Example: Candace was interested in shopping, eating, and dancing, but Ethan was more interested in swimming, camping, and hunting.

Rule 7 Use a semicolon—not a comma—in a series when one or more of the items in the series already contain commas.

Example: The firm has branch offices located in Fort Lauderdale, Florida; Pueblo, Colorado; and Montgomery, Alabama.

Example: Certification tests are scheduled for Friday, May 14, Monday, May 31, and Wednesday, June 16.

PROOFREAD AND MARK 11-2

Use the appropriate proofreader marks to correct the errors in the use of the semicolon. If the sentence is correct, write **C** to the left of the number.

1. Knowing the rules is one thing; applying them is another.
2. The rules of business etiquette are not well known, it takes time to learn to apply the rules properly.
3. The jury, after six weeks of testimony, deliberated for nine days, but it did not reach a verdict until Friday.
4. The last order of the season was sent this morning, therefore, we will close an hour earlier today.
5. Next year we will vacation in Aspen, Colorado, Hilo, Hawaii, or Hartford, Connecticut.

THE COLON

A colon shows anticipation. It alerts the reader that what follows the colon will explain what came before it.

Rule 8 Use a colon before items such as a list, a series, or an explanation of what came before the colon.

Note: If the items appearing in a vertical list are not complete sentences, do not capitalize the first word in each item. Omit periods after the items unless one or more of the items is a complete sentence, a long phrase, or a dependent clause.

Example: Determine the following points for each career:
nature of the work
satisfaction from the job
advancement opportunities

Example: The job requirements are these: experience working in a medical office, ability to work independently, competence in using spreadsheets, and superior communication skills.

Example: Evaluate potential employers in terms of the following factors
1. Are there opportunities for advancement?
2. Are the salary and fringe benefits attractive?
3. Does top management support the position?

In the following example, a colon is used after the first clause because the second and third independent clauses explain the first one.

Example: The representative says the resort has it all. It has an excellent location, and it has outstanding food and entertainment.

Do not use a colon to introduce a list following a preposition or verb. Do not capitalize lists that are not in vertical form unless each item is a complete sentence.

Example: The secretary has the responsibilities of (1) keying the report, (2) sending a cover memo with the final results to the manager, and (3) filing the hard copy.

Example: The group includes Jessica, Antonio, Lan, and Herman.

Rule 9 Use a colon in the following situations: after the salutation of a letter that uses mixed punctuation, within ratios, and between hours and minutes. When time is expressed exactly on the hour, it is not necessary to include the colon and the zeros.

Example: Dear Mrs. Yelle:

Example: The portions are 3:1 olive oil and water.

Example: The flight leaves at 1:49 p.m.

Example: Report to the principal's office at 3 p.m. sharp.

Example: Every dollar contributed will be matched 1/1.

Example: Set your alarm for 5;00 a.m.

11-3

PROOFREAD AND MARK

Use the appropriate proofreader marks to correct the errors in the use of the colon. If the sentence is correct, write **C** to the left of the number.

1. Study the following requirements of each project.

1. short-term benefits.
2. five-year requirements.
3. long-term potential.

2. We will require the following information to complete the order. the catalog number; the date of delivery; and the method of payment.

3. Do you have revenue estimates for: the quarter ending March 31, the quarter ending June 30, and the quarter ending December 31?

4. The list of duties includes opening incoming mail, distributing priority mail, and resetting timers.

5. The Executive Committee will meet at 9:00 a.m. and reconvene after lunch at 1 30 p.m.

THE APOSTROPHE

The apostrophe is used to form contractions, the possessive case of nouns, and the plural forms of some words and letters. Watch for errors in the use of the apostrophe.

Rule 10 Add an apostrophe and *s* (’*s*) to form the possessive case of singular nouns not ending in an *s* sound.

Example:	the committee’s decision	(the decision of the committee)
Example:	the manager’s office	(the office of the manager)
Example:	year’s end	(the end of the year)
Example:	Marcia’s children	(the children of Marcia)
Example:	The books cover is torn.	
Example:	The companys warehouse is located in Milpitas.	

Rule 11 Add an apostrophe and *s* (*'s*) if a new syllable is formed in the pronunciation of the possessive.

Example: Congress's vote (the vote of Congress)

Example: Chris's car (the car owned by Chris)

Example: Mr. Harris' report

Example: Mrs. Lopez' plans

Add only an apostrophe if an extra syllable would make a word ending in an *s* sound hard to pronounce.

Example: Mr. Andrews' suit (the suit belonging to Mr. Andrews)

Example: Ms. Phillips' proposal (the proposal submitted by Ms. Phillips)

Example: Mrs. Marcos doctor

Example: Miss Burroughs investments

Rule 12 Add only an apostrophe to form the possessive case of plural nouns that end in an *s* sound.

Example: the girls' pep club (the pep club of the girls)

Example: the students' behavior (the behavior of the students)

Example: The candidate's names must be on file.

***Thomas's* coin collection includes many rare pieces.**

Rule 13 Add an apostrophe and *s* (*'s*) to form the possessive of plural nouns that do not end in an *s* sound.

Example: Women's organizations (organizations of women)

Example: the alumni's reunion (the reunion of the alumni)

Example: The sheeps' wool was sheared.

Example: The childrens' favorite fruits are apples and bananas.

Rule 14 Add an apostrophe and *s* (*'s*) only to the final name when an item is jointly owned by more than one person.

Example: Dan and Carolyn's wedding (the wedding of Dan and Carolyn)

Example: Yoko and Maria's boutique (the boutique of Yoko and Maria)

Example: Jan's and Terry's ice cream is the best.

Example: For superior service, take your vehicle to Tom's, Dick's, and Harry's Auto Shop.

When two names indicate separate ownership, each name is possessive.

Example: Eric's and Carrie's companies (two companies, separate ownership)

Example: Bill and Judy's signatures (each signature is separate)

Rule 15 Use the apostrophe to form the contraction of two words. Place the apostrophe at the point of the missing letter(s).

Example: don't (do not) haven't (have not)

Example: it's (it is) you're (you are)

Example: who's (who is) I'll (I will)

Example: Theyre not here yet. But were going to start because its getting late.

Rule 16 Use an apostrophe to form the following: (1) the plurals of most figures, even though it is also acceptable to omit the apostrophe; (2) the plurals of some capital and lowercase letters of the alphabet (to avoid misreading an expression for a word); and (3) acronyms. An **acronym** is a word formed from the initial letters of a group of words. Acronyms may be formed with or without periods.

Example: 6's (or 6s) 45's (or 45s) dot your i's (*not* "is")

Example: T's (or Ts) A's (*not* "As") I's (*not* "Is")

Example: SADD's (or S.A.D.D.'s) monthly meeting will be held May 3, 20—.

Rule 17 Use the apostrophe as a symbol for feet in measurements. (The quotation mark is the symbol for inches.)

Example: 4' x 8' (4 feet by 8 feet)

Example: 6'2" tall (6 feet 2 inches tall)

An apostrophe or quotation mark after a number, when used to indicate feet or inches, requires a straight apostrophe or quotation mark, not a curly or curved mark.

11-4

PROOFREAD AND MARK

Use the appropriate proofreader marks to correct the errors in the use of the apostrophe. If the sentence is correct, write **C** to the left of the number.

1. Mr. Arness's computer equipment will be delivered in Brians' van by years end.
2. Your evaluation of Professor Cummings lecture was positive.
3. Sam's and Ivan's acceptance of Ann and Sarah's recommendation was predictable.
4. Do'nt forget to write clearly; your 7s look like 1s, and your es look like is.
5. The company's fiscal year ended October 31, 20—.

OTHER PUNCTUATION ERRORS

UNDERSCORING AND ITALICS

Both underscoring (underlining) and *italics* are marks of emphasis. Italic type is the preferred means of giving special emphasis to words and phrases and to literary titles and artistic works. The following examples show the use of the underscore when italics are not available. Any space between consecutive words should be underscored. However, a punctuation mark immediately following a word or phrase is not underscored (except periods within abbreviations).

Rule 18 Use the underscore to set off titles of complete literary works, such as books, magazines, newspapers, movies, plays, or other artistic works.

Example: I subscribe to Time and the Wall Street Journal.

Example: We have purchased the videotape of The Sound of Music; we will tape Sister Act when it airs on television.

Example: My subscription to Quick Cooking expires in November.

Example: I saw Crazy for You on Broadway this summer.

Rule 19 Use the underscore to emphasize or identify special words or phrases.

Example: Choose a computer that offers ease of use and compatibility.

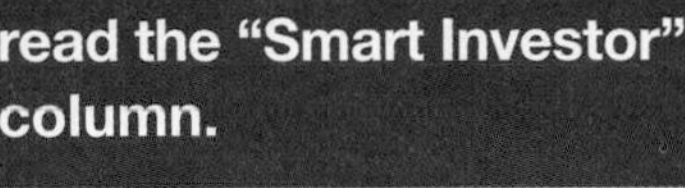

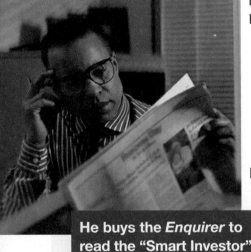

He buys the *Enquirer* to read the "Smart Investor" column.

Example: The report may now be considered a fait accompli.

Example: I said I was not going!

Example: Where were you going at that time of night?

QUOTATION MARKS

Quotation marks are used primarily to enclose direct quotations.

Rule 20 Use quotation marks to enclose all parts of direct quotations and words used in an unusual way.

Example: "The solution," announced the speaker, "is quite obvious."

Example: I heard Cindy tell Brad, "Get lost." So he did.

Example: Bookworm and nerd are not necessarily complimentary nicknames.

Example: Come after school, Richie said, and we'll study for the exam.

Rule 21 Use quotation marks to set off parts of complete works, such as chapters within a book, titles of articles and feature columns within magazines or newspapers, titles of essays, short poems, sermons, unpublished works, or songs.

Example: The most popular column in the *Enquirer* is "Ask the Editor."

Example: Be prepared to discuss the questions from Chapter 13, "Preparing Resumes and Application Letters."

Example: One of my favorite sections in the magazine is called Ombudsman.

Rule 22 Use quotation marks with other punctuation marks in the following manner:

- **Periods are placed *inside* quotation marks.**

  Example: The editor said, "Please send all chapter drafts by Priority Mail."

- **Commas are placed *inside* quotation marks.**

  Example: "When I fly," I said, "I plan to fly first class."

- **Exclamation marks and question marks are placed *inside* the quotation marks when the punctuation mark applies *only* to the quoted material.**

  Example: Mara exclaimed, "Watch out!"

  Example: Marquetta replied, "What did you say?"

- **Exclamation marks and question marks are placed *outside* the ending quotation mark when the exclamation or question applies to the entire sentence.**

  Example: Why did you just ignore Lauralee after she told you "Get out!"?

- **Semicolons and colons are placed *outside* the ending quotation mark.**

  Example: The memorandum to employees used the word "cheap"; the word should have been "inexpensive."

  Example: Please send me the following items from the folder marked "Confidential": the proposal salary schedule, Bruce's evaluation, and the new employee contract.

11-5

PROOFREAD AND MARK

Use the appropriate proofreader marks to correct the underscore and quotation mark errors . If the sentence is correct, write **C** to the left of the number.

1. Please send me copies of your most recent issue of the Avid Gardener and the Garden Gate.
2. The allocation covers daily expenses <u>and</u> lodging.
3. "We have an answer, the host said, to your first question."
4. No one has ever told me I am over the hill, I wonder if it's true!
5. The article titled Internet Anxiety was very informative.

✤ Train your eye to check the terminal punctuation of each sentence.

✤ Check to be sure that the punctuation mark conveys the proper meaning. If in doubt, ask the originator.

✤ Check to be sure that the closing quotation marks have not been omitted.

SPELLING AND WORD USAGE CHECK

Compare the words in Column A with the corresponding words in Column B. Use the appropriate proofreader marks to correct the misspelled or misused words. If both columns are correct, write **C** to the left of the number.

Column A	Column B
1. cooperate	cooperite
2. criterea	criteria
3. curriculum	curriclum
4. development	developement
5. emphasis	emphasis
6. evaluate	evauluate
7. libility	liability
8. minamum	minimum
9. plaque	plaqeu
10. procedure	proceedure
11. reguard	regard
12. volumne	volume
13. Any one can enter.	Anyone may qualify.
14. Flo rises colorful irises.	Please raise your hand.
15. Don’t lean on me.	I only eat lien meat.

PROOFREADING APPLICATIONS PART A

11-7

BUSINESS LETTER

Proofread the following letter, and correct all errors using the appropriate proofreader marks.

THE NEW CAPITOL THEATRE
35 Central Avenue
West San Jose, CA 95128-1469
(408) 555-6749 • Fax: (408) 555-6752

May 15, 20--
Mr. & Mrs. Frank Doolittle
3429 Oak Meadow Road
San Jose, CA 95134-3428

Dear Mr. & Mrs. Doolittle:

Do you remember those lein days in the twenties and thirties. Do you remember dating in high school and enjoying the Saturday matinees at the local Bijou? the Biograph? the Orpheum or the Strand. Do you recall the anticipation as you walked to the theatre. The never-ending wonder of those crystal chandeliers and mirrored walls. The enticing smell of popcorn. The luxurious feeling of sinking into a cushioned seat?

Well, this grand environment is not "gone with the wind". It's alive and well, and you can see it all at the New Capitol Theatre, a once-popular landmark in San Jose.

Yes, the New Capitol has been rebuilt literally from the ground up. The developement of this replica of the original Capitol Theatre, which opened in April 1926, took three years to complete, and due reguard was given to restoring all the luxurious ambiance that was so exciting in the heyday of the flapper era. We spared no expense in refurbishment.

Enphasis was also given in restoring two pleasant amenities that were so much a part of moviegoing in the past; (1) the usher who guided you to your seat with a pinpoint flashlight and (2) the washroom attendant who was always ready with a needle and thread and who would give an emergency mending with a minamum of fuss. Our principal new policy will be to evauluate and show the best films of the twenties and thirties.

The enclosed flyer announces our opening double feature, "Footlight Parade" and "Gold Diggers of 1933," and includes a brief review of each movie. You may have seen the original showing, you may have enjoyed the revivals, or you may have watched them on late night TV.

If you know the way to San Jose, come join us for the joy of reminiscence. May we also suggest that you dress in appropriate costume of the twenties and thirties? You will find that the—good old days—were more than fodder for trivia games.

Rah. Rah. The good old days are here again.

Sincerely,

Darryl Kraft, Owner-Manager
New Capitol Theatre

wit

Enclosure; Opening Flyer

PROOFREADING APPLICATIONS — PART B

11-8

SIMPLIFIED MEMORANDUM

Proofread the following memo, and correct all errors using the appropriate proofreader marks.

THE NEW CAPITOL THEATER MEMORANDUM

May 25, 20--

Theatre Staff

THE CURTAIN RAISES AT THE NEW CAPITOL THEATRE

Congradulations ! The grand reopening of our show case theatre the NEW CAPITOL went off faultlessly. From the opening ceremonies in the foyer to the last strains of the song "'Til We Meet Again," it was 1926 all over again.

The double bill of "Gold Diggers of 1933" and "Footlight Parade" were an inspired choice. The volumn of mail response from the audience was over whelming. I understand there were a run on these films at the vidio stores today and we can expect that will continue. We are evauluating proceedures to tie in this reopening with reguard to other historical events of the twenties and thirties.

Were you among those in the audience who excepted our invitation to wear evening clothes apporpriate to the era. The enphasis was on the twenties, and many arrived at the theatre in antique cards we have the Antique Car Society to thank for this. Fortunately the wheather that evening was mild.

I know that many of you are old-movie buffs, in fact many of you have indicated to me personaly that you have extensive collecttions of movies from the twenties and thirties. I will apperciate your suggestions with reguard to future bookings. We do'nt want to limit ourselfes to movies of these two decades but right now this is where the greatest interest lies. It has been suggested that a placque commemorating this occassion be installed and we are liening in that direction.

We apprecaite any suggestions that might rise concerning publicity and suport from locale merchants.

Again thank you for your corperation.

Darryl Kraft, Owner-Manager

wit

11-9

ANNOUNCEMENT

Proofread the following announcement, and correct all errors using the appropriate proofreader marks.

HOLY FAMILY PARISH
555 Newhall Street
San Jose, CA 93334-3248

THE CONTEST OF THE CENTURY

Sponsored by San Jose's New Capitol Theatre

Guess the grass revenue of the top movie money-makers of the last fifty years and you will win a fabulous cash prise while helping you parish underwrite the developement of the summer curriclum of programs for the whole family. When you coperate, we all win!

Listed here are the names of motion pictures that has grossed enormuos sums on there first runs. All you have is to do to guess the total revenue of each movie on its first run; right down to the last dollar.

Remember you need to evaulate the first run only. Obviously the first run of Gone with the Wind, which came out at the tail end of the depression will be substancially lower and seem like peanuts when compared with the blockbuster "Batman."

The proceedure to enter is simple. Any one can enter, but only one entry per family, please. List the movie titles and dollar amounts on a 3' x 5' card, and then mail it in an envelop to Holy Family Parish. There address is as follows 555 Newhall Street San Jose CA 93334-3248. Thats all you have to do! No other criterea!

Good luck!

THE PICTURES:	Gone with the wind	Star Wars
	Batman	Sound of Muzic
	Ben Hur	The Wizard of Oz
	The God Father	Singing in the Rain
	The Brige on the river Kwai	Dick Tracy
THE PRIZES	Fist:	$5,000
	Second:	$2,500
	3rd:	$1,000

Fr. Patrick O'Brien, Pastor

COMPUTERIZED PROOFREADING APPLICATIONS

ANNOUNCEMENT

1. Load file CPA11-10 from the TMPL11 subdirectory on your template CD. (This is a computer copy of Application 11-9.)
2. Proofread (use a proofreader card) and correct all errors on the screen copy that you have indicated with proofreader marks in Application 11-10. Use the spell check if it is available.
3. Produce the announcement in correct format following the standard procedures described in the previous chapters.

MANUSCRIPT PARAGRAPHS

1. Load file CPA11-11 from the TMPL11 subdirectory on your template CD.
2. Proofread the manuscript page and correct all errors using the appropriate proofreader marks.
3. Produce the manuscript page following the standard procedures.

E-MAIL MESSAGE

1. Load file CPA11-12 from the TMPL11 subdirectory on your template CD.
2. Proofread the e-mail message and correct all errors using the appropriate proofreader marks.
3. Produce the e-mail message following the standard procedures.

CUMULATIVE REVIEW APPLICATIONS NO. 4

CRA4-1

ESSAY

Proofread and correct all errors using the appropriate proofreader marks.

CALIFORNIA, HERE I COME!

At approximatly 160,000 square miles California is the third largest state; following Alaska and Texas. It's topography ranges from desserts to some of our highest mountain range. Its coast line is one of the longest and in some peoples' minds the most spectacular in the United states.

The wheather is a topic of enphasis in limitless conversations, expecially in the arid regions. Large areas of the state are subject to drougt, some times lasting as long as six or seven years. The tempratrue is hot to mild in the Southern half of the state, and mild to cold in the northern half. The average temprature in Los Angles for instance ranges from 66 degrees in the Winter to eighty-four degrees in the Summer. In San Francisco, the temperature ranges from 60 degreees in the winter to seventy-two degrees in the summer.

Farming is an extremely large industry. The state rises vegetables fruits and nuts, and nursery items, which accounts for a large volumn of the nations agricultral output.

California's transportation system is dependant on its road ways, particurlay it's well-known freeway system. The first freeway (from downtown Los Angeles to Pasadena), was completed in 1940. Of course the frequent gridlock driving sitution can some times become a libility to motorists. Californians have a love affair with the automobile and they refuse to abandon it no mater what the alternitive of mode transportation might be.

CUMULATIVE REVIEW APPLICATIONS NO. 4

Two of the world's most famous briges are the Golden Gate Bridge between San Francisco and Marin country and the San Francisco-Oakland Bay Bridge. Both are outstandingly beautiful and has been tourist attrractions for many years. 20 persons was asked the question, what is your favorite city in which to spend your vacation? Nine out of ten answered "The City by the Bay—San Francisco".

Reguarding the gold rush of 1848 it made an indelable impression on the histery of California. The tiny villages of San Francisco and Sacramento became major metropoltan centers almost over night because of the gold.

Tourism is a major industry throughtout the State. One of the most visited areas is the town of Hollywood. From a tiny rustic hamlet adjacent to Los Angeles, the town grew into a thriving city on the basis of it's almost eternal sunshine, which fostered the developement of the early motion pichture industry at the turn of the century.

To die-hard Californias, California is "heaven on earth". To visiters from out of state who say "Its a nice place to visit, but I would'nt want to live there. You don't really mean it, do you. Aren't you just a little bit envious.

California has it all; perfect weather, spectacular outdoors, healthy living, and an endless variety of entertainment and activities. What more could any one ask. There are many faces of California, the truth lies somewhere in between.

California, here I come.

CRA4-2

MANUSCRIPT

Proofread and correct all errors using the appropriate proofreader marks.

"THE STAFF OF LIFE"

Bread is called the "staff of life", and it is the most universal food known to man.

The idea of bread did not raise into the mind of the caveman Like mankind itself, bread evolved, and the developement of bread was a slow evolution. It took hundreds of years for primative man to discover how to grow the many varieties of things that could be used for baking bread, such as the following. Oats, barley, rye, wheat, etc.

Basically bread is made through the process of applying heat to a mixtue of flour or grain meal and water. There are three kind of bread—flat bread (raised by the action of baking powder), yeast bread (rised by the action of yaest) and quick bread (unleavened). The next logical proceedure for the mixture was to bake them over a fire. The first bread was an accident: A mixture of grain and water was left to near the fire resulting the first product that could reasonbly be called bread.

Yeast bread is the most poplar in the United states. Flat bread is widely used in central America, the Orient and India. Because of the low cost of preperation whole grain bread was predominent in most parts of the world until the begining of this century. White bread become popular when its cost of preparation decreased. About the same time the production of bread moved from the home to commercial bakeries.

CUMULATIVE REVIEW APPLICATIONS NO. 4

The production of bread remained substancially same for the many years. In the early forties the eddition of nutrients into commercial baking helped reduce various deseases around the word.

The best bread is the bread that can be eaten with nothing added. When I eat at a restrant my first bite is always without butter. If that goes well, I shout "sensational". Then I'm home free!

Godo bread should be a happy blending of tastes; The crust should be firm, the texture tender. The center of the loaf light and delicate.

Considering the variety of breads availble in groceries today and the reasonable cost of bread. You will agree that the staff of life is one of the world's best bargins.

CHAPTER 12

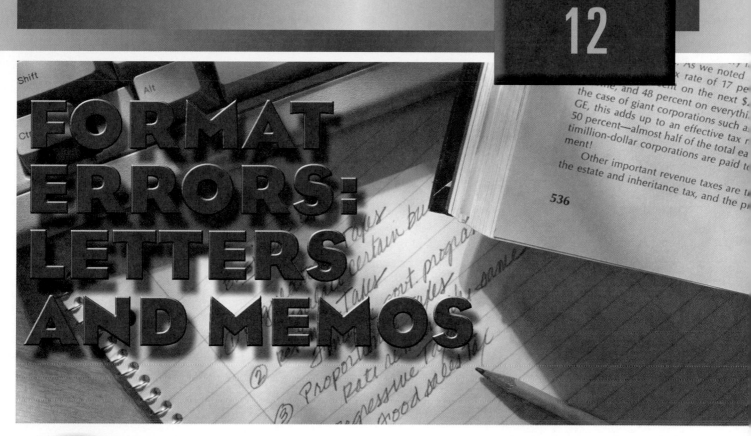

FORMAT ERRORS: LETTERS AND MEMOS

It is estimated that approximately 20 percent of the adults in the U.S. are functionally illiterate; they cannot read, write, or calculate above the eighth grade level. People who are illiterate are unable to read the daily newspaper, read a story to their children, or read the correspondence, memos, electronic messages, or business reports that businesses need to operate.

Business calls illiteracy one of its most serious problems. An illiterate employee may cost a company thousands of dollars because he or she is unable to read a simple letter or manual. One such employee caused $250,000 worth of damage to an engine because he did not understand the repair manual that came with the machine. The problem of illiteracy costs business and industry billions of dollars every year!

Objectives

- Identify format errors in block and modified block style letters.
- Identify format errors in interoffice memorandums.
- Use the appropriate proofreader marks to mark format error corrections.
- Spell correctly 12 frequently misspelled words.
- Use correctly 3 pairs of commonly misused words.

CHAPTER 12

FORMAT ERRORS: LETTERS AND MEMOS

FORMAT

The layout of copy on a page is referred to as **format.** Some formatting considerations include margin settings, spacing between paragraphs, and the organization of document parts. It may also include underlining, capitalizing, and boldfacing letters or words.

Is format important? Yes, it is. The format of a document should enhance the message—not detract from it. The document presentation should reflect the competency of the sender. If a document has a "sloppy" appearance or if the format makes a document difficult to read, the document reflects negatively on the sender. On the other hand, a document that is formatted attractively and printed on high-quality stationery indicates quality and a professional attitude. It is an indication that the sender is a person you can work with and trust.

In this chapter you will learn to recognize incorrectly formatted business letters and interoffice memorandums. Use the following proofreader marks to correct errors in format.

	MARKED COPY	CORRECTED COPY
Begin new paragraph. ¶	site of the building. ¶ The size of each block is	site of the building. The size of each block is
Do not begin new paragraph. No ¶	put in place. No ¶ Are they to be single or	put in place. Are they to be single or
Center.] [	]BASIC OBJECTIVES[	BASIC OBJECTIVES
Align copy. ||	||construction of the new school. I agree that they should be delivered soon.	construction of the new school. I agree that they should be delivered soon.
Make bold. ∿∿	Use the new fax.	Use the **new** fax.

	MARKED COPY	CORRECTED COPY
Move to the left.	If we can be of	If we can be of
Move to the right.	The crew will need it.	The crew will need it.
Move up.	If you like to give would	If you would like to give
Move down.	for His trip provides stops	His trip provides for stops

12-1

PROOFREAD AND MARK

Use the appropriate proofreader marks to revise the copy in the second column according to the instructions in the first column.

1. Center heading. SUMMARY

                to be present

2. Move down. If it is possible
3. Move left. Several people in our company
4. Do not begin new paragraph. I would like to do so.
   The presentation of the award
5. Move up. Mr. John Thomas

   334 West Draxten Boulevard

FORMAT ERRORS: LETTERS AND MEMOS

LETTERS

Letters are documents used to communicate with persons, such as customers or clients, outside the organization. Therefore, proper format is especially important. Proofreading a letter for correct format includes checking three things: (1) the overall balanced appearance; (2) the correct placement, spacing, and sequence of letter parts; and (3) the consistency in the format of the letter style.

BALANCED APPEARANCE

A good proofreader judges whether the overall appearance of a letter creates a favorable or unfavorable impression. Overall balance is achieved when the left and right margins are approximately even and the top and bottom margins are balanced. To achieve vertical balance, the top margin is adjusted to reflect the length of the letter.

Proper balance may be attained by using either standard placement or variable placement. **Standard placement** uses the same margins regardless of the length of the letter. Current practice is to use a standard 6-inch line for all letters and to vary the position of the dateline according to the length of the letter.

In **variable placement**, the side margins and the dateline vary depending upon the length of the letter (margins of 1 to 2 inches; dateline on line 14-18). The longer the letter, the narrower the margins and the higher the date is placed on the page. For example, a short letter of less than 100 words would be formatted with 2-inch side margins and the date on line 18.

12-2

PROOFREAD AND MARK

Proofread the following letters for their overall balanced appearance. Use brackets to show whether the copy should be moved right, left, up, or down.

1.

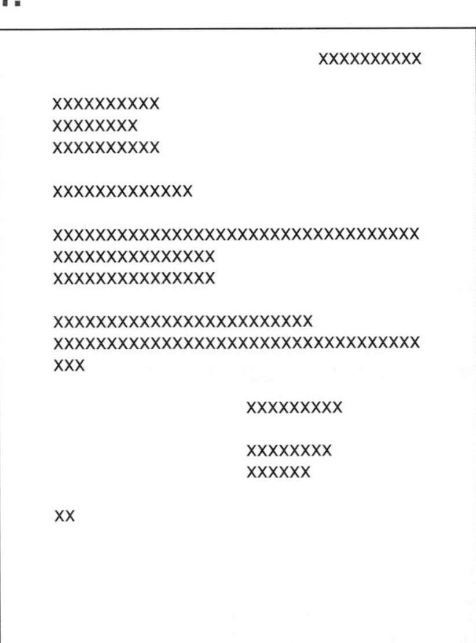

2.

xxxxxxxxxx

xxxxxxxxxx
xxxxxxxx
xxxxxxxxxx

xxxxxxxxxxxxx

xxxxxxxxxxxxxxxxxxxxxxxxxxxxxxxxxx
xxxxxxxxxxxxxxx
xxxxxxxxxxxxxxx

xxxxxxxxxxxxxxxxxxxxxxxx
xxxxxxxxxxxxxxxxxxxxxxxxxxxxxxxxxx
xxx

xxxxxxxxx

xxxxxxxx
xxxxxx

xx

3.

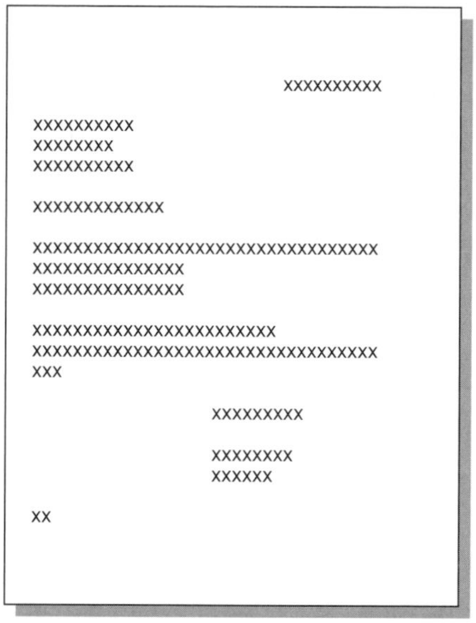

```
                                   xxxxxxxxxx

xxxxxxxxxx
xxxxxxxx
xxxxxxxxxx

xxxxxxxxxxxxx

xxxxxxxxxxxxxxxxxxxxxxxxxxxxxxxxxx
xxxxxxxxxxxxxxx
xxxxxxxxxxxxxxx

xxxxxxxxxxxxxxxxxxxxxxxx
xxxxxxxxxxxxxxxxxxxxxxxxxxxxxxxxxx
xxx

                  xxxxxxxxx

                  xxxxxxxx
                  xxxxxx

xx
```

4.

```
                                   xxxxxxxxxx

xxxxxxxxxx
xxxxxxxx
xxxxxxxxxx

xxxxxxxxxxxxx

xxxxxxxxxxxxxxxxxxxxxxxxxxxxxxxxxx
xxxxxxxxxxxxxxx
xxxxxxxxxxxxxxx

xxxxxxxxxxxxxxxxxxxxxxxx
xxxxxxxxxxxxxxxxxxxxxxxxxxxxxxxxxx
xxx

                  xxxxxxxxx

                  xxxxxxxx
                  xxxxxx

xx
```

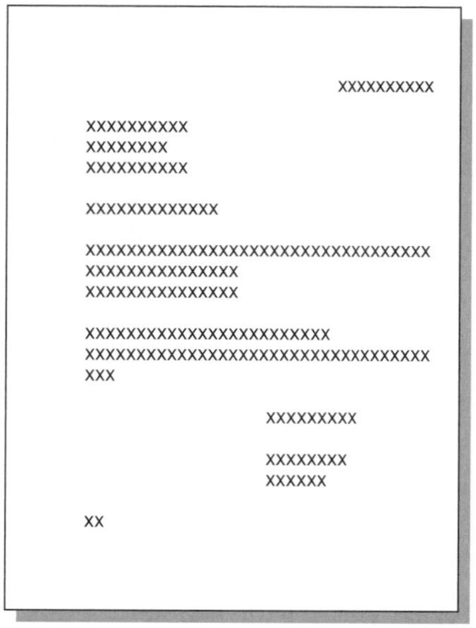

LETTER PARTS

Most letters are prepared using the same basic letter parts arranged in the same sequence. If any letter part is omitted, the sequence of the other parts should not be affected. When proofreading letters, check to make sure that all the required letter parts are present and that they are in the correct sequence. Also check that the proper spacing has been used above and below each letter part. The eight basic letter parts include the following items:

1. Heading
2. Dateline
3. Letter address
4. Salutation
5. Body
6. Complimentary close
7. Writer's name and official title
8. Reference initials

Other letter parts, such as the attention line, the subject line, and notations, may be added as needed.

HEADING

In business letters, the heading is usually preprinted on letterhead stationery. The printed heading includes the name of the company, address, telephone number, fax number, electronic address, and company logo. This heading is placed only on the first page of a multiple page letter.

J & E Company, Inc.
279 Highland Park Court
Charlotte, NC 28208-4233
(704) 555-1234 • Fax: (704) 555-4321
E-Mail: JECompany@email.com

If a letter is to be printed on plain paper, the sender's return address should be included on the lines immediately above the date. There is no blank line between the address and the date.

279 Highland Park Court
Charlotte, NC 28208-4233
December 19, 20--

DATELINE

The dateline includes the month, day, and year. It is positioned at least a double space below the printed letterhead. The line on which the date begins varies with the length of the letter.

LETTER ADDRESS

The letter address includes the personal title, name, and complete mailing address of the receiver. If the letter is addressed to an individual, the individual's personal title (*Mr.*, *Mrs.*, *Ms.*, *Miss*, *Dr.*, etc.) is included as a sign of courtesy. Use *Ms.* when a woman prefers that title or when her preferred title is unknown. The letter address is positioned at the left margin four to six lines below the date.

The letter address is used as the mailing address on the envelope. Should the letter be sent in a window envelope, the letter address may be keyed in all capital letters and without punctuation. The alert proofreader should always check that the city, state, and ZIP Code are correct. (The Appendix contains a list of two-letter state abbreviations.) One space is recommended between the two-letter state abbreviation and the ZIP Code.

Ms. Gloria Ruiz
Del Sol, Inc.
379 North River Road
Dallas, TX 75212-3682

MS GLORIA RUIZ
DEL SOL INC
379 NORTH RIVER ROAD
DALLAS TX 75212-3682

ATTENTION LINE

This may be included in the letter address to direct the letter to a particular person within the company. The attention line is positioned as the second line of the letter address.

Del Sol, Inc.
Attention Personnel Director
379 North River Road
Dallas, TX 75212-3682

Many companies today eliminate the attention line and instead insert the person's name or title as the first line of the letter address.

12-3

PROOFREAD AND MARK

Proofread the following list of cities and states by comparing the states in Column A with their two-letter state abbreviations in Column B. If the state abbreviation in Column B is not correct, use the appropriate proofreader mark to show what correction should be made. If the abbreviation is correct, write **C** to the left of the number.

Column A	Column B
1. Cedar Falls, Iowa 50613-1822	Cedar Falls, IA. 50613-1822
2. Cincinnati, Ohio 45213-0733	Cincinnati, Oh 45213-0733
3. Bloomer, Wisconsin 54724-9125	Bloomer, WS 54724-9125
4. St. Cloud, Minnesota 56303-0658	St. Cloud, MI 56303-0658

	Column A	Column B
5.	Scottsville, Kentucky 42164-0848	Scottsville, KN 42164-0848
6.	Minot, North Dakota 58701-8829	Minot, ND 58701-8829
7.	Newton, Kansas 67114-2642	Newton, KA 67114-2642
8.	Towanda, Illinois 61776-4931	Towanda, LI 61776-4931
9.	South Bend, Indiana 46616-0037	South Bend, ID 46616-0037
10.	Fort Pierce, Florida 34982-5641	Fort Pierce, FA 34982-5641

SALUTATION

The salutation is the friendly "hello" of the letter. Depending upon the relationship between the sender and the receiver, the salutation may be formal or informal. The salutation should agree with the first line of the letter address in number and gender. If the letter is addressed to a company, you might use the salutation "Ladies and Gentlemen." If the letter is addressed to an individual or position/title, the salutation should be that person's name or position/title.

Letter Address	**Salutation**
ABC Corporation 555 State Avenue Jamestown, MI 49427	Ladies and Gentlemen
Ms. Kay Leonard 90 West Boulevard St. Ansgar, IA 50472	Dear Ms. Leonard
Personnel Director ABC Corporation 555 State Street Jamestown, MI 49427	Dear Personnel Director

The salutation is placed at the left margin a double space below the last line of the letter address. A colon follows the salutation when mixed punctuation is used; the colon is omitted when open punctuation is used. The following examples illustrate various situations:

To an individual (open punctuation):	Dear Mr. Monroe
To an organization (mixed punctuation):	Ladies and Gentlemen:
To an individual whose gender is unknown (mixed punctuation):	Dear Sir or Madam:

Only when you know the receiver on a personal basis should you use the receiver's first name in the salutation.

SUBJECT LINE

The subject line, an optional letter part, states the main topic of the letter. It is positioned at the left margin a double space below the salutation. It is usually keyed in all capital letters without punctuation. An alternate form includes the word *subject*.

Dear Ms. Hackbart:	Dear Mr. Dortch
APRIL MADNESS SALE	Subject: Award Winners

BODY

The body contains the message of the letter. It begins a double space below the salutation (or subject line—if one is included). The body is single-spaced with one blank line between paragraphs.

The body should include at least three paragraphs. This makes the letter more attractive. If the message is long, the body may extend to more than one page. In a multi-page letter, maintain a 1-inch bottom margin on the first page, and begin each succeeding page with a heading. The heading consists of the receiver's name, the date, and the page number. The most efficient format for the second-page heading is the single-line style. In this format, the heading begins on line 6 and the body continues on line 8 (which is a double space below the heading).

Mr. Genaro Morales, November 12, 20––, Page 2

office supply items on pages 45 through 53 will be available

COMPLIMENTARY CLOSE

The complimentary close is the social "good-bye" of the letter. It is placed a double space below the last line of the body. Only the first word is capitalized. The punctuation mark used in the complimentary close **must** agree with the punctuation mark used in the salutation. A comma follows the complimentary close when mixed punctuation is used (meaning a colon was used after the salutation); the comma is omitted when open punctuation is used (meaning no colon was used after the salutation).

Mixed punctuation:	Dear Dr. Reed: Sincerely,
Open punctuation:	Dear Dr. Reed Sincerely

While several forms of the complimentary close are in use—sincerely yours, cordially, truly yours, very truly yours—the trend is to use only the word *sincerely*.

WRITER'S NAME AND OFFICIAL TITLE

The writer's keyed name and job title are positioned on the fourth line below the complimentary close. The job title may be positioned on the same line with the keyed name or immediately below, whichever gives the best balance.

Sincerely,	Sincerely
Georgina Mendez Conference Coordinator	Emi Mori, Secretary Social Committee

REFERENCE INITIALS

The initials of the document specialist are keyed in lowercase letters at the left margin a double space below the writer's name and title.

Georgina Mendez
Conference Coordinator

tah

When the writer of a letter keyboards his or her own letter, reference initials are not needed.

NOTATIONS

Other items may be included with a letter. If so, an enclosure notation is keyed below the reference initials. The items enclosed may also be listed. If a copy of the letter is to be sent to other persons, a copy notation is included. Either *c* or *pc* may be used, followed by the names of the persons who will receive a copy. A postscript would be the last notation in a letter. As shown below, all of these letter parts are positioned at the left margin a double space below the preceding part. *See the following example:*

are anxious to work with you.

Sincerely,

Theodore Klements, Head

mri

Enclosure: Price List

c Andres Miranda

The deadline for the discount is…

12-4

PROOFREAD AND MARK

Proofread the following letter parts and correct all format errors using the appropriate proofreader marks. If there are no format errors, write **C** to the left of the number.

1. to discuss your proposal.

   Sincerely,

   Dawn Reinertson

   pc Jarod Sampson

   tis

2. Ms. Gail Jaeckin
   763 Jackson Street South
   Anchorage, AK 99501-0942

   Dear Ms. Jaeckin

      HOLIDAY SHOPPING PLANS

   Yes, it is time to make your...

3. Pavement Prices Co.
   9473 Chestnut Boulevard
   New Orleans, LO 70118-3811

   Dear Sir or Madam

4. Miss Sally Schneiter
   Eastern Pines Resort
   856 Valley View Street
   Portland, ME 04107-0341

   Dear Sally:

5. Mr. Larry Stelter, President
   Comfort Homes, Inc.
   257 Hampton Avenue
   Wilmington, DE 19899-3169

   Ladies and Gentlemen

6. and is enclosed for your use.

   Sincerely,

   Jim Wenisch
   Sales Department
   tbe

7. Mr. Oscar Perea
   Rancho Nuevo
   849 North Pike Road
   Columbia, SC 29205-1492

   Dear Miss Perea

8. MS. MIWAKU YOSHINO
   SWEET SUGAR REFINERY
   4715 OAHU AVENUE
   HILO, HI 96720-4186

   Ladies and Gentlemen

9. and return the enclosed card by June 30.

   Sincerely,

   Nancy Jungers
   National President

   Enclosures

   AK

10. August 11, 20--

    Dr. Barbara Ericson
    Hairs and Ribbons
    7593 Bradley Circle
    Nashua, NH 03063-0269

    Subject: Award Winners

LETTER STYLES

Letters may be prepared in different styles. The two most common letter styles are the block style and the modified block style. The **block style** is quick and easy to format because all letter parts begin at the left margin. This style is very popular because there are no paragraph or line indentations.

The traditional **modified block style**, however, is still widely used. In the modified block style, the dateline, complimentary close, and writer's name and official title begin at the center of the page. Paragraphs may be either blocked or indented; however, blocked paragraphs are the most popular in the business community.

When proofreading letters, check that the letter format has been applied consistently throughout. Also check that either open or mixed punctuation has been used consistently. Figures 12-1 and 12-2 illustrate the two letter styles.

Figure 12-1

Block Letter Style with Mixed Punctuation

GRAND WRITING BROTHERS INC.
39179 West Outer Drive • Knoxville, TN 37921-2648
Telephone: 615-555-6622 • FAX: 615-555-6623
E-mail: Writing@email.com

May 19, 20--

Ms. Myrtle Dallman
874 South Ash Avenue
Montgomery, AL 36117-1749

Dear Ms. Dallman:

BLOCK STYLE LETTER, MIXED PUNCTUATION

When all parts of a business letter start at the left margin, the style is called the block style. The block style is efficient because no tabs are required.

This letter also illustrates mixed punctuation. The salutation is followed by a colon, and the complimentary close is followed by a comma.

The block style appeals to firms that look for efficient ways to handle business correspondence.

Sincerely,

Janet R. Zunder
Communications Specialist

tbe

Figure 12-2

Modified Block Letter Style with Open Punctuation

GRAND WRITING BROTHERS INC.
39179 West Outer Drive • Knoxville, TN 37921-2648
Telephone: 615-555-6622 • FAX: 615-555-6623
E-mail: Writing@email.com

May 19, 20––

Ms. Myrtle Dallman
874 South Ash Avenue
Montgomery, AL 36117-1749

Dear Ms. Dallman

Subject: Modified Block Style Letter, Open Punctuation

The modified block style is similar to the block style except that the date, complimentary close, and closing lines begin at the center. Many businesses prefer this style because it has a more balanced appearance.

This letter also illustrates open punctuation. There is no colon after the salutation and no comma after the complimentary close.

The modified block style continues to be a favorite of many firms. Do you think it represents the traditional image?

Sincerely

Janet R. Zunder
Communications Specialist

tbe

INTEROFFICE MEMORANDUMS

Interoffice memorandums (memos) are informal documents used for communication among persons within the same organization. Because these provide internal communication only, writers are generally not as concerned about enhancing the company image as they are with letters. However, employees are judged by their coworkers and supervisors, not only on their ability to compose clear and correct documents, but also on their ability to proofread carefully. Therefore, care must be taken by the proofreader to be sure the format is accurate.

Generally, memos address only one topic and include the following parts: receiver's name, sender's name, date, subject of the memo, body or actual message, and reference initials.

Some companies have replaced interoffice memorandums with electronic mail. Electronic mail will be discussed in Chapter 15.

FORMAL MEMORANDUM

The formal memo includes four printed headings: TO, FROM, DATE, and SUBJECT. The printed memo forms can be a full page or a half page.

Side margins are 1 inch. The first line of the body begins a double space below the subject line. The paragraphs are blocked and single-spaced. The initials of the document specialist are included a double space below the last line of the body. Memos are usually signed or initialed by the sender. Figure 12-3 illustrates the format of a formal memo.

Figure 12-3

Formal Memo Format

GRAND WRITING BROTHERS INC. Interoffice Memorandum

TO: Support Staff

FROM: Kathy Haack KH

DATE: April 12, 20--

SUBJECT: Format for Memos

This memo illustrates the formal format. It is designed for use on printed interoffice memorandum forms. If plain paper is used, the headings TO, FROM, DATE, and SUBJECT must be keyed.

1. Side margins are approximately 1 inch.

2. The message begins a double space below the printed headings.

3. Paragraphs are single-spaced, and a double space (one blank line) is left between them. Enumerations are treated as numbered paragraphs.

4. Reference initials are keyed a double space below the last line of the body.

The memo may be signed or initialed by the originator.

tbe

SIMPLIFIED MEMORANDUM

The simplified format is designed to be efficient. Unlike the formal format, the headings TO, FROM, DATE, and SUBJECT are not keyed. The parts of the memo are arranged in the same sequence as those of a letter. The spacing between the parts of the simplified memo and those of a letter are also identical. Figure 12-4 illustrates the simplified memo format.

Figure 12-4

Simplified Memo Format

GRAND WRITING BROTHERS INC. Interoffice Memorandum

April 12, 20--
QS
Support Staff

SIMPLIFIED FORMAT FOR MEMOS

This memo illustrates the simplified format. It is designed for use on plain paper. The style is compatible with printers because text does not have to be aligned with printed headings.

1. The side margins are 1 inch. The date begins at the left margin on line 10.

2. The name of the receiver is positioned a quadruple space below the date.

3. The subject is keyed in all capital letters a double space below the name of the receiver.

4. The body begins a double space below the subject line. The body is single-spaced with a double space between paragraphs.

5. Enumerations are formatted as blocked paragraphs.

6. The sender's name is keyed a quadruple space below the body or message.

7. Reference initials are keyed a double space below the name of the sender.

QS
Kathy Haack

tbe

PROOFREAD AND MARK

12-5

Proofread the following formal memo, and correct all format errors using the appropriate proofreader marks.

GRAND UNION COLLEGE INTEROFFICE MEMO

TO: JoEllen Eustis, Head Librarian

FROM: Michael Eggersgluess, Management Department

DATE: October 8, 20--

SUBJECT: Research Reports

Thank you for your interest in our Business

Communications class project. Each student was
asked early in the semester to prepare a research report with
several parts to be included.

The reports that have come in are well done; and
when we receive permission from the authors,
we will be placing them on reserve in the library.
tos

✤ In addition to the body, remember to proofread the special parts of a letter or memo. Also check to be sure that no parts have been omitted.

✤ When preparing more than one letter, be sure that each letter or memo is inserted into the correctly addressed envelope. Check to be sure that all enclosures are, in fact, enclosed with the letter.

✤ When proofreading a letter for format, check that one letter style and one punctuation style have been used consistently throughout.

12-6

SPELLING AND WORD USAGE CHECK

Compare the words in Column A with the corresponding words in Column B. Use the appropriate proofreader marks to correct the misspelled or misused words. If both columns are correct, write **C** to the left of the number.

Column A	Column B
1. beginning	begining
2. priviledge	privilege
3. salary	salery
4. pertinent	pertnent
5. similar	similiar
6. safety	safety
7. technical	technicle
8. especialy	especially
9. transferred	transfered
10. submited	submitted
11. accomodate	accommodate
12. established	establishd
13. We'll loose the game.	Don't lose the keys.
14. Don't quite the team.	He quit his job.
15. an interesting devise	The new device works well.

PROOFREADING APPLICATIONS PART A

12-7

BUSINESS LETTER

Proofread the following letter for all errors, including errors in balance, letter parts, and letter style. The letter should be formatted in modified block style with mixed punctuation. Mark the corrections using the appropriate proofreader marks.

CITY FUNDERS ASSOCIATION OF NEW ENGLAND (CFANE)
3790 Poplar Boulevard • Providence, RI 02915-1388
Telephone: 401-555-7421 • Fax: 401-555-7425

October 23, 20--

Arlene Andross, President
Grand Apple Equipment Corporation
2469 North River Boulevard
Hartford, CT 01609-2331

Organizational Meeting

Ladies and Gentlemen:

The organizational meeting of the new Board of Governors of the City Funders Association of New England has been scheduled for for Tuesday afternoon, November 20. The meeting will be held in the Baker Room of the Grant Street Hotel begining at 2:00 p.m.

On behalf of the Nominating/Elections Commitee, it is my priviledge to welcome you to the CFAEN board. We look forward to your technicle assitance in helping meet the goal for our annual fund drive and identify those projects and activites in the areaa that are most in need of financial assitance.

Other issues that may be address at future meetings include fund saffety, salery issues, security devises and other similiar topics that are pertnent to our board.

Sincerly

Angeline Tigner, President

t is

PROOFREADING APPLICATIONS PART B

12-8

BLOCK STYLE LETTER

Proofread the following letter prepared in the block style with open punctuation. Correct all errors using the appropriate proofreader marks.

CORNSBURG DISTRIBUTING COMPANY
976 Oak Lane NE
Salt Lake City, UT 84115-3199
(801) 555-1011 Fax (801) 555-1012

Mr. Gary Heitner
Mountain View Advertising
15 South Jackson Way
Albuquerque, MN 87108-2713

Dear Ms. Heitner;

At the recent meeting of our mrketing staff, it was decided that your company should be contacted for infromation about advertising rates for our campaign in the state of New Mexico. Late this summer we will be introducing our newest line of packing boxxes at outlets through out the western U. S.

In each of the states we will be asking one add agency to be responsible for promotion within that state. You are one of the agencies we are consideriing for the state of New Mexic. We were especialy impressed with the add campaig your developed for the General Electric Company last year. We were quiet impressed with your technical expertise.

Enclose is a report on what needs to be shared with our potental customers. May we have your response within the next fourteen days so we can accomodate their wishes.

Sincerely

Luisa Diaz, Head
Marketing Department

BE

SIMPLIFIED MEMO

12-9

Proofread the following simplified memo for all errors, including errors in format. Mark the corrections using the appropriate proofreader marks.

GENERAL MANUFACTURING, INC. *Interoffice Memorandum*

November 30, 20--

Aurelia Rivera

Recognition of staff

President Yuan has recieved several letters of commendation on the excellent job that you did at the national convention last week. We have submited copys of you letters to Personnel to be placed in your personnal file. Congratulations!

Please complete the Enclosed form by Fri. so that we will have the information we need for the nest issue of General Notes. This news letter will be published at the end of next weak. Don't loose out on this oportunity to high light the excellent work you did!

Would you also send us a photo graph that we might use with the artical.

Jane Davies Thomas

tih

COMPUTERIZED PROOFREADING APPLICATIONS

12-10 BLOCK STYLE LETTER

1. Load file CPA12-10 from the TMPL12 subdirectory on your template CD. (This is a computer copy of Application 12-8.)
2. Proofread (use a proofreader card) and correct all errors on the screen copy that you have indicated with proofreader marks in Application 12-8.
3. Produce the letter in correct format following the standard procedure described in previous chapters.

12-11 FORMAL MEMORANDUM

1. Load file CPA12-11 from the TMPL12 subdirectory on your template CD.
2. Proofread the memo, and correct all errors using the appropriate proofreader marks.
3. Produce the memo following the standard procedures.

12-12 MAIL MESSAGE

1. Load file CPA12-12 from the TMPL12 subdirectory on your template CD.
2. Proofread the e-mail message and correct all errors using the appropriate proofreader marks.
3. Produce the e-mail message following the standard procedures.

CHAPTER 13

FORMAT ERRORS: REPORTS AND JOB SEARCH DOCUMENTS

Your letter of application in a job search is similar to a sales letter. The purpose of this letter is to match your qualifications with the employer's needs in the best way possible. Because of its importance, your letter must be perfect—no errors. Consider the impression you might make on a potential employer if these errors were found in your letter:

- I have worked in sales since 1098.
- I am enclosing my resume, along with other important parts of me.
- I have taken the following curses in my studies: keyboarding, business law, communications, and entrepreneurship.

Objectives

- Recognize format errors in reports.
- Recognize format errors in job search documents.
- Use the appropriate proofreader marks to indicate corrections in format.
- Spell correctly 12 frequently misspelled words.
- Use correctly 3 pairs of commonly misused words.

REPORTS

Reports are used to provide or analyze information and to communicate within a company or with other companies. Business reports can be used for financial, managerial, operational, sales, planning, forecast, and other informational reporting. There is a standard format for most reports, just as there is for letters and resumes. School reports, such as themes, book reports, and term papers, are usually prepared in the standard report format as well.

Reports may be formatted as unbound, left-bound, or top-bound documents. The most common format is the unbound report. Although the spacing and arrangement of report parts may vary somewhat from writer to writer, you will review the basic unbound format in this chapter.

REPORT PARTS

When proofreading a report, check closely for consistency and correctness among report parts. For example, check that the spacing above and below similar headings is the same throughout the report. Report parts vary, depending upon the length and formality of the report. The basic parts, however, include the title page, the body, and the bibliography.

Title Page

The title page includes the title of the report, the writer's name and school or organization, and the date. Figure 13-1 illustrates the format and spacing of a title page in an unbound report.

Body

The body is the message of the report and begins with the **main heading**—placed approximately 2 inches from the top. If there is a **secondary heading**, it is centered a double space below the main heading. The main heading is the title of the report, also found on the title page, and the secondary heading provides further information about the message of the report. To make the information easy to read, the body is organized under one or more levels of headings. The first level of headings is called a **side heading**, and the next level of headings is called a **paragraph heading**. Figure 13-1 illustrates an acceptable format for side and paragraph headings.

Enumerations are often used to emphasize certain facts or present information in an easy-to-read format. Although enumerations may be prepared in various ways, the block style is the easiest to format. Enumerations in block style are indented five spaces from the left margin and single-spaced.

Margins and spacing should be consistent throughout the report. For an unbound report, the side and bottom margins are 1 inch. The top margin for the first page is 2 inches; on all other pages, the top margin is 1 inch. Generally, reports are double-spaced and paragraphs are indented $\frac{1}{2}$-inch. Pages are numbered beginning with the second page. The page number appears 1 inch from the top and is followed by a double space.

2 inches
from top ⟶ FORMAT FOR UNBOUND REPORTS

5.3 inches from top ⟶ by

Karen E. Mikelson

Eastern Cottonwood College

8.6 inches from top ⟶ April 19, 20--

2 inches ⟶ FORMAT FOR UNBOUND REPORTS

Side margins: 1"

General Guidelines

Quadruple-space ⟶ Indention: .5 inch

When proofreading reports, the proofreader's responsibility includes checking for all mechanical errors, including format errors. Although this is a big responsibility, the writer has ultimate responsibility for the correctness of the report.

⟵ Double-space

The writer is responsible for the correct presentation of the paper in its entirety—all the preliminary, illustrative, and reference matter as well as the body of the text.[1]

⟵ Double-space

Follow these guidelines to format unbound reports.

⟵ Double-space

Spacing and Margins ⟵ Side Heading

Reports may be either single- or double-spaced. School reports, formal reports, and manuscripts are usually double-spaced. Business reports are often single-spaced.

Regardless of the spacing, the top margin for the first page is 1.5 inches. The top margin on all other pages is 1 inch. Side and bottom margins are about 1 inch. Paragraphs ae indented five spaces. Quoted material that is four or more lines is single-spaced and indented five spaces from the left margin.

Headings

For ease of reading, information is organized using various levels of headings.

⟵ Double-space

———

⟵ Double-space

[1]Kate L. Turabian, A Manual for Writers of Term Papers, Theses, and Dissertations. 6th ed. (Chicago: The University of Chicago Press, 1996), 230.

1 inch at right margin ⟶ 2

Paragraph heading

Main heading. Center a main heading (or title) in all capitals over the line of writing. If the heading has two or more lines, allow one blank line between them. Leave three blank lines between the heading and the first line of the body.

Secondary heading. If the title includes a secondary heading, it is centered a double space below the main heading, The main words are capitalized.

Side Headings. Side headings begin even with the left margin and are underlined. The main words are capitalized.

Paragraph headings. All paragraph headings are indented and underlined. Only the first word is capitalized. The heading at the start of this paragraph is an example of a paragraph heading.

Page Numbers

It is not necessary to number the first page. All other pages are numbered in the upper right corner on line 4. A double space follows the page number.

Guidelines for Dividing Copy

Follow these guidelines when dividing words and paragraphs within the body of a report:

1. Divide words according to the word division rules.
2. If it is necessary to divide a paragraph between two pages, at least two lines of the paragraph should appear on each page.

2 inches from top ⟶ REFERENCES

Side margins: 1"

Quadruple-space ⟶ Indention: .5 inch

House, Clifford R., and Kathie Sigler. Reference Manual for the Office. 8th ed. Cincinnati: South-Western Educational Publishing, 1995.

Robinson, Jerry W., Jack P. Hoggatt, Jon A. Shank, Arnola C. Ownby, Lee R. Beaumont, T. James Crawford, and Lawrence W. Erickson. Century 21 Keyboarding, formatting, and Document Processing. 6th ed. Cincinnati: South-Western Educational Publishing, 2000.

Turabian, Kate L., A Manual for Writers of Term Papers, Theses, and Dissertations. 6th ed. Chicago: The University of Chicago Press, 1996.

Figure 13-1

Unbound Report Format, Including Title Page, Sample Pages, and References Page

References

If references have been used in writing the report, they are listed at the end. The references may be placed a quadruple space after the last line of the body of the report *or* on a separate page. The references are listed under an appropriate heading, such as REFERENCES, SOURCES, WORKS CITED, or BIBLIOGRAPHY. As seen in these examples, the heading is typed in all caps.

Each entry is single-spaced, with a double space between entries. The first line of each entry begins at the left margin, but all other lines are indented five spaces from the left margin. This is called the **hanging indent style**. Figure 13-1 illustrates a *REFERENCES* page.

Because of the increased use of electronic sources as references, you should also know how to document electronic citations. An electronic citation includes the following reference components: Author (Date). "Title of Work." *Title of Complete Work*. Available: URL [Date you accessed this site].

Peng, Yeo (December 1997). "Tips for Reading Faster." *Executive World* [Online]. Available: ***http://www.informatics.edu.sg/ics-sin/business_letters.htm*** [January 3, 2000].

DOCUMENTATION

When using another person's ideas or quoting statistics or other specific information, the writer must indicate the sources from which the information was taken. Reference to the originator adds credibility to the report and gives credit to the originator. The most common means of documentation for business writers include textual citations, footnotes, and endnotes. More formal documentation styles include the MLA and APA styles of notation.

Textual Citations

Textual citations (also called textnotes or parenthetic in-text citations) have grown in popularity. They usually include the last name of the author(s), the date of publication, and the page number. Textual citations are placed in parentheses within the body of the report. The complete references are then listed in alphabetical order by author surnames under the heading REFERENCES, SOURCES, or BIBLIOGRAPHY at the end of the report. (See the section entitled "References.") If the report in Figure 13-1 had used a textual citation instead of a footnote, the reference would have appeared as follows:

When proofreading reports, the proofreader's responsibility includes checking for all mechanical errors, including format errors. Although this is a big responsibility, the writer has ultimate responsibility for the correctness of the report.

> **The writer is responsible for the correct presentation of the entire paper—all the preliminary, illustrative, and reference matter as well as the text. The person preparing the manuscript, if other than the writer, is responsible for accurate transcription of the copy, the layout of the components as illustrated in chapter 14, and the general appearance of the final manuscript, but not for content (Turabian, Grossman, and Bennett, 1996, p. 240).**

The Modern Language Association (MLA) and the American Psychological Association (APA) styles of citation are used in formal reports. The MLA style is used primarily in literary works and lists in parentheses the author's last name and the page number (*Author 53*). The APA style is used primarily by writers in the social sciences and lists in parentheses the last name of the author, the year of publication, and the page number (*Author, 20xx, p. 53*).

Footnotes

Footnotes are numbered consecutively throughout the report. They appear at the bottom of the page on which the references are cited. A $1\frac{1}{2}$-inch divider line separates the footnote from the body. Superscripts are used to number footnotes. If a printer cannot format superscript figures, the number may be placed within brackets [1]. Figure 13-1 illustrates the format for footnotes.

If you are using the footnote feature of your word processing program, the feature will automatically position your footnotes in the correct place at the bottom of the page.

Endnotes

Endnotes are essentially the same as footnotes. But, unlike footnotes, endnotes are listed together on a separate page at the end of the report.

If you are using the endnote feature of your word processing program, the endnotes will automatically appear at the end of your document.

Check APA's Web site (www.apa.org) for additional information about using the APA documentation style.

Check MLA's Web site (www.mla.org) for additional information about using the MLA documentation style.

13-1

PROOFREAD AND MARK

Proofread the following paragraph from a bound report. Use the appropriate proofreader marks to correct the errors. If the line is correct, write **C** to the left of the number.

1. Deere & Company, with Headquarters in Moline Illinois is
2. one of the worlds oldest and respected most companis. Deere
3. & Com. manufactures, distributes and finance a full line of
4. agriculturel equipment, as well as a braod range of
5. construction and forestry equipment.

JOB SEARCH DOCUMENTS

Three documents are crucial to a person's application for employment—a resume (also called a data sheet or vita), an application letter, and (following an interview) a follow-up letter. Because of the importance of these documents in the employment process, each should show the employer the highest standard of work of which the applicant is capable. Since each document should be submitted without error, careful proofreading is crucial.

RESUME

Prospective employers use resumes to screen individuals for an interview. As such, the resume should summarize a person's background in several important sections—personal, education, work experience, and related activities. Other sections might include your career objective, summary of qualifications, computer experience, and references.

The most common resume formats are chronological, functional, and combination. The **chronological format** lists your employment history in reverse chronological order, with your most recent employment first. This resume emphasizes your work stability and experience with specific companies.

The **functional resume** focuses attention on your skills or qualifications rather than on your past employment history. Applicable skills may come from various areas such as communication, organization, management, human relations, or computer software. The functional resume is appropriate for applicants who lack related work experience or who have gaps in their employment history.

The **combination resume** takes advantage of the best features of both the chronological and the functional resume. The combination resume emphasizes the applicant's skills or qualifications and also includes a complete job history.

Personal

This section is at the top of the page and includes the applicant's name, address, and telephone number. If you have an electronic address (such as your own Web page or personal e-mail account), you may want to include it here. No other personal information should be given unless it relates directly to the job.

Education

This section should include the name and address of the schools attended—the most recent one listed first (reverse chronological order). Only the city and state are needed as the address. It is also appropriate to include in this section the dates you attended each school, your GPA, and those courses that have provided special preparation for the desired position.

Work Experience

In this section, you should list any previously held jobs, even though they may not directly relate to the desired job. Whether you have worked in agriculture, a service industry, or an office position, a prospective employer is interested in your experience in working with people, your attitude toward work, and your values. Work experience shows the prospective employer that you know how to take initiative and responsibility for your actions.

Related Activities

This section shows your involvement in organizations and athletics during your years in school, as well as any awards, honors, or scholarships you may have received. Include the name of the organization or group, as well as the time you were a member, and indicate any officer positions you may have held. Include only those activities that are related to the position you want.

Optional Sections

While your resume can include any information you want, try to limit the resume to one page. What differentiates you from all other applicants? If the information is not important to an employer, it should not be included on your resume.

Since a majority of jobs today require specific computer experience, consider having a separate section that identifies your computer experience. You might also include this information under "education."

While a separate "references" section was important in the past, most employers today are not interested in a list of references until later in the interview process. For example, an employer might request a list of references from the top candidates. Instead of listing references on your resume, take a separate list with you to the interview. Each entry on this list should include the name and courtesy title of the person, her/his official title (coach, teacher, principal, supervisor), complete mailing address, and telephone number. Always ask for permission before listing someone as a reference.

Teacher's may be used as references if they give you their permission.

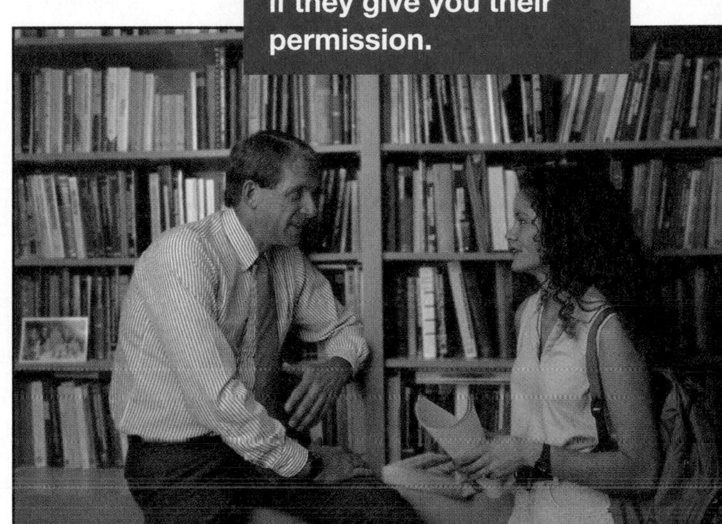

Many companies now request a resume as an electronic submission (also called a cyber resume). The computer looks for key words and phrases during the scanning process and selects only those resumes that included those key words. The information on your resume should be formatted in such a way that the reader will be able to understand it easily. Figure 13-2 illustrates a correctly formatted resume.

APPLICATION LETTER

The application letter should be keyed on plain paper with a return address, as described in Chapter 12. The body of the letter should have only three or four paragraphs.

You should begin the first paragraph by telling the reader where you heard of the position (placement office, newspaper ad, counselor, teacher, etc.), exactly what you understand to be the title of the position, and that you are a candidate for the job.

In the middle paragraphs of the letter, you should briefly tell the reader about your interest in and background for the job. Discuss your key qualifications, education, and work experience as they relate to this position; do not repeat everything listed on your resume. In this section, you should also state that you are enclosing your resume.

Because an interview is a crucial aspect of any employer's decision process, you should ask for an interview at the reader's convenience in the last paragraph. It is appropriate to suggest specific dates. If you end the paragraph by calling attention to your address and telephone number on the "enclosed resume," it will be logical for the reader to read the resume in more detail. Figure 13-3 shows a sample application letter.

BRADLEY B. ANDERSON
218 South Andrew
Whitewater, WI 53190-1118
(608) 555-2423
E-Mail: Name@email.com

EDUCATION

Northview Public Schools, Whitewater, Wisconsin. 2000 – 2004
(Will receive high school diploma, May 2004)
Graduated with High Honors (3.65 on a 4.00 scale)

Special Preparation:
Completed courses in English, math, science, and business
Key at 65 words per minute

COMPUTER SOFTWARE EXPERIENCE

Experienced in using the following software applications:
Word, PowerPoint, Microsoft Excel, Microsoft Access, and PageMaker

WORK EXPERIENCE

Administrative Assistant, Dayton Office Supplies, Inc., Fort Atkinson, Wisconsin, May 2002 – December 2004
Worked 15 hours each week after school and on weekends

Responsibilities:
- Answered telephones
- Deposited cash
- Stocked and ordered supplies
- Trained employees in using Word and PowerPoint

RELATED ACTIVITIES

National Honor Society, 2004
Student Council Senior Class Representative, 2004
Future Business Leaders of America
President, 2002, and Publicity Committee Chair, 2003
Volleyball and Soccer, 2003

Figure 13-2 *Sample Resume*

218 South Andrew
Whitewater, WI 53190 1118
May 23, 20--

Ms. Deborah Wetzell
Human Resources Department
Hummel Manufacturing
37 Main Street
Whitewater, WI 53190-4498

Dear Ms. Wetzell:

Miss Edna Reyes, my business teacher at Northview High School, told me about the opening you have at Hummel Manufacturing for a technical assistant. Please consider me an applicant for this position.

As you will see from the enclosed resume, I will graduate next week from Northview High School. In addition to advanced courses in English, math, and science, I worked with Miss Reyes in training students in word processing and desktop publishing. I am comfortable working with most software applications, and I am a quick learner.

This semester I have worked part time at Dayton Office Supplies, Inc. During the time I worked there, I was given increased responsibilities. I was also commended by my supervisor for my human relations skills and technical competence in using software applications.

I would appreciate the opportunity to discuss with you my qualifications for this position. I will telephone you next week to request an appointment, or you may call me at your convenience at (608) 555-2423.

Sincerely,

Bradley B. Anderson

Enclosure: Resume

Figure 13-3

Sample Application Letter

FOLLOW-UP LETTER

After you have had an interview, it is important to send a short thank-you note to the interviewer expressing your appreciation and explaining again your interest in the job. Your thank-you note should be sent within 24 hours after the interview. Figure 13-4 illustrates a sample follow-up letter.

Figure 13-4

Sample Follow-Up Letter

218 South Andrew
Whitewater, WI 53190-1118
June 2, 20--

Ms. Deborah Wetzell
Human Resources Department
Hummel Manufacturing
37 Main Street
Whitewater, WI 53190-4498

Dear Ms. Wetzell:

Thank you for meeting with me yesterday about the technical assistant position at your company. Your description of what the job would require was very helpful in learning what would be expected of me. I particularly liked the opportunity to tour the company and meet with members of your technical team.

As a result of our meeting and the tour, I am even more interested in being a part of the "Systems Team" and helping Hummel Manufacturing meet its objectives.

If you need additional information, please let me know. I'm excited about the possibility of working for your company.

Sincerely,

Bradley B. Anderson

✤ Technical material and legal descriptions should be proofread in pairs.

✤ When proofreading a lengthy report, proofread all similar parts as a separate step. For example, check the format of all side headings; then check all paragraph headings. Check separately the continuity and sequence of all numbered pages, tables, and figures.

✤ When preparing a multi-page document, prepare a style sheet to show how unusual features, such as names, titles, or terminology, will be handled.

13-2

SPELLING AND WORD USAGE CHECK

Compare the words in Column A with the corresponding words in Column B. Use the appropriate proofreader marks to correct the misspelled or misused words. If both columns are correct, write **C** to the left of the number.

Column A	Column B
1. commission	comission
2. quantity	quanity
3. tomorrow	tomorrow
4. financial	finantial
5. preperation	preparation
6. offerred	offered
7. permissable	permissible
8. approximately	approximatly
9. disatisfied	dissatisfied
10. guarantee	guarentee
11. knowledgeable	knowledgeable
12. counselor	counseler
13. He alluded the police.	The answer eluded her.
14. They did not alot the money.	Please allot the quotas.
15. Rainy whether is ahead.	the weather forecast

13-3

INTERNATIONAL VOCABULARY

Compare the Spanish words in Column A with the corresponding words in Column B. If the word or phrase in Column B is different from the word or phrase in Column A, use the appropriate proofreading marks to correct Column B. If the words in both columns are the same, write **C** to the left of the number.

Column A	Column B
1. entrevista	entervista
2. cualidad	cualidad
3. reasumir	reasimir
4. trabajo	trebajo
5. aventura	aventora

PROOFREADING APPLICATIONS PART A

13-4

REPORT

Proofread the following report for all errors, including errors in format. Mark the corrections using the appropriate proofreader marks.

WALES

One of the parts of Great britain that is not too well known is the country of Wales. It is is located on a peninsula directtly across the irish sea from Ireland. The peninsula is approximately 130 mile long from North to South and approximately 95 miles from east to west at its widest pont. Wales is part of Great Britain, with scotland and England being the other two parts. To the east of Wales is the country of England and to the northeast or it (and to the north of England) is Scotland.

Geography

Wales is a very mountainous country with Mount Snowdon at 3,500 feet in northern Wales being the highst point in England and Wales. Slate quarrying was a magjor source of employement in northern Wales for many many years. In recent years, ohter types of building materials have replaced slate and it is no longer as prominent in the Welsh economy.

In the mountainous part of southern Wales is located some of the world's finest coaflields for steem coal. Many persons have gained an impression of coal miners and their way of life in Wales from scenes in the move, <u>How Green Was My Valley</u>. The movie, based upon the book by the same name by Richard Llewellyn was sit in the Rhondda Valley of southern Wales. Over the years, as alternate forms of energy were developed, the demand for steam coal decreased and today very few of the mines are still open.

Language

One of the distinctive features of wales is it's language—Welsh. Many persons consider it to be an extremly difficult language to learn until they find out that "w" and "y" are considred vowels. Some of the sounds of Welsh letters are different from english. For example, an "f" is pronounced like a "v." In a word like "Gymanfa", the pronounciation is "Gah-mahn-vah."

Some other unique sounds in the Welsh language are the ones for "dd" and "ll." Teh "dd" is pronounced like the "th" in the english word "the." Therefore, in proncing the Welsh word "Eisteddfod," the middle syllable is "teth" rether than "ted."

The "ll" sound requires that the speaker plac the tip of her/his tongue at the top of the back side of the front teeeth and then carfully blow out each side. This technique is used twice in pronouncing the name of the city "Llangollen" amd tje author "Llewellyn."

Conclusion

Much more could be writen about this small country and its contribution to msic, the arts, politics, the economy, etc. It is a "region of great ... beauty."[1]

---

[1]The Encyclopedia Americana, International Edition, S.V. "Wales"

PROOFREADING APPLICATIONS PART B

13-5

APPLICATION LETTER

Proofread the following letter and correct all errors using the appropriate proofreader marks.

433 Spring Street
Idaho Falls, ID 83403-9044
June 15th, 20--

Mr. Lawrence Herbert
Personnel Division
CAS Financial Services
1005 Underwood Ave.
Idaho Falls ID 83403-4980

Dear Mr. Lawrence:

Mr. Mario Guzman, counsilor at Lexington High School, has infromed me that you have an opening for an assistant bank teller. Because I am very interested in working in the finantial services industry, please consider me a candidate for the positoin.

As you will see form the enclose resume, I have alot of related work experience. I worked for Northwest Bank on a part-time basis for approximatily two years. I also worked as a telemarketing representitive where I offerred warranties/guarantees to prospective customers. In this position I learned the importance of accuracy, dependibility, and working quickly. None of my pass employers have been disatisfied with my work.

I would appreciate the opportunty to meet with you the first week of July to discuss how I can be a part of you company's team. I will call your office next week to see if an appointment can be made. If you wish to contact me before that that day, mmy address and telephone number are at the top of the resume.

SIncerly

Micaela Rivera

Enclosure: Resume

RESUME

13-6

Proofread the following resume and correct all errors using the appropriate proofreader marks.

MICHAELA Rivera
433 Spring St.
Idaho Falls, ID 83403-49800
(804) 555-6293 E-Mail: Rivera@email.com

Education:

Lexington High Schol, Idaho Falls, Idaho, 20xx – 20xx
Received high school diploma, May 20xx
Graduated with high honors (3.99 on 4.00 scale)

Special Courses

Desktop Publishing, Business Communications, Business Law, and Economics

COMPUTER EXPEREINCE:

Familair with the following software applications: PageMaker, WordPerfect, Microsoft Work, and Micorsoft Access, and PowerPoint

SCHOOL Activites:

Varsity Basketball, 20xx–20xx; Captain, 20xx–20xx
Spanish Club, 20xx–20xx; Vice President, 20xx–20xx
Lexington Business Club, 20xx–20xx

WORK EXPEREINCE

Northwest Bank, Idaho Falls, ID
Assistent Teller, Worked 20 hours per week, 20xx – 20xx
Responsibilities:

- Served customers
- Balanced night deposits
- Completed aplication fomrs

Brickhof Telemarketing Communiations, Idaho, Falls, Idaho
Customer Service Representitive, 20xx – 20xx
Responsibilities:

- Answered customre questions
- Sold warranties and guarantes

COMPUTERIZED PROOFREADING APPLICATIONS

13-7

APPLICATION LETTER

1. Load file CPA13-7 from the TMPL13 subdirectory on your template CD. (This is a computer copy of Application 13-5.)
2. Proofread (use a proofreader card) and correct all errors on the screen copy that you have indicated with proofreader marks in Application 13-5. Use the spell check if it is available.
3. Format the letter in blocked style with the appropriate top and side margins. Produce the memo following the standard procedures described in the previous chapters.

13-8

TWO-PAGE REPORT

1. Load file CPA13-8 from the TMPL13 subdirectory on your template CD.
2. Revise the report according to the rough draft shown on pages 221 and 222. In addition, proofread for other errors that may have been missed, including format errors.
3. Format the document as a two-page unbound report; add a page number. Position the footnote on the appropriate page of the report.
4. Proofread the report carefully on the screen before printing it.
5. Save and print the report.
6. Proofread the printed report following these steps:
   a. Check closely for all mechanical errors, including format errors.
   b. Compare the printed document to the rough draft to be sure that you made all of the corrections.
   c. Check the format.
7. Correct any errors you may have missed and reprint the report.

13-9

E-MAIL MESSAGE

1. Load file CPA13-9 from the TMPL13 subdirectory on your template CD.
2. Proofread the e-mail message and correct all errors using the appropriate proofreader marks.
3. Produce the e-mail message following the standard procedures.

BASIC BUSINESS COMMUNICATION

In resent years there has been an explosion of technological changes in the way information is processed. Almost every week, for example, one reads about new types of copmuters, changes in printers and chips, and the development of new software. One of the most resent developements is the use of voise recognition technology. Now you words type automatically! The words "user friendly" are used to describe the easy with which the new technological techniques and equipment can make it easier to work with infromation.

However, beneath all of the technological advances is the the need for a basic skill in communications. A person may know how to use the equipment; however, if he/she doesn't have a basic understanding of how to use basic language skills, the technlogical advances have little meaning. An example of this basic need involves the preparation of business letters. As has been presented earlier in this text, prfreaders need to be careful in checking the format of letters. However, an even more important concept is that the work originator unerstands some of the complexities of writing the letters. "Quantity" in writing is not important, but "quality" is important.

Basic Letter Sequences One basic fact that word originators must understand is the importance of using the right sequence of ideas in a letter to make it have the most impac on the reader. When a person decides to write a letter, some the of first questions to be answered are "What will be the impact on the reader? Will he/she be pleased with the content? Will he/she be disappointed? Will he/she be nuetral in his/her reaction?" The answers to those questions provide a clue as to the sequence that the writer should use in creating the commnunication.

Ductive Sequence. If the writer assumes that the reader's reaction will be neutral or plasant, the correct sequence of ideas is the deductive one. With this sequence, the writer starts with the "positive news" or answer in the first sentence. This then is followed with details that elaborate on the "positive news". The letter sequence concludes with a pleasant ending or even "resale" to encourage the person to consider even more goods and services. One can not alude to things which aren't clear.

Inductive Sequence. If the writer assumes that the reader will be disapointed with the mesasge, the writer should use the inductive squence. This squence starts with a neutral beginning and is followed by an explanation of the reasons that led to the negative result. To further lesson the impact on the reader, the negative answer should be placed in the middle sentence in the middle paragraph.

Careful attention to the sequence of ideas in a business letter will make the message even more effective and the commnication will have it's maximum impact. As Bell states "You should equip yourself with the knowlege and creativity to meet communication needs as they arise."[1]

---

[1]Arthur H. Bell, Business Communication: Toward 2000 (Cincinnati: South-Westrn Publishing Company, 1992), 5.

CHAPTER 14

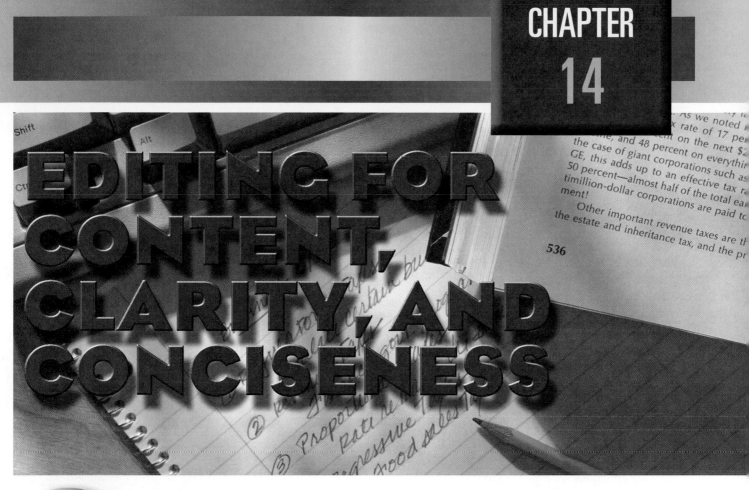

EDITING FOR CONTENT, CLARITY, AND CONCISENESS

Like the letter of application in the job search, your resume briefly summarizes your qualifications for the job for which you are applying. This document, too, must be perfect—without *any* errors. How do you think a prospective employer might react to the following statements in your resume?

- Attended the University of Ohio from 1892–1997.
- Graduated Magna Cum Loud.
- A position which allows me to use my superior commuter skills.
- My GPA at night is 3.2 (4.0).

Objectives

- Edit a message for completeness, correctness, and consistency in content.
- Edit a message for conciseness by avoiding redundancy and eliminating unnecessary modifiers.
- Edit a message for clarity by using simple—not difficult—words, by avoiding trite, overused expressions, and by presenting ideas logically.
- Distinguish between active and passive voice.
- Spell correctly 12 frequently misspelled words.
- Use correctly 3 pairs of commonly misused words.

CHAPTER 14

EDITING FOR CONTENT, CLARITY, AND CONCISENESS

WHAT IS EDITING?

As you know, **proofreading** is the process of locating mechanical errors that may occur because of incorrect keying, spelling, capitalization, grammar, punctuation, abbreviation, word division, number usage, and formatting. **Editing** involves checking copy to see that every aspect of the content is correct and that the message is clear, concise, and complete. Editing may also require changing words, correcting errors, or rewriting parts of the document text.

Editing and proofreading are two distinct activities and must be performed separately. The objectives of both, however, are the same—to improve the quality of the final copy and to make the intended message clear so that no possibility of misunderstanding or misinterpretation exists. Once copy is edited, however, it must be proofread a second time for accuracy. It is impossible to edit the content of the message and proofread for mechanical errors at the same time.

EDITING FOR CONTENT

Editing for content involves checking to see that the message is accurate. All facts, figures, and calculations must be correct. If errors in content exist, the reader may lose confidence in the writer. Correctness shows competence and regard for the reader.

The best way to locate content errors is to read the document carefully, at a natural, unhurried rate, and concentrate on what you are reading. As you read, be alert for the following types of content errors:

- **Incomplete information (omission of essential information).**
- **Incorrect facts (names, dates, addresses, numbers, etc.).**
- **Inconsistency in the way material is written (style and format).**
- **Incorrect usage of words, especially homophones (words that sound alike but differ in spelling and meaning). Examples: cite, site, sight; right, rite, wright, write; sell, cell; sail, sale.**

It is important to realize that the editing changes may vary due to the proofreader's understanding and interpretation of the material's message. Therefore, the proofreader must be alert to make sure that the editing changes retain the message the writer intended to convey.

COMPLETE INFORMATION

Editing a message for completeness means checking to see that all necessary information is included. How puzzling it is to discover that the enclosures mentioned in a letter have not been included. How frustrating it is not to be able to make a business decision because important information has been omitted. When possible, answer the "who, what, when, where, and why" information in bulleted items rather than in long, drawn out sentences.

To assure completeness, reread the message and check to see that dates, addresses, times, and other factual information are included. Make sure that any enclosures mentioned in the letter are indeed enclosed.

Check for omissions of copy by comparing the final copy with the rough draft or the original document source. Reading the wrong column or the wrong line causes material to be omitted, especially in long or complex documents. Skipping a word or a whole line also leads to omissions. Likewise, if information has been transferred from one document to another, double-check to make sure that nothing has been omitted.

To avoid omissions in tables or lists, use a helpful device such as a card, a ruler, or a piece of paper. Laying the straight edge of the card, the ruler, or the paper under the line you are reading will help focus your attention.

CORRECT FACTS

"The meeting will be held from Wednesday through Friday, September 15-18." This statement is confusing; since *Wednesday* is *September 15*, *Friday* is definitely not *September 18*. Did the writer intend to say *Wednesday through Saturday*, *Tuesday through Friday*, *September 15-17*, or *September 16-18*?

Incorrect facts may appear in numerical data (dates, amounts, ZIP Codes, Social Security numbers, serial numbers, identification numbers, stock numbers, and addresses).

Unusual, unfamiliar, and foreign names (*Papadopulos*, *Teutschel*, *Shimabukuro*) as well as similar sounding names (*Johnson*/*Johnston*) need to be checked for accuracy. Names are easily misspelled, especially because they can be spelled in so many different ways. Note the various ways the following names can be spelled:

Andersen, Anderson
Brown, Browne, Broune, Braun
Cain, Caine, Cayne, Kane, Kaine, Kayne
Carol, Carole, Carrol, Carroll
Hernandes, Hernandez
Smith, Smithe, Smythe
Schmid, Schmidt, Schmit, Schmitt
Schneider, Schneiter, Snider, Snyder
Tomson, Thomson, Thompson

Never assume you know how to spell a name; always check to see that the spelling used in the original document source is correct. In a business letter, for example, check the addressee's name in the letter address, in the salutation, within the body, and on the mailing envelope.

Locating incorrect facts is not easy. It requires concentration and attention to detail. Whenever possible, the document should be checked against the rough draft or the source document. If you are not sure about the accuracy of a statement, write a question mark next to the copy and in the right margin to alert the writer that the message is unclear and that the statement should be revised.

CONSISTENCY

Consistency means that all similar ideas are handled in the same way. Related ideas should be expressed in the same grammatical form (parallel structure). Likewise, format within a document should be consistent. Although enumerations may be either blocked at the left margin or indented, all enumerations within a document should be formatted in one style.

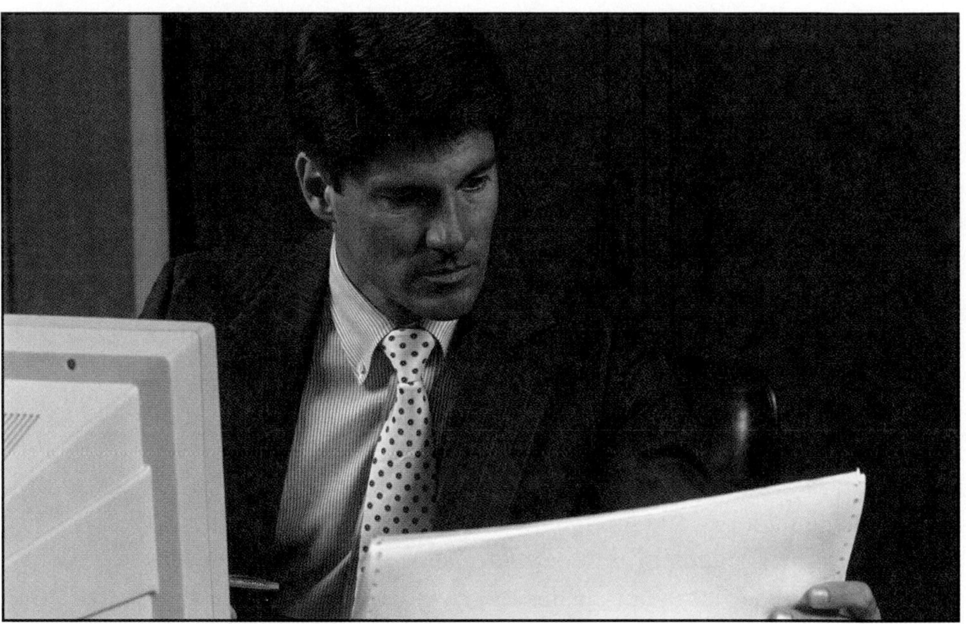

CORRECT WORD USAGE

The proficient proofreader should be able to determine whether the correct words are used so that the reader will understand the writer's message. **Word usage** refers to how language is used to convey best the intended meaning. Words that sound alike but which are spelled differently and have different meanings (homophones) must be checked carefully. Study these sentences and notice how the italicized words are used.

There is no solution in *sight*.

The *sights* of London are breathtaking.

The *site* of the new building is convenient to public transportation.

He was *cited* for speeding.

Note: Answers to the exercises in this chapter will vary because often there is more than one acceptable answer. Remember that you must retain the meaning intended by the writer.

14-1

PROOFREAD AND MARK

Using the factual information as a reference, edit the message for content errors. Correct the message using the appropriate proofreader marks. Write the revised message on the blank lines.

Speaker	**Dr. Jeanette Rachut, Stanford Graduate School of Business**
Topic	**"Preparing for Global Literacy"**
Location	**Foothill College, Johnston City**
Date	**Thursday-Friday, March 21-22, 20--**
Time	**2:30 p.m. to 5:30 p.m., Thursday** **4 p.m. to 6:30 p.m., Friday**
Completion	**Certificate awarded for two-day attendance**
Fee	**$25 for one day; $40 for two days**

The three-day conference, "Preparing for Global Literacy," is scheduled for Friday-Saturday, March 14-15, at Foothill College in Johnson City. Friday's session will be from 4:30 to 6:30 p.m. and Saturday's session from 3:00 to 5:30 p.m. The workshop will be conducted by Miss Jeanette Rachute, noted professor at Stanford Business School.

14-2

PROOFREAD AND MARK

Edit the following message for completeness. On the blank lines, list any important but missing information that you believe would make the message clearer.

Here are your travel arrangements for the three-day meeting at Foothill College on March 21-22. You will fly Liberty Airlines and earn frequent flyer miles. I know you like to stay at the Royal Court Hotel. Let me know if these arrangements are satisfactory.

____

____

____

EDITING FOR CLARITY

It is important to check that the words used to write messages do not confuse the reader and that ideas are presented in a clear, logical manner.

CLEAR AND SIMPLE WORDS

Clear and simple words are not only easier to write but also easier to read. Such words help the writer say exactly what he or she means. When writing, do not use words that you would not ordinarily use when talking to that person face to face. Clear messages are more likely to be understood as they were intended. When proofreading a document, follow these guidelines to correct unclear messages.

Use Familiar Words

Familiar words increase understanding. Difficult words annoy the reader and distract him or her from concentrating on the message. To achieve clarity, substitute a simpler word for a difficult one. Compare the difficult words in the first column with the simpler words in the second column.

DIFFICULT WORDS	SIMPLER WORDS
alternative	choice
germane	appropriate, fitting
optimum	best
oblivious	unaware

DIFFICULT WORDS	SIMPLER WORDS
provincial	unsophisticated, narrow
remuneration	pay
sagacious	keen, shrewd
substantiate	prove
verbose	wordy

Use Precise Words

Words have different meanings for different people. For example, *average* to one person may mean *mediocre*; to another person, it may mean *normal*. To a customer waiting to receive an order, the word *soon* may mean *tomorrow*; to the retailer, who must first obtain the merchandise from a supplier, *soon* may mean *within ten days*. When editing a message for clarity, use words that will help convey the exact meaning.

APPROPRIATE WORDS

Some words and expressions are outdated or overused. Inappropriate words and expressions do not impress a reader. They imply that the writer did not try hard enough to express ideas in a simple-to-understand manner. Apply the following guidelines to help make a message clear.

Avoid Cliches

Cliches are ready-made expressions. They are dull, overused, sometimes old-fashioned, and trite. Avoid cliches and use language that is more appropriate. Cliches are especially confusing to people whose first language is not English. Here are some examples of cliches.

stick-in-the-mud
bark up the wrong tree
be as poor as a church mouse
bite off more than one can chew
jump on the bandwagon
keep one's head above water
keep one's nose to the grindstone
the bottom line
the head honcho or the big enchilada
the tip of the iceberg
throw in the towel
turn over a new leaf
a day late and a dollar short

Eliminate Overused Words and Expressions

Replace overused words and expressions with exact words. In the following examples, notice that the words in the second column are more direct and clearer than those in the first column.

OVERUSED EXPRESSIONS	EXACT EXPRESSIONS
acknowledge receipt of	received
at your earliest convenience	immediately, tomorrow, Friday
due to the fact that	because
enclosed herewith	here is
enclosed please find	enclosed is
in the near future	within _ days
in the event that	should, if
pursuant to your request	as requested, you asked
under separate cover	in another package, separately
would like to recommend	recommend
thanking you in advance	thank you

LOGICAL ORGANIZATION

Well-organized messages are easy to read and understand. All ideas within a business letter, for example, should generally support one primary purpose. Likewise, each sentence within a paragraph should focus on one central idea or concept. When editing for clarity, ask yourself these questions:

- **Is the main idea or purpose of the message clear to the reader?**
- **Does each paragraph express one idea?**
- **Do all the paragraphs support the main idea of the message?**
- **Is there a logical relationship that binds all the parts of the message together?**
- **Does one idea flow easily into another?**

14-3

PROOFREAD AND MARK

Edit the following message for clarity using the appropriate proofreader marks. Write the revised message on the blank lines.

Enclosed herewith is the information pursuant to your request of February 10. In the event that you find this germane for your business trip next month, I would like to recommend the optimum accommodations in the city.

PROOFREAD AND MARK

Edit the following message for clarity using the appropriate proofreader marks. Write the revised message on the blank lines.

So that you won't be barking up the wrong tree, I have listed two lodging alternatives where you will be most comfortable. Remember to obtain receipts for your expenses to substantiate business expenses to the head honcho so that you can be remunerated for out-of-pocket expenses.

14-5

PROOFREAD AND MARK

Edit the following message for clarity using the appropriate proofreader marks. Write the revised message on the blank lines.

Due to the fact that fiscal budget preparations will begin in the near future, the bottom line is that we must have all the essential facts regarding operations before the first meeting.

____

____

____

____

____

____

EDITING FOR CONCISENESS

Conciseness means saying only what is necessary to send the intended message to a reader. Conciseness requires eliminating unnecessary words or repetitious ideas. Businesspeople appreciate messages that make each word count. Concise messages have impact.

UNNECESSARY WORDS OR MODIFIERS

Follow these guidelines to achieve conciseness:

- **Delete phrases such as *I believe* or *in my opinion*. Generally, what is stated is the writer's belief. However, such expressions can serve the purpose of conciliation or diplomacy. They can soften criticism too.**
- **Revise sentences that begin with *There is/are* or *Here is/are* whenever possible.**
- **Avoid using unnecessary modifiers; say *unique*, not *absolutely unique*; or *perfect*, instead of *almost perfect* or *nearly perfect*.**

Note how the words in the right column have greater impact than those in the left column.

WORDY	CONCISE
at the present time	now
basic fundamentals	basics
come to the conclusion	conclude
consensus of opinion	consensus
true facts	facts
during the time that	while
each and every	each, every (never use both)
end result	result
feel free to	please
in spite of the fact that	even though
in the near future	soon, on (exact date)
past history	history
free gift	gift
in the amount of	for (give exact amount)

ACTIVE VERSUS PASSIVE VOICE

Voice indicates whether the subject is performing the action or receiving the action of the verb. The **active voice** portrays the subject as performing the action and assigns responsibility to someone or something. For example, in the sentence "The accountant wrote the report," the subject *accountant* is performing the action of the verb.

The **passive voice** portrays the subject as receiving the action of the verb. "The report was written by the accountant" is expressed in the passive voice and shows the subject *report* receiving the action of the verb. The passive voice is also used to de-emphasize a negative message. Generally, business messages are written in the active voice. As the examples on the following page illustrate, the active voice is forceful and concise.

ACTIVE VOICE	PASSIVE VOICE
The instructor selected the software for the course.	The software for the course has been selected by the instructor.
Verify the facts before writing the report.	The facts should be verified before the report is written.
You did not submit your report on time.	Your report was not submitted on time. (de-emphasizes the negative message)

Active voice: The council members reached an agreement.

Passive voice: An agreement was reached by the council members.

14-6

PROOFREAD AND MARK

Edit these sentences to make them more concise. Rewrite each sentence on the blank lines. Convert sentences written in the passive voice to the active voice.

1. There are several ideas that I would very much like to introduce at the staff meeting.

2. In my opinion, this report lacks the basic fundamentals needed to come to the conclusion that the budget be increased.

3. As a result of last week's increase in sales, all sales staff may anticipate receiving bonuses in the near future.

4. The past history indicates that the agents are always late whenever they must submit their reports.

5. It is my personal opinion that we should continue on with the project.

✤ Read the document at a normal, unhurried pace when editing, so that you can concentrate on what you are reading.

✤ Wait a few minutes before you edit your own writing. You may find mistakes that you would otherwise have overlooked.

✤ Edit the document for one specific purpose at a time. For example, first check the accuracy of facts. Then check for completeness; then for conciseness; and, finally, for clarity.

✤ Proofread for mechanical errors after you have edited the document.

SPELLING AND WORD USAGE CHECK

Compare the words in Column A with the corresponding words in Column B. Use the appropriate proofreader marks to correct the misspelled or misused words. If both columns are correct, write **C** to the left of the number.

Column A	Column B
1. adequate	adquate
2. admissable	admissible
3. capacity	capacity
4. continueing	continuing
5. dependant	dependent
6. familiar	familar
7. miscellaneous	miscellanous
8. practise	practice
9. referrence	reference
10. resturant	restaurant
11. accessable	accessible
12. immediately	immedaitely
13. Lay the book on the desk.	Lay down and rest.
14. Can I leave now?	I may attend the conference.
15. I maybe late.	It may be too late.

PROOFREADING APPLICATIONS — PART A

14-8

BUSINESS LETTER

Edit the following letter for correctness, conciseness, and clarity in content. Supply additional information, if necessary, to make the message more complete and clearer. Then proofread the letter for mechanical errors. Facts: Letter was addressed to Mrs. Helga Schneider, 14923 Eastlake Street, Tempe, AZ 85273-4211, in block style with open punctuation. Refer to the Appendix, if necessary.

Family Fitness and Health
724 Great Bend Avenue • El Paso, TX 79905-1472
(505) 555-2904 • Fax: (505) 555-2909
E-Mail: ***Fitness@email.com***

June 31, 20—

Mrs. Hilda Sneider
14913 Eastlake Street
Temple, AZ 85273-4122

Dear Ms. Sneider:

I'm sure you're familar with the routine: Start a diet on Monday and abandon it on Friday. If dieting didn't work last weak, last month, or last year, it isn't logical that it will work today, tomorrow, or anytime. Stop barking up the wrong tree!

I'm not going to suggest another try for the brass ring. What I am going to suggest is that you have the capasity and determination to seas the opportunity and practise sensible dieting. You must keep your nose on the grindstone and turn over a new leaf. Jump on the bandwagon and join us in the development of a lifestyle that will maintain good health at a sensible level. We will show you how to eat the rite kinds of foods in adquate amounts, whether at home or in a resturant, to keep hunger at bay. You must lie down certain rules to avoid becoming dependant on the continueing gain-and-loss cycle that makes life unbearable for you and everyone else around you.

Hilda Sneider, June 31, 20—, Page 2

Pursuant to your request, enclosed herewith are copies of our brochure and several recent flyers covering some of the topics we discuss at our seminars.

After you become familar with the enclosed information, please fill in the form attached and send it to me at your earliest convenience. May be by joining us, you will finally be able to shed that extra wait, trim a few inches, and improve your health and lifestyle.

With referrence to cost, the bottom line is the financial commmitment of the $5 enrollment fee. There are no miscelaneous charges, nothing to buy, and no salesperson will solicit.

Let us here from you today!

Yours truly,

Anita Lopez, President

Enclosures

rpm

PROOFREADING APPLICATIONS PART B

14-9

BROCHURE

Edit the following brochure text for correctness, clarity, and conciseness. Then proofread for mechanical errors.

SENSIBLE EATING ON THE ROAD

Don't be a stick-in-the-mud about your eating habits while traveling. Jump on the bandwagon and follow these guidelines.

Its one thing to follow a sensable diet while you're at home where every thing is familar. When you travel you must practise a different dicsipline.

With referrence to air or land travel, begining tommorrow try these miscellanous rules regarding meals on the plain or in resturants. They are healthful and easy to follow.

Eat a good, healthy breakfast ever morning. A healthy breakfast includes hole wheat toast, serial (hot or cold with skimmed milk), and fresh fruit—not canned.) Some company cafterias offer low calorie breakfasts. Substitutions are admissable and acceptable. Special dietitic menus are sometime avaialble on airlines so check on this before the flight date.

If your hours for mealtime is later than usual, counting lunch as dinner and keep the entree on the lien side is a cleaver devise. The amount of food served in resturants at lunch is usually smaller than at dinner—and it costs less too. Use salad dressing sparingly. If the meal is being presented in the familar buffet style, take one only small serving. Dont go back for seconds; let your stomach do the eating, not your eyes.

Develope a habit of eating healthful snacks, such as fresh fruits and vegetables and keep them handy. You can use them to keep your head above water between meals. Speaking of water, drink lots of it; it fills you up. The fact of the matter is that you should drink eight cup of water each day. Water is a great substitute for those sweet, syrupy soft drinks. If possible, avoid caffiene as it stimulates you appetite and can cause nervousness and insomia.

Try having a large salad for lunch or dinner with due regard for calories and use good judgement in selecting a dressing. When eating salads, keep in mind that the bottom line for counting calories will always be dependant on the kind of dressing you select.

Make this a continueing program, never throw in the towel. Eat rite and stay healthful!

14-10

MANUSCRIPT

Edit the following manuscript for correctness, clarity, and conciseness. Then proofread for mechanical errors.

TOO MUCH OF A GOOD THING?

Someone once said: "Too much of a good thing is wonderful." While this may be treu for some things to much of a good thing may cause injuries when it come to exercise. No pain, no gain! Wright?

Wrong! Strenouous exercise is good exercise but pain is a signal to stop while youre ahead. Stop imediately when there is great pain! Its quality that counts—not quanity. Saffety is of primary importance. Turn over a new leaf, for tommorrow is another day.

Be careful in hot wheather. Ask your doctor for adquate guidelines relative to your age and be aware of your limitations. Exercising when you're dehydrated is especially hard on the heart. A flash of pain may be just the tip of the iceberg and a signal to slow down or stop all together. Continueing beyond your capasity is foolish and dangerous to your health, but don't throw in the towel just yet.

Preperation is important. It is permissable to drinking a glass of water before you exercise and have more when you feel thirsty. Salt Intake is dependant on amount of exercise. In most cases, additional salt is no needed during exercise. Prevent salt loss by drinking salty liquids or add a little extra table salt to your food. You should be familar with your own salt capasity. That's the bottom line.

A resent study suggests that 30 minutes of moderate-intensity physical activity, most days of the week, is suficient for sedentary people. Get on the ball! You need to find a way to incorporate 30 minutes of of moderate activity (walking, stair-climbing, raking leaves, wash the car) in to your day.

Practise make perfect, but don't bit off more than you can chew. If you have been away from working out on a particular exercise for a while, watch it. Don't jump in with both feet. Starting slowly and build up strength and endurence. Consult with a qualified instructor about a personnal exercise program of exercise. Do'nt insist on continuing if you are tired or injured. Use good judgement to gain the maximum benifits.

If your find that exercise has become exccessive, if you feel the need to do it without regard to the consequences, if it is interfering with your other activties—lay back and consider—you maybe doing yourself more harm then good.

Exercise should be enjoying and beneficial. Be aware that is it never too late for you. Its too much of a good thing to ignore. Star today and get back on the road to good health!

COMPUTERIZED PROOFREADING APPLICATIONS

14-11

MANUSCRIPT

1. Load file CPA14-11 from the TMPL14 subdirectory on your template CD. (This is a computer copy of Application 14-10.)
2. Edit the text for correctness, conciseness, and clarity, using the marked copy for Application 14-10. Then proofread for mechanical errors. Use a proofreader card and the spell check if it is available.
3. Produce the manuscript following the standard procedures described in the previous chapters.

14-12

EXCERPT FROM NEWSPAPER COLUMN

1. Load file CPA14-12 from the TMPL14 subdirectory on your template CD.
2. Edit the text for correctness, conciseness, and clarity. Then proofread for mechanical errors. Use a proofreader card and the spell check if it is available.
3. Produce the document following the standard procedures.

14-13

E-MAIL MESSAGE

1. Load file CPA14-13 from the TMPL14 subdirectory on your template CD.
2. Edit the text for correctness, conciseness, and clarity. Then proofread for mechanical errors. Use a proofreader card and the spell check if it is available.
3. Produce the document following the standard procedures.

CUMULATIVE REVIEW APPLICATIONS NO. 5

CRA5-1

BUSINESS LETTER

Proofread and correct all errors using the appropriate proofreader marks. Facts: Letter was addressed to Mr. Jose Farentino, 4089 Avenida del Sol, Crescent City, SC 19895-8616, in modified block style with indented paragraphs and mixed punctuation.

TWENTIETH CENTURY BUSINESS COLLEGE
400 Broadway • Crescent City, SC 29847-1532
(803) 555-6872 Fax: (803) 555-6877
E-Mail: ***Century@email.com***

Mr. Jose Farantino
4098 Avedina Del sol
Crecsent City, NC 29895-6816

Dear Mr. Jose

Dean Lila Quiring informed me that you have completed all of requirements for the advanced course in Bussiness Adminstration and are now submiting your application for employement to a number of inter national companeis reccommended by our placement Department.

Congradulations! I am confidant that you will be sucessful in obtaining employement within a very short time.

While obtaining employment is your primery concern at the present time I strongly encourag you to take the long view and to consider your carreer in relation to other factors that will come into play as you mount the ladder of success—your work, your family, you continueing education, and your social life. Your work. Due to the fact that work is going to be the majer factor in your life in the begining. You must be prepared to make adjustments, if not sacrifices, to accomodate yourself to the exigencies and requirments of your chosen field. You may be asked to work a few hours of uncompensated overtime, you may have to come in early and leave late on an occassional weekend when the work load is heavy, or you may be forced to post pone a vacation during the busy season. This is the name of the game; and it may be well the pattern for many years into the future, at least untill you establish yourself in your carreer. Don't be a stick-in-the-mud—take it in stride and come up smiling.

Your family. Must come first when it comes to matters of physical and mental healthy. But there's no denying the fact that there will be times when you will have to make a hard decision concerning the little league game you promised to attend but can't, the school play staring your daughter that gets lost in your're busy schedule, and the class reunion your wife was looking foreward to but had to cancell because of an unexpected visit by your company president.

Continueing education. An invalueable tool in your career path. It prepares you for greater responsiblity and keeps you up-to-date on the changes and developements in youre choosen field. Take advantag of this oppurtunity becaues this is as good as it gets!

Your social life. Socialising is the name of the game in many businessess. Train yourselves to be not only an interesting dinner partner but also an desireable one. Learn how to initiate or hold a conversation; take the time to learn, if not master, the basic dance steps, and an interest in art and music and painting should be developed. Not only are these things enjoyable in and of themselves; they can also be a factor in your carreer developement as well as position advancement.

Remember, that a carreer is more than an occupation, it is a way of life that have a bearing on the lives of everyone with who you come in contact with. There are alternatives to be made; and if made wisely they will sustain you and thru a life time.

Again, congradulations! I wish you the very best in what I am confident will by a very succesful career.

Sincerely,

Eldon R. Goodenough, Ph.d.
President

Enclosure

tcp

CRA5-2

MANUSCRIPT

Proofread and correct all errors using the appropriate proofreader marks.

CATS—<u>FELIS DOMESTICUS</u>

Once called misterious and unpredictible, the cat has emerged to become the most poplar household pet in America. There is approxmately fourty-two million pet cats in the United States today. For those who like cats, they are the ideal pet. For those who dislike cats, they are anathema.

Cats are thought by some to bring good luck and by other to bring bad luck. Whatever you beleive I'll bet you like most people will at least pause when a black cat cross youre path.

Cats are known to be individaulists. While the may make good pets, they are never totaly under the controll of there owners. They give much in return and contrary to popular beleif, they are more in need of constant care than dogs. The owner of a cat take on a considerable responsability to insure that his pet is well fed, well grommed, trained well and looked after well by a veterinerian.

The egyptians are generally credited with domesticating the cat first. Gradually, they were carried to the middle east and the far east and while they were thought to be sacred by the Egyptians. They were considered to be value pets by other cultures. Earned their keep by controlling mice and rats. The live span of a cat range between ten to fifteen years. There are many exceptions and cats have been known to servive for as long as twenty-five to thirty years.

In chosing a new kitten or cat, you should look for several thing that indicate good health and temperiment. First of all, the cat should have cleaer bright eyes. Runny eyes, sneezing or a nasal discharge can indicate a respiratory infectoin. The mouth and gums should be pink, with not evidense of ulcers or soars. Your new cat or kitten should be friendly and comfortible with people. Beware of a cat that frequentely runs and hides or sleeps moer than normal SOME TIPS FOR KAT KARE

Feeding. What to feed, how much to fed and how often to feed are common concerns of first time cat owners. First you should out find what you cat has been eating. Weather you feed dry, canned or semimoist food, be sure to purchased a product that meets the standarsd establish by the association of American Feed Control Officials (AAFCO). If you feed a diet that meet the AAFCO standards you can be sure your cat is receivng an adequate supply of vitimins and minerals. You should also remember that chocolate is toxic to cats. And caffeine can also cause problems.

Grooming. Cats should comb an owner's fur daily, even though they do much of their own grooming. By brushing or combing your cat regularly, you keep it's coat clean, shiny and sleek. For long-hair breeds, such grooming is required to prevent matting and especially for hair balls. If a cat can not rid himself of a hair ball by himself, surgury maybe required.

Training. Training is not only essential but a very important part of a cats' developement. Start early, even before a kitten is a year old. Don't attemp to teach your cat tricks, as you would a dog. Rather, teach what is permitted and what is not permitted such as scratching furnture and pulling on drapes. Provide a scratching post, two posts is even better.

All training should be done with rewards—verbal praise or food. The use of a litter box should be taught early. Learn the means by which cats communicate with other animals, with humans, and between themselves.

CHAPTER 15

PROOFREADING AND EDITING ON COMPUTER

Technology is changing the way we work, both personally and professionally. Spell checkers, grammar checkers, on-line dictionaries, and voice recognition technology all work to make tasks easier for us. But is the technology always right? How accurate was the spell check in the following?

- Isn't technology grate!!
- Know won knows better than me what a difference it makes. Me own spell checker tells my that my righting is perfect. I've maid know errors!
- This whey I don't have too rely on some won else proof reading me work for me.
- So you sea, bee smart and play the game.
- Let you spell checker due you work for you!

Objectives

- Understand and apply the principles of on-screen proofreading.
- Increase your productivity level in preparing written business documents.
- Improve the quality of your written business documents.

CHAPTER 15

PROOFREADING AND EDITING ON COMPUTER

INTRODUCTION

The increased use of computers and information processing programs has made the task of creating written materials easier and faster. However, the speed with which information is processed through computers and printers has placed a heavy responsibility for accuracy upon the operators of such equipment. The need for proficient proofreading and editing skills is critical when using a computer.

Most word processing programs have a feature that can merge addresses with a "shell" document to create instantaneously personalized sales letters for distribution to hundreds or even thousands of persons. If errors exist in the shell document, all of the merged letters will have the same errors. Consequently, customers receiving these letters will have a poor impression of the company. The result may be fewer sales; or, in some cases, the company may have to send out corrected copies of the letter, which would substantially increase the cost of the mailing.

ON-SCREEN PROOFREADING

The types of errors found in on-screen copy are the same as hard copy errors, so the same proofreading skills are applied. However, there is a major difference between hard copy proofreading and on-screen proofreading. In hard copy proofreading, proofreader marks are written on the hard copy to identify the errors. In on-screen proofreading, when an error is located on the computer screen, the proofreader corrects the error immediately, saving time that would otherwise be spent rekeying. The diligent proofreader who detects and corrects all the errors in the on-screen copy will produce a printed hard copy that is free of errors the first time. Several tools and tips can simplify on-screen proofreading.

SPELL CHECK

The **spell-check** feature, found in most information processing software programs, should be performed first—after saving the document. With this feature, the program compares the spelling of each on-screen word with the words in a dictionary stored within the computer's memory. If the on-screen word matches the stored dictionary word, the computer moves to the next word. If it does not, the on-screen word is highlighted. At this point, the operator must either purposely ignore the highlighted word and continue with the spell check or correct the misspelled word by selecting one of the suggested choices listed in the memory dictionary. The computer will not automatically correct the misspelled word; the operator must choose the correct word.

The spell check is an extremely valuable tool for the proofreader. However, the spell check will not locate inappropriately used but correctly spelled words, such as homophones. For example, in the following paragraph, the spell-check feature would identify only one incorrectly spelled word. However, seven incorrect words appear in this copy. Can you find the errors?

> At the meering held last weak, the members decided that their should bee a committee too prepare a proposal four expansion of the west central office located inn Los Angeles, California.

GRAMMAR CHECK

The **grammar check** is a feature of some software programs that allows proofreaders to identify and correct grammar errors in their written documents. The grammar check program may be employed after the spell check program. Depending upon the specific program, a grammar check program will analyze the material on the screen for various aspects of writing, including correctness of grammar, sentence structure, punctuation, and spelling.

Grammar check software lets you select the checking style that is best for your writing style. In addition, German, French, and Spanish versions are available from some companies.

CURSOR MOVEMENT CHECK

A third step in on-screen proofreading is to use the cursor. When proofreading on-screen copy, the proofreader should use the cursor and the directional arrow keys to move through the copy. A simple technique is to proofread on-screen material by moving the cursor down one line at a time. When the cursor is at the bottom of the screen, continuing to move it down will bring a new line to the bottom of the screen. A line at the bottom of the screen is easier to proofread because there are no words below the line (see Figure 15-1).

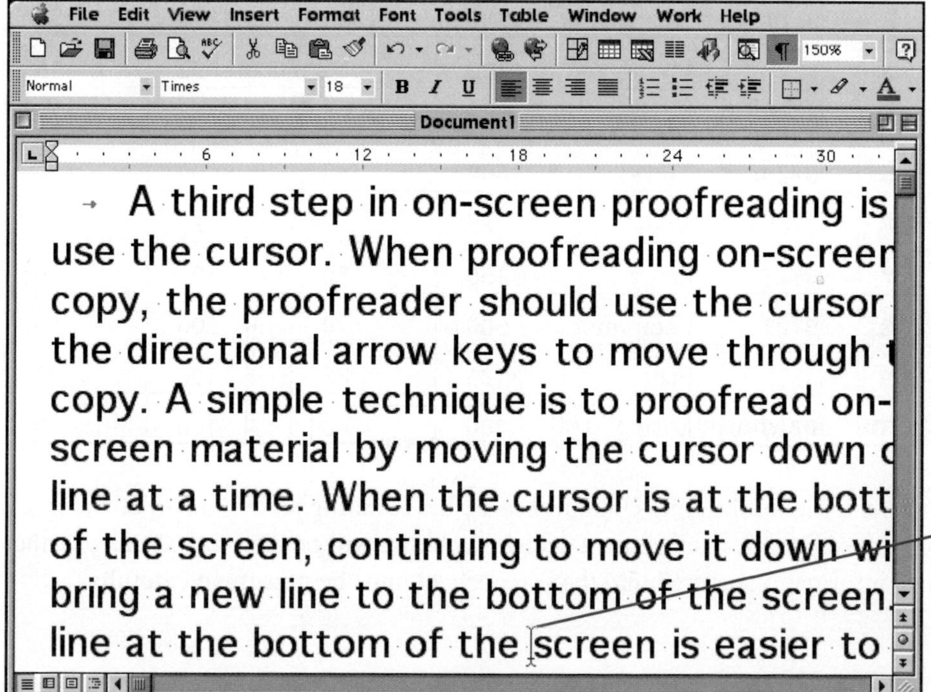

Figure 15-1

On-Screen Editing In Word Processing Program

PRINT PREVIEW

Most word processors have a feature to preview the document before it's printed. By using **print preview**, you can see if the margins, formatting, spacing, etc., are correct. You will also see if the document fits on one page or two; if two, you will either make adjustments to fit the document on one page or create a second page header (for a letter or memo) or footer (for a report). Using print preview before printing a document saves time and paper.

INFORMATION PROCESSING TOOLS

When proofreading on or off screen, you will deal with information processed in a variety of ways with a variety of software programs. Familiarizing yourself with formats such as the spreadsheet and database will help you proofread more effectively.

SPREADSHEET

An important tool in business management is the **spreadsheet** (also called a columnar worksheet). Basic information is entered into columns and rows. The spreadsheet program processes the information through a variety of calculations, and additional data is generated in other columns and rows, as shown in Figure 15-2.

Figure 15-2

Sample Spreadsheet

	A	B	C D	E F	G H	I J	K L
1	**1**	**Acct. No.**	**Title**	**Budget**	**Used/Sep**	**Bal. 9/30**	**Used/Oct**
2	**2**	3721	Supplies	1500	250	1250	150
3	**3**	3722	Phone	100	10	90	15
4	**4**	3723	Fax	50	5	45	7
5	**5**	3724	Travel	1000	0	1000	0
6	**6**	3725	Dues	25	0	25	0
7	**7**	3726	Mags.	150	50	100	0
8	**8**	3727	Lecturer	500	0	500	0
9	**9**	3728	Film	125	25	100	20
10	**10**	3729	Misc	100	0	100	0

If the basic information contains errors, the resulting analyses will be incorrect; consequently, management decision making will be affected. Therefore, the basic information entered into the spreadsheet must be proofread carefully.

DATABASE

Another electronic tool used in processing information is a **database**. The database format is a structured way to store basic information such as names, addresses, and telephone numbers; product data; or information on services performed. The bits and pieces of the information are entered into fields. These fields form a separate record for each customer, person, or company. All of the records become the database; and the operator can use various commands to rearrange, sort, or select information from the database.

A crucial step in the preparation of a database is keying the initial information. Uncorrected errors will result in incorrect data. Each record should be carefully checked against the original information and all errors corrected.

VOICE RECOGNITION SOFTWARE

Voice recognition software gives you the ability to transfer your spoken words directly into text. As you speak into a microphone connected to your computer, the soundcard takes the sound of your voice and transfers your speech into written form.

Since each person has a unique voice profile, the software must first learn your voice pattern. Most programs first ask you to speak a sample list of words or sentences into the microphone. As you practice your speech skills, the software learns your voice and unique way of speaking. The success rate for the software depends on your computer's speed, but it's not unusual to have an accuracy rate of 95 percent or higher.

Both continuous speech (normal speaking speed) and discrete speech (slight pauses between each word) versions are available. Continuous speech versions are faster and easier to learn.

ELECTRONIC MAIL (E-MAIL)

Electronic mail, or e-mail, is the most widely used Internet service. E-mail is convenient and easy to use as it allows you to electronically send, receive, and store written messages. Anyone with Internet access can send and receive messages 24 hours a day, almost instantaneously.

In order to use e-mail, you need special software and an e-mail account. You must also know your receiver's e-mail address. E-mail addresses are similar to a postal address in that the e-mail address enables the computer to deliver your message to the right person. Everyone has a unique e-mail address. The first part is the receiver's individual name; the second part comes after the @ sign and is called the site or domain name. The domain name identifies the name of the Internet service provider.

It is important to remember that e-mail is not private. Numerous court cases have determined that company e-mail messages belong to the company, not the individual. If a subpoena is issued to your Internet service provider, everything you have done or said can be traced. E-mail does not disappear. It can usually be traced back to the person who sent the message.

PROOFREADING AND EDITING ON COMPUTER

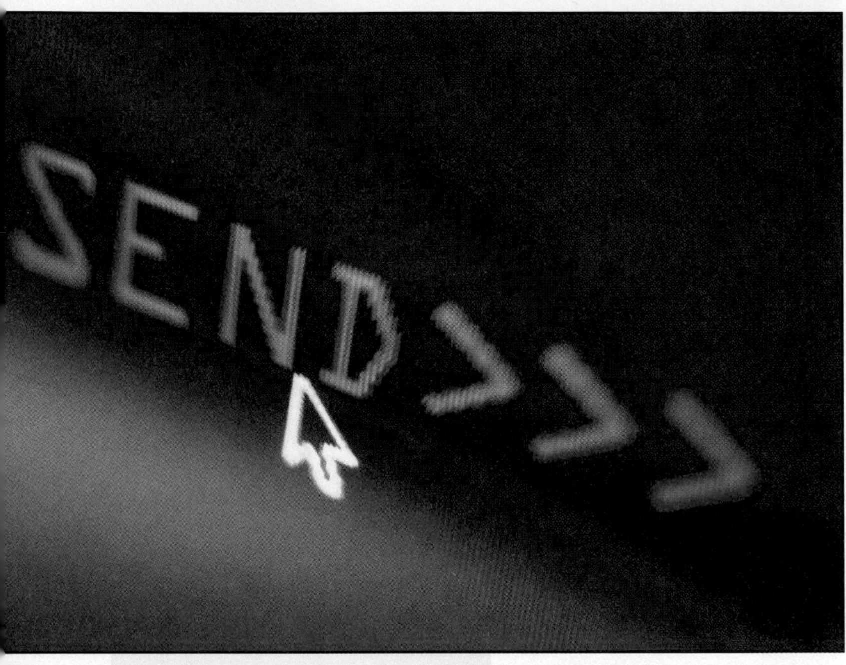

Although e-mail generally uses a more conversational tone than other traditional forms of communication, you still need to use good communication skills to prevent misunderstandings. In writing an e-mail message, consider the following points:

◆ Your e-mail messages represent you, and first impressions are important.

◆ Correct spelling, grammar, and punctuation are still important.

◆ Write descriptive subject lines.

◆ Use short paragraphs and keep your message short.

◆ Consider carefully what you write because it is a permanent record that can be forwarded to others.

◆ Do not type in all caps. This is often perceived as *shouting*.

◆ Do not attach large files (over 50K) without first receiving permission from your recipient.

◆ When forwarding messages, put your comments at the top of the message.

◆ Do not overuse acronyms like BTW (by the way), IMHO (in my humble opinion), or ROFL (rolling on floor laughing).

◆ Do not use e-mail for information that is highly sensitive or confidential.

◆ Be aware of format.

✤ To make on-screen proofreading easier and faster, use a proofreader card, a 3" x 5" or 5" x 7" file card, a ruler, or the edge of a sheet of paper.

✤ Use the cursor and proofread the bottom line of the on-screen copy, advancing only one line at a time.

✤ Do not rely solely on spelling and grammar checkers to find and correct errors in your electronic communications. Remember to check for misused words that are spelled correctly.

✤ Proofread and edit your e-mails as you would any other written correspondence.

COMPUTERIZED PROOFREADING APPLICATIONS

In this chapter, the exercises will give you an opportunity to proofread on-screen documents. In some cases, you will proofread the on-screen copy against a hard copy draft. Proofread the on-screen copy very carefully. Your goal should be to print an error-free document the first time.

15-1 BUSINESS LETTER

Load file CPA15-1 from the TMPL15 subdirectory on your template CD. Proofread the letter on the screen, and make all corrections before printing the hard copy. Follow the standard procedures for proofreading the hard copy—revising, resaving, and reprinting.

15-2 INTEROFFICE MEMORANDUM

Load file CPA15-2 from the TMPL15 subdirectory on your template CD. Proofread the memo on the screen, and make all corrections before printing the hard copy. Follow the standard procedures for proofreading the hard copy.

15-3 SHORT REPORT

Load file CPA15-3 from the TMPL15 subdirectory on your template CD. Proofread the report on the screen, and make all corrections before printing the hard copy. Follow the standard procedures for proofreading the hard copy.

15-4 STATISTICAL REPORT

Load file CPA15-4 from the TMPL15 subdirectory on your template CD. Proofread the report on the screen by comparing it with the handwritten draft (on page 254); make all corrections before printing the hard copy. Follow the standard procedures for proofreading the hard copy.

OFFICE FURNITURE AND EQUIPMENT COMPARISON

Central City Competitors

Model No.	Description	Our Price	Store A	Diff +/-%	Store B	Diff +/-%	Store C	Diff. +/-%
DC-10	Desk Chair	$ 75	$ 90	+20%	$ 95	+26%	$ 70	-07%
DT-21	Desk	320	410	+28%	580	+81%	300	-06%
CT-28	Computer Table	250	220	-12%	340	+36%	250	None
CR-42	Calculator	15	20	+33%	28	+87%	20	+33%
FC-58	File Cabinet	75	65	-13%	90	+20%	70	-07%
ET-61	End Table	90	90	None	120	+33%	75	-17%
DL-36	Desk Lamp	45	50	+11%	75	+67%	45	None
TR-32	Desk Tray	10	12	+20%	15	+50%	9	-10%
FM-15	Floor Mat	70	75	+07%	90	+28%	65	-07%
FC-62	File Cabinet	90	85	-06%	110	+22%	85	-06%

NEWS ARTICLES 15-5

In using desktop publishing programs, the writer and/or the editor will often create separate articles that are then imported to specific locations on the newsletter page. Load file CPA15-5 from the TMPL15 subdirectory on your template CD. Proofread the two articles, and make all corrections on the screen before printing the hard copy. Follow the standard procedures for proofreading the hard copy.

EDITED MEMORANDUM 15-6

Load file CPA15-6 from the TMPL15 subdirectory on your template CD. Using the following list of changes, make corrections and changes in the document. Proofread the material, and make any additional corrections on the screen before printing the hard copy. Follow the standard procedures for proofreading the hard copy.

CHANGES IN MEMO:	
SUBJECT line:	Insert "Proposed" between "for" and "Denver."
New Paragraph 1:	Insert the following as the first paragraph: On May 1, the Management Council asked for information about the sales potential in the Denver metropolitan area. Contacts were made to conduct a survey.
Old Paragraph 1 becomes new Paragraph 2:	In line 3, add "representatives of" between "by" and "City." In line 4, change "3" to "four." In line 4, add "eastside" between "the" and "shopping." In line 5, change "survey instruments" to "questionnaires."
Old Paragraph 3 becomes new Paragraph 4:	Start paragraph with "Because of national radio and television advertising," In line 2, insert "the names of" between "with" and "several." In line 2, delete "However,"
Last paragraph:	In line 1, insert "major" between "A" and "conclusion." In line 2, insert "viable" between "a" and "market." In line 3, delete "the process of opening" and replace it with "determining the feasibility of establishing."

15-7

MERGED DOCUMENTS

Load file CPA15-7A from the TMPL15 subdirectory on your template CD; you will merge the names and addresses in this list with the shell document in file CPA15-7B. Then load file CPA15-7B, proofread the shell document, and make all corrections. Merge and print the letters.

15-8

SPREADSHEET

Load file CPA15-8 from the TMPL15 subdirectory on your template CD. Proofread the spreadsheet against the basic data that follows. Make corrections on the screen and print a hard copy. Follow the standard procedures for proofreading the hard copy.

Data for Spreadsheet:

Grayer: January-1348; February-1235; March-1436; April-1371; May-1368; June-1384

Burnes: January-932; February-742; March-991; April-1122; May-973; June-873

Ashby: January-562; February-491; March-590; April-530; May-492; June-503

Weston: January-1732; February-1622; March-1978; April-1368; May-1567; June-1473

Milton: January-1436; February-1288; March-1222; April-1250; May-1242; June-1303

15-9

DATABASE

Load file CPA15-9 from the TMPL15 subdirectory on your template CD. Proofread each record in the database against the information given on the registration cards that follow. Make corrections on the screen and print a hard copy. Follow the standard procedures for proofreading the hard copy.

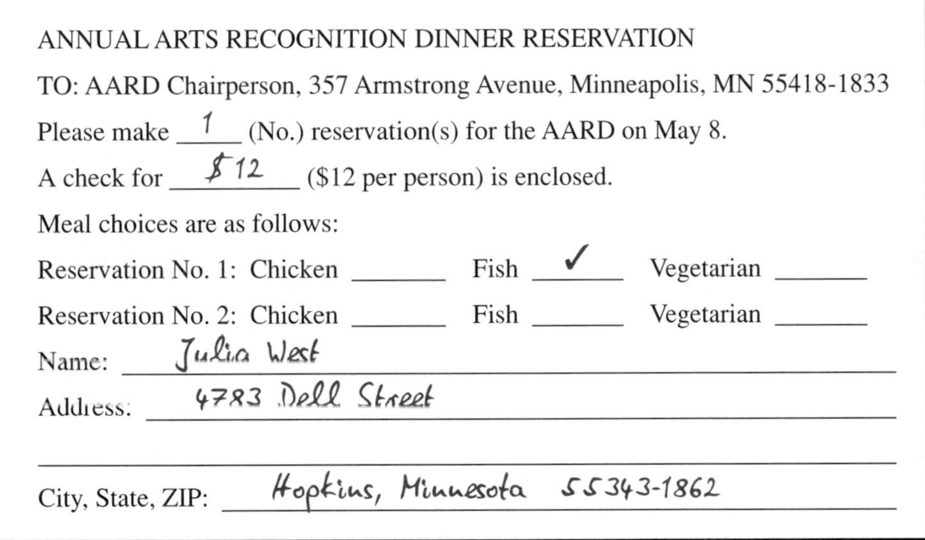

ANNUAL ARTS RECOGNITION DINNER RESERVATION

TO: AARD Chairperson, 357 Armstrong Avenue, Minneapolis, MN 55418-1833

Please make 1 (No.) reservation(s) for the AARD on May 8.

A check for $12 ($12 per person) is enclosed.

Meal choices are as follows:

Reservation No. 1: Chicken ____ Fish ✓ Vegetarian ____

Reservation No. 2: Chicken ____ Fish ____ Vegetarian ____

Name: Julia West

Address: 4783 Dell Street

City, State, ZIP: Hopkins, Minnesota 55343-1862

ANNUAL ARTS RECOGNITION DINNER RESERVATION

TO: AARD Chairperson, 357 Armstrong Avenue, Minneapolis, MN 55418-1833

Please make 2 (No.) reservation(s) for the AARD on May 8.

A check for $24 ($12 per person) is enclosed.

Meal choices are as follows:

Reservation No. 1: Chicken ✓ Fish ____ Vegetarian ____

Reservation No. 2: Chicken ____ Fish ✓ Vegetarian ____

Name: Don Fern

Address: 27624 7th St.

City, State, ZIP: Edina, MN 55424-2388

ANNUAL ARTS RECOGNITION DINNER RESERVATION

TO: AARD Chairperson, 357 Armstrong Avenue, Minneapolis, MN 55418-1833

Please make 2 (No.) reservation(s) for the AARD on May 8.

A check for $24 ($12 per person) is enclosed.

Meal choices are as follows:

Reservation No. 1: Chicken ____ Fish ✓ Vegetarian ____

Reservation No. 2: Chicken ____ Fish ____ Vegetarian ✓

Name: Jim Gappa

Address: 18321 Fern

City, State, ZIP: Crystal, MN 55428-1381

ANNUAL ARTS RECOGNITION DINNER RESERVATION

TO: AARD Chairperson, 357 Armstrong Avenue, Minneapolis, MN 55418-1833

Please make 2 (No.) reservation(s) for the AARD on May 8.

A check for $24 ($12 per person) is enclosed.

Meal choices are as follows:

Reservation No. 1: Chicken ✓ Fish ____ Vegetarian ____

Reservation No. 2: Chicken ✓ Fish ____ Vegetarian ____

Name: Hal Torres

Address: 832 Carl St.

City, State, ZIP: St. Paul, Minnesota 55125-2162

ANNUAL ARTS RECOGNITION DINNER RESERVATION

TO: AARD Chairperson, 357 Armstrong Avenue, Minneapolis, MN 55418-1833

Please make 2 (No.) reservation(s) for the AARD on May 8.

A check for $24.00 ($12 per person) is enclosed.

Meal choices are as follows:

Reservation No. 1: Chicken ✓ Fish ____ Vegetarian ____

Reservation No. 2: Chicken ✓ Fish ____ Vegetarian ____

Name: Elsa Birr

Address: Box 83

City, State, ZIP: Byron, Minnesota 55920-0083

ANNUAL ARTS RECOGNITION DINNER RESERVATION

TO: AARD Chairperson, 357 Armstrong Avenue, Minneapolis, MN 55418-1833

Please make 1 (No.) reservation(s) for the AARD on May 8.

A check for $12 ($12 per person) is enclosed.

Meal choices are as follows:

Reservation No. 1: Chicken ______ Fish ______ Vegetarian ✓

Reservation No. 2: Chicken ______ Fish ______ Vegetarian ______

Name: Sumio Wakui

Address: 11362 Mill

City, State, ZIP: Mound, MN 55364-2183

ANNUAL ARTS RECOGNITION DINNER RESERVATION

TO: AARD Chairperson, 357 Armstrong Avenue, Minneapolis, MN 55418-1833

Please make 1 (No.) reservation(s) for the AARD on May 8.

A check for $12 ($12 per person) is enclosed.

Meal choices are as follows:

Reservation No. 1: Chicken ✓ Fish ______ Vegetarian ______

Reservation No. 2: Chicken ______ Fish ______ Vegetarian ______

Name: Sara Mead

Address: 628 Point Street

City, State, ZIP: Barrow, Wisconsin 54812-1371

ANNUAL ARTS RECOGNITION DINNER RESERVATION

TO: AARD Chairperson, 357 Armstrong Avenue, Minneapolis, MN 55418-1833

Please make 2 (No.) reservation(s) for the AARD on May 8.

A check for 24.00 ($12 per person) is enclosed.

Meal choices are as follows:

Reservation No. 1: Chicken ______ Fish ✓ Vegetarian ______

Reservation No. 2: Chicken ______ Fish ______ Vegetarian ✓

Name: Ruth Palo

Address: 34 N. 8th

City, State, ZIP: Durand, WI 54736-8034

ANNUAL ARTS RECOGNITION DINNER RESERVATION

TO: AARD Chairperson, 357 Armstrong Avenue, Minneapolis, MN 55418-1833

Please make 2 (No.) reservation(s) for the AARD on May 8.

A check for $24.00 ($12 per person) is enclosed.

Meal choices are as follows:

Reservation No. 1: Chicken ______ Fish ______ Vegetarian ✓

Reservation No. 2: Chicken ______ Fish ______ Vegetarian ✓

Name: Mark Maas

Address: Box 135

City, State, ZIP: Aitkin, MN 56431-0135

ANNUAL ARTS RECOGNITION DINNER RESERVATION

TO: AARD Chairperson, 357 Armstrong Avenue, Minneapolis, MN 55418-1833

Please make 2 (No.) reservation(s) for the AARD on May 8.

A check for $24.00 ($12 per person) is enclosed.

Meal choices are as follows:

Reservation No. 1: Chicken ✓ Fish ______ Vegetarian ______

Reservation No. 2: Chicken ✓ Fish ______ Vegetarian ______

Name: Jane Pahl

Address: Box 322

City, State, ZIP: Baldwin, WI 54002-0322

ANNUAL ARTS RECOGNITION DINNER RESERVATION

TO: AARD Chairperson, 357 Armstrong Avenue, Minneapolis, MN 55418-1833

Please make 2 (No.) reservation(s) for the AARD on May 8.

A check for $24 ($12 per person) is enclosed.

Meal choices are as follows:

Reservation No. 1: Chicken ______ Fish ______ Vegetarian X

Reservation No. 2: Chicken ______ Fish ______ Vegetarian X

Name: Dana Wu

Address: Rt. 3

City, State, ZIP: Hudson, Wisconsin 54016-0329

the EDITOR ONLINE

Instructions: You work in the main office of The Editor Online, a new organization that edits and publishes books and then promotes them through Internet Web sites and bookstores. The company is based in Columbus, Ohio, but works with staff across the nation via computer. Your responsibilities include proofreading internal and external company documents. This simulation includes a group of these documents prepared by the staff at The Editor Online:

- Isabel Aponte, Project Manager
- Kevin Sampson, Editor

Use the appropriate proofreader marks to show what corrections should be made. Each document is identified by number.

Objectives

- Demonstrate an understanding of the importance of accurate proofreading through the careful review of typical business documents.
- Identify a variety of proofreading errors.
- Use appropriate proofreader marks to show what corrections should be made.

Document 1

WEB PAGE

the EDITOR ONLINE

Authors! Are you fed up with tradtional publishers? Unless you have already have written a string of best-sellers, these publishers just aren't interested, right? It's just to expensive for them to take on an unknown author.

The Editor Online is changeing that. In fact, we are changing the whole Publishing ind-ustry. New technology now allows us to print one book a time, on demand. This means that bookstores and online catalogs can by one book at a time from us. In this way, they can meet there customers' needs without carrying a large inventory of books that they might not sell. At no cost to them, they can list books from from many authors—including you!

To help sell your book, The Editor Online has fromed partnerships with the organiza-tions below. These partnerships will assure that your potential readers know about your book and can eazily order it.

- ***Books.com***, the leading online sourse of books
- ***Books-r-Us***, one of the nation's largest bookstores
- ***Douglas Edwards, Inc***, the World's largest book holesaler and distributor. Bookstores nationwide rely on Douglas Edwards to fill there book orders.

If you're not quiet ready to publish, The Editor Online can help. You can use our ***chat rooms*** to talk with othr authors, published and to-be-published. you can subscribe to our ***newletter*** to keep up up with current trends in the Online publishing industry.

Our staff reviews ever submission to determine whether it's ready for public-ation. You will be notified within two weeks of our decision. In most case, we can work with you to strengthen any weak points in your manuscript. Their is a small fee for this editorial guidance.

The basic cost for publication are only $350, which includes the creation of a proffessional cover for your book. If you book is not selected for publication, your check or credit card payment will be processed. You pay nothing at al!

For information on submiting your manuscript to The Editor Online, click on ***Submissions***.

Submissions

You can submit your manuscript to The Editor Online though the mail or online. As you you choose which method to use, consider these two factors:

Payment method: If you are paying the $35 fee by check, you must mail your submission. If you want to e-mail your submision, you can pay by credit card over our secure line.

Manuscript length: If the computer file for your Manuscript is larger than 4.5 megabites, please mail the disk to us.

Booth mail and online submissions require the three components below. To receive more information or to download documents, click on the the highlighted phases.

1. A signed ***publishing contract***(You can download it sign it, and mail it to us. Or you can indicate your agreemnet with the contract terms online.)

2. a completed ***submission form*** (You can also download and compete this form. Or you can complete it online and submit it.)

2. ***Payment*** (Send a check or your credit card number if you are maliing your submission. For online submissions, enter your credit card numbers on out secure line. Remember: The Editor Online will not process your chek or credit card payment unless we select your book to be published.)

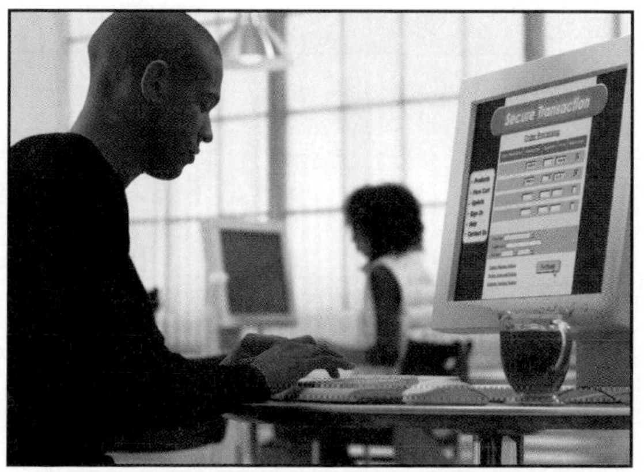

Document 2

E-MAIL CONFIRMATION TO MIA NELSON

Directions: Proofread the e-mail message against the completed form below. Correct any errors you find.

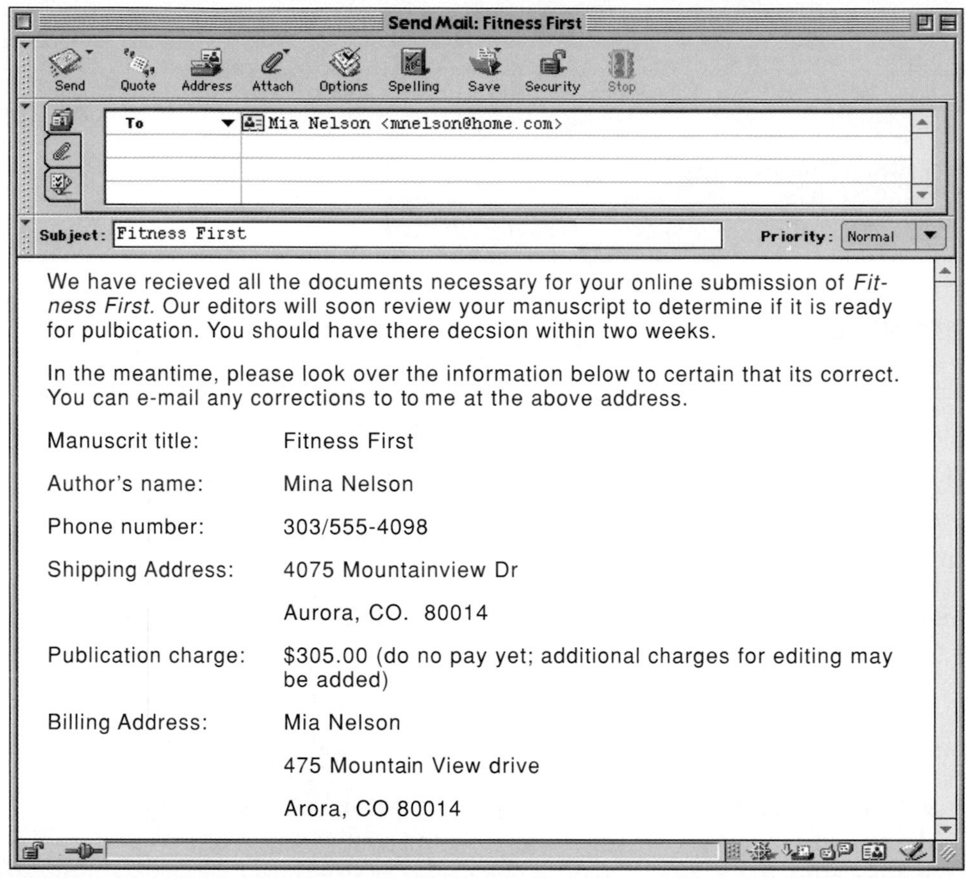

Send Mail: Fitness First

Send | Quote | Address | Attach | Options | Spelling | Save | Security | Stop

To: Mia Nelson <mnelson@home. com>

Subject: Fitness First   Priority: Normal

We have recieved all the documents necessary for your online submission of *Fitness First.* Our editors will soon review your manuscript to determine if it is ready for pulbication. You should have there decsion within two weeks.

In the meantime, please look over the information below to certain that its correct. You can e-mail any corrections to to me at the above address.

Manuscrit title:	Fitness First
Author's name:	Mina Nelson
Phone number:	303/555-4098
Shipping Address:	4075 Mountainview Dr
	Aurora, CO. 80014
Publication charge:	$305.00 (do no pay yet; additional charges for editing may be added)
Billing Address:	Mia Nelson
	475 Mountain View drive
	Arora, CO 80014

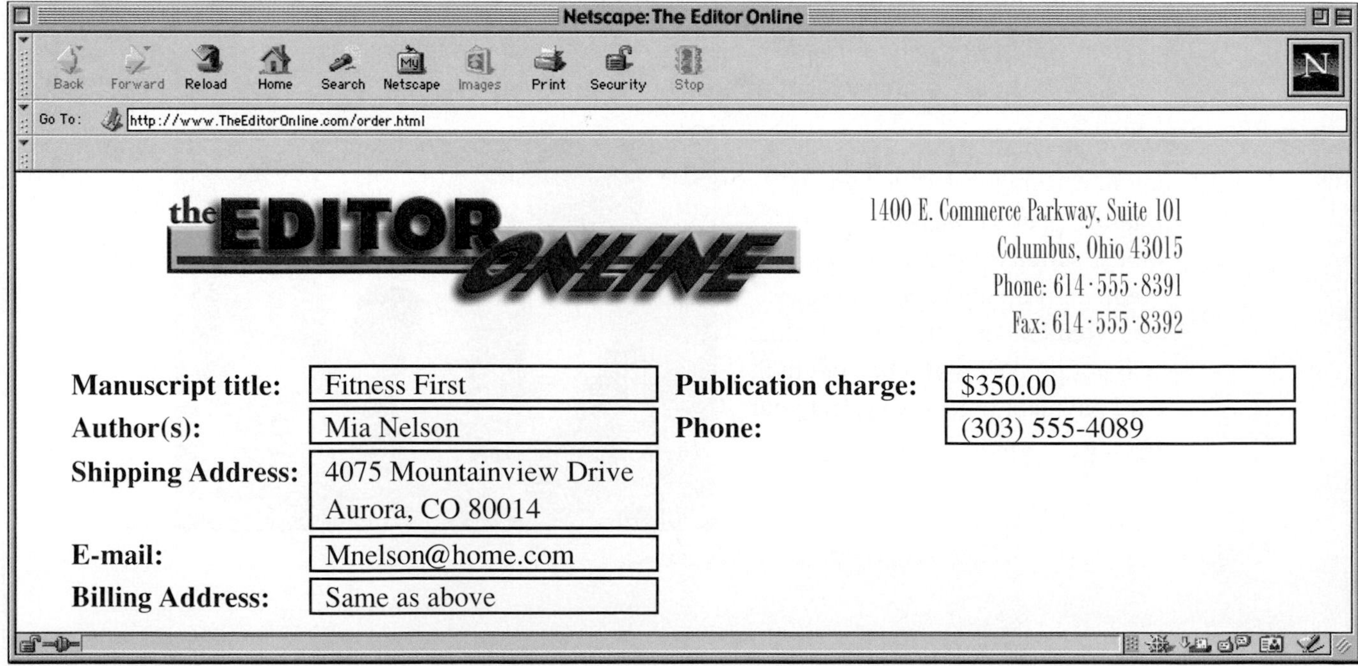

Netscape: The Editor Online

Back | Forward | Reload | Home | Search | Netscape | Images | Print | Security | Stop

Go To: http://www.TheEditorOnline.com/order.html

the EDITOR ONLINE

1400 E. Commerce Parkway, Suite 101
Columbus, Ohio 43015
Phone: 614·555·8391
Fax: 614·555·8392

Manuscript title:	Fitness First	**Publication charge:**	$350.00
Author(s):	Mia Nelson	**Phone:**	(303) 555-4089
Shipping Address:	4075 Mountainview Drive Aurora, CO 80014		
E-mail:	Mnelson@home.com		
Billing Address:	Same as above		

Document 3

ACCEPTANCE LETTER TO MIA NELSON

1400 E. Commerce Parkway, Suite 101
Columbus, Ohio 43015
Phone: 614·555·8391
Fax: 614·555·8392

March 11, 20--

Mia Nelson
4077 Mountainview Drive
Aurora, CO 80041

Deer ms. Nelson:

Thank you again for submitting you manuscript to The Editor Online. We are pleased to tell you that *Fitness First* has been excepted for publication. Please see my initial comments, that appear on the next page. Your editor will be Kevin Sampson, whom has been with The Editor Online since it began. He will soon be in touch with you with his' detailed feedback.

The immediate concern of our production staff are the book's length. We print our books in a six- by nine-inch format. This means that the submtited manuscript must be at least 108 pages long. About forty thousand words. I'm estimating that your manscript is less then 30,000 words. After reading my initial evaluation, the best approach might be to add more examples to bring the manuscript up to 40,000 words. Of course you can also add more diagrams and photographs. Kevin will be in touch with you to get you input.

Its important that we work together to make your book as good as it can be. Our authors are generally very pleased with the books which we publish.

Sincerely,

Isabel Apont, ph.D
Project Manger

Initial Evaluation: *Fitness First* **Date: March 10, 20--**

Organization
- [x] smooth, logcial presentation
- [x] Titles and subtitles follow table of contants
- [x] detailed appendix
- [ ] needs more work

Book Elements
- [x] interesting opening
- [x] Periodic summarys or reviews
- [ ] apropriate graphics
- [ ] one or more elements needs more work

Content
- [ ] geared to intended readers
- [ ] to detailed
- [x] Too few examples
- [ ] in appropriate examples
- [ ] needs more work

Writing Style
- [x] consistant use of active voice
- [ ] two much pasive voice
- [ ] Needs more work

Grammer
- [ ] few errrors
- [x] moderate number of errors
- [ ] Needs more work

Sales Prediction
- [ ] should appeel to a wide audience
- [x] Somewhat narrow market: YOUNGER AUDIENCE

Recommendations
- [x] excepted to be published
- [x] will need some auther revisions (See above comments.)
- [ ] rework and resubmit, following above comments
- [ ] does not meet The Editor Online standards

Document 4

MEMO TO KEVIN SAMPSON

INTEROFFICE MEMORANDUM

From: Isabel Aponte, Project Manager
To: Kevin Sampson, Editor
Date: March 13, 20--

Subject: New Manuscript: *Fitness First*

Please review my initial evaluation which I have attached. *Fitness First,* as you will see is basicly a solid manuscript. The author needs just more examples to help explain their main points Many of these examples could be incorperated as photographs.

To begin you might suggest that Mina review other fitness books to note their use of examples and graphics. Either *Fit At Fifty* by Jim Hoffman or *More Than Muscles* by Shirley Coons are good choices. One of my favorite sources are *Shape Shop* by Sue McCormick.

The author also needs to show how her fitness recommendations will help readers meet there own needs. She must explain how a series of exercises for example will benefit a reader in his daily life. As a first-time author, I believe Mina can overcome these problems with your asistance. You might have her to re-write chapter one and submit it to you to make sure she's on the right track.

As I noted on my evaluation Mina's manuscript also contains to many grammar errors. Many of these mistakes would be caught by a grammar checker so you might recommend that she use one.

Kevin please let me know if I can help with this manuscript. I look forward to reading Mina's 2nd draft.

DOCUMENT 5

LETTER AND EDITED MANUSCRIPT TO MIA NELSON

Directions: Proofread and edit Kevin's letter and the two pages of manuscript that follow it.

1400 E. Commerce Parkway, Suite 101
Columbus, Ohio 43015
Phone: 614·555·8391
Fax: 614·555·8392

march 17, 20––

Mia Nelson
4077 Mountainview drive
Aurora, COL 80041

Dear Ms Nelson,

The project editor and I are both pleased with your 1st draft. I would like to make some recommendations concerning changes that will farther strengthen your manuscript.

I have enclosed a hard copy of your manuscript with a number of place marked where you might add examples. For additional help, you might read *Fit at Fifty* by Jim Hofman, *More Than Mucles* by Shirley Coons or *Shape Shop* by Sue McKormick. All of these sourses offer germane guidance relating to the use of examples.

Enclosed herewith you will also find 2 pages that I have edited to make the writing clearer and less verbose. Please review these changes and continuing on to make the same kinds of changes in the rest of the manuscript. Do not hesitate for a second to call me if you have any questions about my changes.

Due to the fact that this manuscript must be ready for production by July 1, I need to have your 2nd draft by May 15. Past history tells me that we may need the rest of may and june for other revisions.

I look forward to receiving your next draft.

sincerely

Kevin Sampson

Getting Started

When it comes to exercise and many other challenges some people bite off more than they can chew. They are soon ready to throw in the towel and retreat to the couch again. Exercising should be relaxing, not full of stress.

You are a unique and special Individual, and no one can chose the perfect exercise program for you. Everyone must choose forms of exercise that suit their lifestyle so they will continue doing them. Also remember that exercise spread throughout the weak is more healthful then exhausting workouts on each and every weekend.

Here are 4 reasons why people give up on exercising and ways to overcome them.

1. They don't have enough time. If this sounds familiar, try exercising for short or brief periods several times a day. For example, 3 10-minute walks.

2. They are embarrassed about their bodies or they feel awkward about there coordination. These people can start by exercising at home, following an exercise tape in your V.C.R. Many of these tapes are available for beginning exercisers. Soon they may may feel confidant enough to join a class.

2. They are to tired to exercise. The end result of exercise is more energy. You will experience this youself soon after you begin to exercise regularly.

3. The weather is bad. Too hot or too cold. Regular exercisers learn to be flexable about where they exercise. Even a brisk walk through the Mall can provide exercise if the whether is bad that day.

4. Exercising costs two much. You might wonder what you can do if you can't afford an expensive membership to a fitness club? Your city may have a Community Center that offers free or low-cost exercise programs. You also can also walk some places instead of driving.

Exercise and Stress

Stress is part of most life events, both gigantic and miniscule. Anytime we have to adjust to the events around us, whether positive or negative we experience stress. Stress releases chemical from our pituitary and adrenal glands. These chemicals increase our hart rate and blood pressure. Our breathing rate goes up, our digestion rate slow down. We experiences a sudden rush of energy. Our bodies are preparing to fight a attacker or flee danger. However we often can do either.

When the source of the stress is gone our brains should send a signal to our glands to stop releasing these chemicals. However, sometimes our brains don't not send this signal and we end up in a constant state of stress. We may experience a headaches, backache, or upset stomach. We may feel irritible and be short of patience.

Many people try to cope with stress by smoking, drinking overeating or even oversleeping. Do not control stress effectively. Instead, they can have dangerous side affects.

Exericse controls stress naturally. Its a healthy response to the fight-or-flight impulse. Walking will help relaese the built-up energy. Exercise of many kind will help work off the tension in the muscles! During exercise, the body's glands begin to release chemicals which bring a feeling of well-being instead of stress.

The Relaxation Response

When you feel stress building you can counteract it with a relaxation response.Follow these steps—

1. sit quietly with your eyes closed.

2. slowly relax each mucsle group, starting at your feet.

3. focus on your breathing.

Document 6

E-MAIL ANSWERING MIA NELSON'S QUESTIONS

Directions: Use Kevin's notes, below, to proofread his e-mail message to Mia Nelson on the next page.

Mia's questions:

When will my book be published?

It should be ready for sale online within 60 days. Of course, this time period depends on how long you take to check the proofs that we will send to you.

How much will my book cost?

Soft-cover books such as yours usually range between \$5.99 and \$7.99.

Will my book be sold in the Books-r-Us stores?

There is no guarantee of this, but Books-r-Us does choose several books each month to promote in its stores. Your book might be one of them. Your book will also be available online at Books-r-Us.com.

Will my book be carried by bookstores besides Books-r-Us?

More than 4,500 bookstores nationwide will be able to order your book through the Douglas Edwards, Inc., listings.

Where is The Editor Online located?

We have offices in Columbus, Ohio; San Diego, California; Minneapolis, Minnesota; and Oklahoma City, Oklahoma.

COMPUTERIZED MINISIMULATION

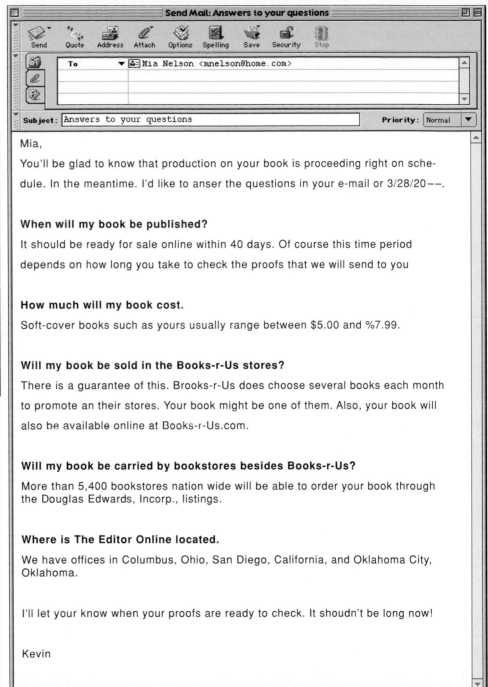

Send Mail: Answers to your questions

Send Quote Address Attach Options Spelling Save Security Stop

To: Mia Nelson <mnelson@home.com>

Subject: Answers to your questions

Priority: Normal

Mia,

You'll be glad to know that production on your book is proceeding right on schedule. In the meantime. I'd like to anser the questions in your e-mail or 3/28/20––.

When will my book be published?

It should be ready for sale online within 40 days. Of course this time period depends on how long you take to check the proofs that we will send to you

How much will my book cost.

Soft-cover books such as yours usually range between $5.00 and %7.99.

Will my book be sold in the Books-r-Us stores?

There is a guarantee of this. Brooks-r-Us does choose several books each month to promote an their stores. Your book might be one of them. Also, your book will also be available online at Books-r-Us.com.

Will my book be carried by bookstores besides Books-r-Us?

More than 5,400 bookstores nation wide will be able to order your book through the Douglas Edwards, Incorp., listings.

Where is The Editor Online located.

We have offices in Columbus, Ohio, San Diego, California, and Oklahoma City, Oklahoma.

I'll let your know when your proofs are ready to check. It shoudn't be long now!

Kevin

COMPUTERIZED PROOFREADING APPLICATIONS

SIM-1

WEB PAGE

Alternate instructions:

1. Load file SIM-1 from the TMPLSIM subdirectory on your template CD. (This is a computer file of Document 1.)
2. Correct any errors in the Web page and the Submissions page that is linked to it. Follow your proofreader marks on Document 1.
3. Proofread both pages on your screen. Use the spell check if it is available.
4. Save and print both pages.
5. Proofread the hard copy. If you find any more mistakes, correct the errors and resave and reprint the page.

E-MAIL CONFIRMATION TO MIA NELSON

Alternate instructions:

1. Load file SIM-2 from the TMPLSIM subdirectory on your template CD. (This is a computer file of Document 2.)
2. Revise the e-mail message, correcting any errors you indicated with proof reader marks. Make sure to check the information against the printed form that Mia completed.
3. Proofread the document on the screen. Use the spell check if it is available.
4. Save and print the e-mail message.
5. Proofread the hard copy. If you find any more mistakes, correct the errors and resave and reprint the message.

ACCEPTANCE LETTER TO MIA NELSON

Alternate instructions:

1. Load file SIM-3 from the TMPLSIM subdirectory on your template CD. (This is a computer file of Document 3.)
2. Revise the letter and initial evaluation, correcting any errors you indicated with proofreader marks.
3. Proofread the documents on the screen. Use the spell check if it is available.
4. Save and print both pages.
5. Proofread the hard copy. If you find any more mistakes, correct the errors and resave and reprint the page.

SIM-4

MEMO TO KEVIN SAMPSON

Alternate instructions:

1. Load file SIM-4 from the TMPLSIM subdirectory on your template CD. (This is a computer file of Document 4.)
2. Revise the memo, making the corrections you have indicated with proofreader marks.
3. Proofread the document on the screen. Use the spell check if it is available.
4. Save and print the memo.
5. Proofread the hard copy. If you find any more mistakes, correct the errors and resave and reprint the page.

SIM-5

LETTER AND EDITED MANUSCRIPT TO MIA NELSON

Alternate instructions:

1. Load file SIM-5 from the TMPLSIM subdirectory on your template CD. (This is a computer file of Document 5.)
2. Revise the letter and two pages of manuscript, making the corrections you have indicated with proofreader marks.
3. Proofread the document on the screen. Use the spell check if it is available.
4. Format the letter in block style with the appropriate top and side margins.
5. Save and print all three pages.
6. Proofread the hard copy. If you find any more mistakes, correct the errors and resave and reprint the page.

SIM–6

E-MAIL ANSWERING MIA NELSON'S QUESTIONS

Alternate instructions:

1. Load file SIM-6 from the TMPLSIM subdirectory on your template CD. (This is a computer file of Document 6.)
2. Revise the e-mail message, correcting any errors you indicated with proofreader marks. Be sure to check the information in the e-mail against Kevin's notes.
3. Proofread the document on the screen. Use the spell check if it is available.
4. Save and print the e-mail message.
5. Proofread the hard copy. If you find any more mistakes, correct the errors and resave and reprint the message.

COMMONLY CONFUSED WORDS

accept *v.* to agree to; to receive
except *prep.* but; other than

addition *n.* process of summing
edition *n.* copies of a published book

advice *n.* recommendation
advise *v.* to give advice; to inform

affect *v.* to influence
effect *v.* to bring about; *n.* result

all ready *adj.* (two words) completely ready
already *adv.* before now or a specified time

all right *adj.* (two words) all correct or appropriate
alright unacceptable spelling of *all right*

allude *v.* to make an indirect reference to something
elude *v.* to avoid or escape notice

a lot *n.* (two words) a large amount; many
alot unacceptable spelling of *a lot*
allot *v.* to allocate or distribute

altogether *adv.* entirely, completely, utterly
all together *adv.* (two words) gathered into a single unit or group; collected in one place

among *prep.* comparison of three or more persons or things
between *prep.* comparison of only two persons or things

any one *adj./pron.* (two words) certain person; use when the pronoun is followed by an *of* phrase: *Any one of us can go.*
anyone *pron.* anybody; any person at all

assistance *n.* help
assistants *n.* helpers

assure *v.* to give confidence to; to feel sure; to convince
ensure *v.* to make sure, certain
insure *v.* to cover with insurance; to guarantee; to secure from harm

can *v.* to be able to do something
may *v.* to be possibile; to give permission

capital *n.* official seat of government; money to invest
capitol *n.* a building in which a legislature meets

cent *n.* 1/100; penny
sent *v.* past tense and past participle of send
scent *n.* a distinctive odor; perfume; a sense of smell

cite *v.* to quote; to acknowledge
sight *n.* a vision; *v.* to see or observe
site *n.* a location

complement *n.* something that adds to or completes a whole; *v.* to complete or make perfect
compliment *n.* an expression of praise; *v.* to praise

cooperation *n.* working together
corporation *n.* a legal entity

correspondence *n.* a communication by exchange of letters
correspondents *n.* those who write letters

council *n.* an assembly of persons
counsel *v.* to give advice or guidance; *n.* a lawyer or group of lawyers; *n.* advice received

currant *n.* small, seedless raisin
current *adj.* up to date; *n.* electricity

dairy *n.* a commercial firm that processes and/or sells milk and milk products
diary *n.* a daily personal record of events, experiences, and observations

device *n.* machine or gadget
devise *v.* to invent or to plan

envelop *v.* to cover with a wrapping
envelope *n.* a paper container for correspondence

farther *adv.* more distant
further *adj.* to a greater degree; additional

foreword *n.* an introduction; preface
forward *adj.* at or near the front; *v.* to send mail

it's contraction of *it is* or *it has*
its *adj.* possessive form of *it*

later *adv.* after
latter *adj.* the second of two

lay *v.* to place or set down an object
lie *v.* to rest; to recline

lean *adj.* thin; not fat; *v.* to slant away from a vertical position
lien *n.* the right to sell property of a debtor

loose *adj.* not fastened; free
lose *v.* unable to find; to fail to win
loss *n.* a person or thing lost; a defeat

may be *v.* to be allowed or permitted to
maybe *adv.* perhaps; possibly

moral *adj.* concerned with goodness or badness of human action and character; *n.* lesson contained in a story or an event
morale *n.* attitude of an individual

personal *adj.* private; pertaining to a particular person
personnel *n.* persons employed; staff of a company

precede *v.* to come before in time or rank
proceed *v.* to go forward

principal *adj.* main; *n.* money that earns interest; *n.* head official of a school; chief
principle *n.* a basic truth; a rule or standard

quiet *adj.* calm; opposite of noisy
quit *v.* to stop; to resign
quite *adv.* completely; considerably

raise *v.* to lift; to move upward; to bring up or rear; to grow things; *n.* an increase in pay
rise *v.* to get up; to move upward by itself; to increase in intensity, volume, or speed

recent *adj.* occurring at a time immediately prior to the present; modern or new
resent *v.* to feel strongly; to feel anger
resent *v.* (past tense of *resend*) sent again

right *adj.* correct, truth, proper; opposite of left
rite *n.* religious or solemn ceremony
write *v.* to form letters of the alphabet on a surface with a tool such as a pen or pencil

seas *n. pl.* a continuous body of salt water
sees *v.* (third person form of *see*) to perceive with the eye; to observe; to view
seize *v.* to grasp suddenly and forcibly; take or grab

some one *n.* a certain person
someone *pron.* a person; somebody

stationary *adj.* immovable; fixed
stationery *n.* writing materials

their *adj.* possessive form of *they*
there *adv.* in or at that place
they're contraction of *they are*

to *prep.* toward; for the purpose of
too *adv.* also; more than enough
two *n.* one more than one

vain *adj.* without success; not resulting in the desired outcome; conceited
vane *n.* a rotating device that indicates the direction of the wind
vein *n.* a blood vessel

weather *n.* conditions in the atmosphere; *v.* to endure
whether *conj.* if

who's contraction of *who is*
whose possessive form of *who* and *which*

you're contraction of *you are*
your possessive form of *you*

FREQUENTLY MISSPELLED WORDS

accessible
accommodate
achieve
acknowledge
acknowledgment
adequate
admissible
advantageous
already
analyze
anxiety
anxious
appropriate
approximately
arrangements
assessment

beginning
believe
business

canceled
capabilities
categories
cautious
censor
changeable
clientele
commission
commitment
committee
communication
compel
compelled
conceited
conference
congratulations
conscientious
conscious
consultant
continuing
controlling
convenience
correspondence
counseling
courteous
criteria
curriculum
customer

decision
defendant
dependent
description
design
desirable
development

efficient
eligible
embarrassed
emphasis
enclosing
equipment
especially
evaluate
exceed
excellent
existence
extension
extraordinary

facilities
faculty
familiar
foreign

government
grievance
guarantee
guidance

harassed
hierarchy

illegible
immediately
impatient
indispensable
installation
institution
interfere
interference
interrupt
irate

jealousy
judgment

knowledgeable

leisure
liability
library
likelihood

maintenance
manageable
mathematics
maximum
mediocre
miscellaneous
misspell
mortgage

necessary
negotiable
noticeable

obvious
occasionally
occurred
occurrence
offered
offering
omitted
opportunity

palette
parallel
partial
participation
pastime
pedestrian
percent
permissible
perseverance
phenomenon
plagiarism
plagiarize
possibility
potential
practice
precede
precedent
preferable
preference
preferential
preferred
prejudice
privilege
proceed
proficient
proficiency
pursue

receipt
receive
recommendations
referred
responsibility
restaurant

salary
schedule
self-confident
separate
session
situation
submitted
substantially
succeed
sufficient

transferred
truly

unanimous
unique
usable
usually

vacuum
vague
vengeance

COMMONLY MISSSPELLED U.S. CITIES

Abilene, TX
Albuquerque, NM
Berkeley, CA
Bismarck, ND
Boise, ID
Butte, MT
Charlotte, NC
Chattanooga, TN
Cincinnati, OH
Cleveland, OH
Decatur, GA or AL
Des Moines, IA
Dubuque, IA
Durham, NC
Everett, WA
Fayetteville, NC or AR
Fremont, CA, NE, or OH
Gainesville, FL or GA
Hialeah, FL
Honolulu, HI
Indianapolis, IN
Milwaukee, WI
Pasadena, CA or TX
Philadelphia, PA
Phoenix, AZ
Pittsburg, CA or KS
Pittsburgh, PA
Raleigh, NC
Roanoke, VA
San Bernardino, CA
San Francisco, CA
Savannah, GA
Schenectady, NY
Shreveport, LA
Sioux City, IA
Sioux Falls, SD
Tallahassee, FL
Tucson, AZ
Worcester, MA

SPELLINGS AND ABBREVIATIONS OF STATES AND U.S. TERRITORIES

Alabama	AL	Indiana	IN	Nevada	NV	South Dakota	SD
Alaska	AK	Iowa	IA	New Hampshire	NH	Tennessee	TN
Arizona	AZ	Kansas	KS	New Jersey	NJ	Texas	TX
Arkansas	AR	Kentucky	KY	New Mexico	NM	Utah	UT
California	CA	Louisiana	LA	New York	NY	Vermont	VT
Colorado	CO	Maine	ME	North Carolina	NC	Virgin Islands	VI
Connecticut	CT	Maryland	MD	North Dakota	ND	Virginia	VA
Delaware	DE	Massachusetts	MA	Ohio	OH	Washington	WA
District of Columbia	DC	Michigan	MI	Oklahoma	OK	West Virginia	WV
Florida	FL	Minnesota	MN	Oregon	OR	Wisconsin	WI
Georgia	GA	Mississippi	MS	Pennsylvania	PA	Wyoming	WY
Hawaii	HI	Missouri	MO	Puerto Rico	PR		
Idaho	ID	Montana	MT	Rhode Island	RI		
Illinois	IL	Nebraska	NE	South Carolina	SC		

LETTER PLACEMENT GUIDE AND REPORT FORMATS

Two different styles of dateline placement and margin width can be keyed for business letters. Style 1 corresponds to the traditional letter placement, where the side margins and dateline vary according to the length of the letter. Style 2 offers easy-to-follow guidelines (1" side margins and a 2" standard or a floating top margin) that are especially suitable for letter preparation using word processing software programs.

LETTER PLACEMENT TABLE

	Style 1		Style 2		
LETTER LENGTH	VARIABLE SIDE MARGINS	DATELINE (FLOATING)	STANDARD SIDE MARGINS	DATELINE (STANDARD)	DATELINE (FLOATING)
Short	2"	Line 18	1"	2"	Line 18
Average	1 1/2"	Line 16	1"	2"	Line 16
Long	1"	Line 14	1"	2"	Line 14

The report formats that follow may be applied to typewriters and word processing software.

REPORT FORMATS

Margin Settings

PLACEMENT	UNBOUND	LEFTBOUND	TOPBOUND
Top margin:			
Page 1	1 1/2" - 2"	1 1/2" - 2"	2" – 2 1/2"
All other pages	1"	1"	1 1/2"
Bottom margin:	1"	1"	1"
Left margin:	1"	1 1/2"	1"
Right margin:	1"	1"	1"
Spacing code:	Reports are usually DS but may be SS.		

INDEX

A

abbreviations, 58-63
acronyms, 171
active voice, 233
addresses
  abbreviating, 60
  commas and, 156
  in letters, 189
  syllabication of, 31
adjectives, commas and, 154
agreement, pronoun and antecedent, 112-115
antecedent
  agreement, 112-115
  collective nouns as, 113
  compound, 114
apostrophe, 169
application letter, 211-212
appositives, 152
attention line, 189
automatic hyphenation, 26

B

balanced appearance, 186
bias-free language, 132-136
block style, 194

C

capitalization, 44-49, 165
case, 115
citations, in reports, 208
cities, U.S., 277
clarity, in editing, 228
clause, 128
cliches, 229
collective nouns, 100-101, 113
colon, 168-169
commas, 148-154
  with dates and addresses, 156
  with direct address and titles, 156
  with direct quotations, 155
company names, abbreviating, 60
comparative proofreading method, 6
compass, capitalizing points of, 48
complements, 95
completeness, in editing, 224
complimentary close, 191
compound
  antecedent, 114
  sentence, 148, 166, 167
  subject, 99
  word, 30
conciseness, in editing, 232
conjunctions, 130, 166, 167
consistency, in editing, 226
content errors, 5
contractions, 169

D

dangling modifiers, 131-132
databases, 21
dates, 31, 46, 156, 188
dependent clause, 128
direct object, 117
direct question, 165
documentation, in reports, 208-209

E

editing
  definition, 224
  for content, 224
  for correct facts, 225
  for consistency, 226
  for clarity, 228
  simplicity and, 228
  for conciseness, 232
  precision and, 229
e-mail, 251-252
endnotes, 209
enumerations, 206
errors, 2
  abbreviation, 58-63
  added copy, 12
  capitalization, 44-49
  content, 5
  incorrect letters, 13
  mechanical, 4
  number expressions, 74-78
  numerical, 16
  omitted copy, 14
  spelling, 10-16
  transposition, 10
  word division, 26-27
exclamation mark, usage, 165

F

factual correctness, 225
follow-up letter, 213
footnotes, 209
format, 184-185
  job search documents, 209-211
  letters, 186-196, 211-214
  memos, 196-199
  reports, 206-209

G

gender, 112
grammar check, 249

H

hanging indent style, 208
headings, 187, 206
helping verbs, 94
homonyms, 10
hyphenation, automatic, 26

I

indefinite pronouns, 101-103, 115
independent clause, 128, 148-149, 166
indirect object, 117
indirect question, 165
information processing tools, 250
interrupting expressions, 152
intervening modifiers, 98-100
introductory elements, 149-151
italics, 172

J

job search documents, 209-214

L

language, bias-free, 132-136
letters, 13, 186-196
linking verbs, 95

INDEX

lists, capitalization in, 44
logical organization, 230

M

marks
  proofreading, 3, 11, 12, 15, 27, 44, 58, 64, 74, 94, 148, 164, 184
  punctuation, 148
mechanical errors, 4
memos, 196-200
modified block style, 195
modifiers, 98-100, 131-132

N

nominative case, 116-117
nonessential elements, 152
nonrestrictive elements, 152
notations, in letters, 192
nouns
  collective, 100-101, 113
  proper, 31, 45
  singular and plural, 97-98, 169
number, 112
numbers, 74-78
numerical errors, 16

O

object of the preposition, 117
objective case, 117-118
on-screen proofreading method, 7, 248-250
organizations, abbreviating, 60

P

parallel structure, 129-130
passive voice, 233
period, usage, 165
person, 112
phrase, 95, 128
  prepositional, 117
  verb, 95
placement, 186
plural nouns, 97-98
possessive case, 119-120, 169
predicate pronoun, 116
prepositional phrase, 117
pronoun(s), 101-103, 112-120
proofreader(s), 3
  card, 5
proofreading
  comparative method, 6
  definition, 3, 224
  importance of, 2
  in relation to editing, 224
  marks, 3, 11, 12, 15, 27, 44, 58, 64, 74, 94, 148, 164, 184
  on-screen method, 7, 248-250
  team method, 7
proper nouns, 31, 45
punctuation marks, 148, 165

Q

question, punctuation for, 165
question mark, usage, 165
quotation marks, 172-173
quotations, 44, 155

R

ratios, punctuating, 168
references, 6, 208
reports, formatting, 206-209
request, punctuation for, 165
restrictive clauses and phrases, 153
resumes, 210-211
root word, 28
rough drafts, 63-64

S

salutation, 168, 190
semicolon, 166-167
sentence(s)
  complete, 94
  compound, 148
  elements, 128-129
  fragments, 96-97
  parallel structure in, 129-130
  structure, 94-96
series, punctuation for, 151, 167, 169
singular nouns, 97-98
spell-check programs, 10, 248
spelling, 10-16, 17
spreadsheets, 250
standard placement, 186
statement of fact, 165
states, U.S., 278
stet, 64
subject, 94, 99, 116
suffix, 28
syllabication, *see* word division

T

tense, 94
time, 62, 168
title page, of report, 206
titles
  abbreviation of, 59
  capitalization of, 47
  commas and, 156
  of works, 172
  syllabication of, 31
transitional expressions, 166

U

U.S. cities and states, 277-278
underscoring, 172

V

variable placement, 186
verb, 94, 95
voice, active and passive, 233
voice recognition software, 251

W

who and *whom,* 118-119
word division, 26-27
word usage, 17, 226
words
  commonly confused, 275-276
  familiar, 228
  frequently misspelled, 277
wraparound mode, 26

Z

ZIP codes, 78-79